"there can be no true creation without opacity"

— Claude Lanzmann
(who made Shoah.
quoted. p. 122

Deborah Anne Kapchan
deborahkapchan@mac.com

The Wherewithal of Life

ETHICS, MIGRATION, AND THE QUESTION
OF WELL-BEING

Michael Jackson

In conversation with Emmanuel Mulamila,
Roberto M. Franco, and Ibrahim Ouédraogo

p. 4. logic of sacrifice
p. 4-5: infatuated with the magicality of our own writing
cf. Taussig. The Corn Wolf

citations are of literature & philosophy

p. 6: allegories; migrant narratives as allegories of life: cf.
J. Clifford.

p. 8 ethical activity =

p. 9 the 'social', the 'cultural' become "intersubjectivity"
[what about milieu?]

p. 10 the social for M-P.

24. quote for listening to Disintegration

35: ethics in context.

36: Sartre and colonialism

56 how immigrants become perceived as monsters

UNIVERSITY OF CALIFORNIA PRESS
BERKELEY LOS ANGELES LONDON

74. acting "for life itself."

83: Michel Serres quote

83 Field work defined

117. ethnography's reasons
118 conversation as ethnographic method
126 characterization, turning a person into a subject
157-58 life as literature. ←
172 migration as oedipal complex
174 culture and identity
179 listening eclipses a sense of self.
187 body proxima
193 life / love as literature ↤
198 literature again, and ethnographic writing

University of California Press, one of the most distinguished university presses in the United States, enriches lives around the world by advancing scholarship in the humanities, social sciences, and natural sciences. Its activities are supported by the UC Press Foundation and by philanthropic contributions from individuals and institutions. For more information, visit www.ucpress.edu.

University of California Press
Berkeley and Los Angeles, California

University of California Press, Ltd.
London, England

Library of Congress Cataloging-in-Publication Data

Jackson, Michael, 1940–
    The wherewithal of life : ethics, migration, and the question of well-being / Michael Jackson in conversation with Emmanuel Mulamila, Roberto M. Franco, and Ibrahim Ouédraogo.
        pages   cm.
    Includes bibliographical references and index.
    ISBN 978-0-520-27670-3 (cloth : alk. paper)—
    ISBN 978-0-520-27672-7 (pbk. : alk. paper)
    1. Anthropology—Philosophy.   2. Ethics—Anthropological aspects.
3. Well-being.   4. Immigrants—Cross-cultural studies.   I. Title.
    GN33.J34 2013
    301.01—dc23   2013008535

Manufactured in the United States of America

22   21   20   19   18   17   16   15   14   13
10   9   8   7   6   5   4   3   2   1

In keeping with a commitment to support environmentally responsible and sustainable printing practices, UC Press has printed this book on Rolland Enviro100, a 100% post-consumer fiber paper that is FSC certified, deinked, processed chlorine-free, and manufactured with renewable biogas energy. It is acid-free and EcoLogo certified.

It was a wrong number that started it, the telephone ringing three times in the dead of night, and the voice on the other end asking for someone he was not. Much later, when he was able to think about the things that happened to him, he would conclude that nothing was real except chance. But that was much later. In the beginning, there was simply the event, and its consequences. Whether it might have turned out differently, or whether it was all predetermined with the first word that came from the stranger's mouth, is not the question. The question is the story itself, and whether or not it means something is not for the story to tell.

PAUL AUSTER, *City of Glass*

CONTENTS

Preamble

IN THE SUMMER OF 2005, en route from Denmark to the United States
to take up yet another visiting academic position, I decided to break my journey in London to look up Sierra Leonean friends and document some of their
experiences of living betwixt and between. One cloudless morning, I accompanied Sewa Koroma on a circuitous tour of the West End, revisiting the sites
of critical events during his first year in the city. At one point, we stopped on
Westminster Bridge to take in the view. Tourist boats were moving up and
down the river, whose muddy banks had been exposed by the ebbing tide.
Ahead of us lay County Hall, where I had been interviewed for a job as a
welfare worker with the homeless in the winter of 1963—a lifetime ago, it   `1963`
seemed, before the London Eye, the Gherkin, and Millennium Bridge were
built, before Sewa was born. Suddenly, as if he were also struggling with similar anachronisms, Sewa exclaimed, "You know, Mr. Mike, I am thinking that
right now my brothers and cousins are all working on their farms back home
in Kondembaia, working hard, but I am here in London, walking these
streets, living this life, this different life." When I pressed Sewa to spell out
the difference between life in his natal village and life in London, he
explained that, although the menial jobs he did in the United Kingdom were
very poorly paid, they were preferable to farming. While farming involved a
repetition of age-old patterns, London offered perennial possibilities of
something different, something new. Yet the life he had left behind haunted
him. He was often "seized" by homesickness. It "took hold" of him and
would not let him go. He would wake at night to dreams of fraternal in-
fighting, and even though he learned to assuage them by praying to Allah in
the way his father had taught him, he struggled to reconcile family obligations with personal ambitions and often felt "small," "stared at," and

"stressed," as if his gains were a sordid boon that could never compensate for what he had given up by leaving his homeland.

That Sewa's ambivalent relationship with both Sierra Leone and Britain should move me so deeply reflected my own transient biography and explains why, after settling in the United States, I continued to explore the origins and repercussions of migration[1]—during return visits to London,[2] in the course of fieldwork with Sewa in northern Sierra Leone in 2008,[3] and finally in the conversations that compose this book.

THE JOURNEYING SELF

In the well-known opening lines of *The Myth of Sisyphus,* Albert Camus asserts that "the fundamental question of philosophy" is "judging whether life is or is not worth living."[4] Although Camus explored suicide as a response to a life that has become insufferable or meaningless, he failed to consider migration as a "way out" or address the dilemma of every migrant for whom life in his or her home place is a kind of social death, yet for whom rebirth in a foreign land may prove illusory. Yet this existential dilemma was anticipated in a letter he wrote to his best friend when he was nineteen. Describing the sea, sun, sand, geraniums, and olive and eucalyptus trees of his natal city, he concluded, "I could never live anywhere but Algiers, although I will travel because I want to know the world, but I'm sure that anywhere else, I'd always feel in exile."[5]

This book is empirically grounded in the experiences of three men whose journeys from the global South to Europe and the United States dramatize, in often harrowing detail, a number of ethical and existential issues that will be familiar to most readers, if for no other reason than that the vicissitudes of attachment, separation, loss, and renewal are unavoidable aspects of every human life. Our lives oscillate between transitive and intransitive extremes. Whether planned or accidental, desired or dreaded, the passage from one place to another, one life stage to another, or one state or status to another often figures centrally in the stories we tell about our lives and who we are. Though we may hanker after hard and fast differences between self and other, human and animal, man and machine, male and female, these boundaries get blurred, transgressed, and redrawn. We morph and migrate, in and out of our bodies, in reality and in our imaginations.[6] Our moments of rest are soon enough disrupted, our settled states disturbed, our minds distracted.

Moveo ergo sum. Along with all living things, *we move through life.* By this I mean not only that we are all bound to die (it is only a question of when) but that we were all once migrants (again, it is only a question of when). These sweeping statements indicate the existential perspective from which I view migration. Rather than treat the migrant as a singular figure—an interloper, anomaly, or alien in our midst—I view the migrant as exemplifying a universal aspect of human existence. Either we are moving or the world is moving—about, under, or above us. To cite the slogan so often seen on vehicles in West Africa, "No condition is permanent."

Although movement, metamorphosis, and mutation are in the nature of things, change does not merely befall us like a bolt from the blue; it is often chosen and embraced, in the hope that we may be carried into a more fulfilling relationship with the world. Whether we construe "the wherewithal of life" as a matter of having wealth or health, fresh water or self-worth, love or lebensraum, food, family, or a future—it tends to be characterized by scarcity. As a limited good, it must be actively sought, struggled for, salvaged, and safeguarded.[7] Critical to these processes of capturing or commanding life is a capacity to *move* to where life appears to be most abundant and accessible, or to *orient* oneself so as to see what other possibilities may exist where one is.[8] This explains why many desert-dwelling Australian Aboriginals readily abandoned a hunter-gatherer economy when they first encountered white pastoralists, choosing to "sit down" on the fringes of cattle stations or mines and exchange their labor for tea, flour, and sugar. Just as nomadic people value both stasis and movement, so sedentary people sometimes grow restive when stuck in the same place or the same rut for too long. In the traditional sand drawings and contemporary acrylic paintings of Aboriginal artists, the recurring icons of circle and line suggest a perennial oscillation between camping and traveling, sitting down and "going walkabout." Dreaming myths recount how totemic ancestors moved far and wide across the partially formed face of the earth, performing ceremony, shaping landforms, imprinting and impregnating the ground with their sweat and their designs. Exhausted by their travels and nostalgic for their natal country, they eventually returned whence they came, sinking back into the ground, to be ritually brought forth again by the dancing, chanting, and clacking boomerangs of the living. Aztec migration narratives echo this archetype. In the early sixteenth-century *Mapa de Cuauhtinchan,* Mesoamerican artists living in the "Place of the Eagle's Nest" depicted, two decades after the Spanish conquest, a labyrinthine journey by their ancestors through sacred landscapes.

By means of this map, subsequent generations would be able to vicariously revisit the critical events that led to the founding of the Aztec world.[9] Like Aboriginal paintings from Central Australia, this Aztec "masterpiece of cultural history and religious memory"[10] can also be read as a cryptic account of a cosmology in which the peregrinations of the ancestors mirror the movement of life energies between microcosm and macrocosm. For the Aztecs, women, captives, and children had to be periodically fed to the sun and their "vital energy transferred" to the cosmos as a kind of "debt payment to the hungry gods" for the expected regeneration of life on earth.[11] This primordial logic of sacrifice, requiring that individual lives be given up for life itself to be renewed, prefigures the rationale for contemporary migration, in which one gives up one's life in a natal *altepetl* or community to gain a more bountiful life across the border, in a foreign place. But the tension between what W. B. Yeats called "one dear perpetual place"[12] and all the other places to which one develops ties or where one finds fulfillment is never completely resolved. How much does one have to sacrifice to have a life worth living? How much can one expect from the powers-that-be in one's search for a just apportionment of the things that make life possible? And as much as one yearns for pastures new, one also yearns, in an alien land, to be at home again or, at least, to recover a balance between being an actor and being acted upon—a balance I refer to elsewhere as "being at home in the world."[13]

Throughout this book, I explore these existential tensions and quandaries through a deep engagement with the three individuals who shared their life stories with me. In each case, the stories unfolded in conversation. I did not so much interview my subjects as collaborate with them, occasionally annotating the experiences they recounted, yet distancing myself from the jargon of migration studies so that *their* voices would be heard and their observations and recollections would determine the course of my own deliberations.[14] Consider, for instance, Jean-François Bayart's 2007 study of global governmentality, where migrants are spoken of collectively as "the drudges of globalization," living a "floating" or "liminal" existence.[15] These are arresting images. But even in Roberto Franco's darkest days working in the fields of Southern California, and despite the long hours Ibrahim Ouédraogo toils for a minimal wage in an Amsterdam kitchen, these men do not *ontologize* themselves as drudges, floating, or liminal, although there are times when these words ring true.[16] If we are to avoid the trap of becoming infatuated with our own intellectual-cum-magical capacity to render the world intelligible, then the vocabulary "we" all too glibly project onto "them" must be

tested continually against the various and changing experiences of actual lives. Otherwise we risk becoming complicit in the social violence that reduces the other to a mere object—a drudge, a victim, a number, assimilated to a category, a class, or a global phenomenon. As John Chernoff notes in his splendid portrayals of West African urban life through the ebullient narratives of "a brilliant but uneducated African woman" who "examines moral ambiguities from a perspective of situational ethics,"[17] most media reports, academic studies, and novels of the educated elite "all have ambitions to elevate generalizations about big social issues" and "it is difficult to get an idea of what life is like at ground level or to get a feeling for the experience of the people who lived there."[18] Ruth Behar's narrative ethnography of a Mexican migrant, whose name translates as "hope," brings home to us how close-grained empirical and ethnographic documentation can speak against the social and discursive violence that creates inequalities of presence, recovering the lived experience that is often lost in the administrative and intellectual discourse of the global North.[19] As Behar puts it in her preface to Esperanza's story, "I can only hope that her story will find *un rinconcito,* a little space somewhere on this side of the border where there are no aliens, only people." I share this same hope for the stories in my book.

THE QUESTION OF LIFE ITSELF

In his author's note to *Heart of Darkness,* Joseph Conrad observes that "it is well known that curious men go prying into all sorts of places (where they have no business) and come out of them with all kinds of spoil." He then refers to this work and another unnamed story as being "all the spoil I brought out from the center of Africa, where, really, I had no sort of business."[20]

Conrad could not have anticipated the irony of his comments, for as a direct consequence of the European colonization of places where people like Conrad had no right to be, countless people from those regions would wind up in the global North, where they would be stigmatized as interlopers and often told to go back to where they properly belonged.[21] Yet the ramifications of Conrad's observations go beyond colonialism. For whether we are speaking of mercenary ambitions for power and profit, ethnographic quests to understand the human condition, utopian longings for an elsewhere or a soul mate, or movements of people from the impoverished South to the global

North in search of work and well-being, ethical questions arise that go beyond historical events, social identities, legal rights, and moral norms.

I therefore begin with the question of life itself, before considering the particular ways in which life is understood and the specific conditions under which it can be accessed, augmented, possessed, preserved, and shared.

For Spinoza, life and death were not absolute poles of being and nothingness, but matters of being more or less alive, since every life form "endeavors to persist in its own being," seeking whatever augments and amplifies its existence, while avoiding all that imperils or diminishes it.[22] Spinoza's concept of the struggle for being is directly relevant to understanding the human impulse to move and migrate, as well as what it means to have a life or the hope of a better life, or to be so destitute of the wherewithal for life that one experiences oneself as socially dead. It also helps us understand the relation between being and belonging, since to be is also to yearn to be with others, to experience one's being as integrated with and integral to a wider field of being, and to know that one's own particular life merges with and touches the lives of others—predecessors, successors, contemporaries, and consociates, as well as the overlapping worlds of nature, the cosmos, and the divine.

Migrant narratives are, in many ways, allegories of human existence, in which the hope that our lives may be made more abundant, for ourselves and those we love, constantly comes up against the limits of what we may achieve and the despair into which we may be plunged when we find ourselves unable to achieve that state of well-being and flourishing that Aristotle called *eudaimonia.*

Spinoza's ethics also touches on the relation between a particular form of life—human, animal, or plant life, or different human lives—and life itself. Accordingly, ethics concerns the ways species life or individual lives are struggled for and sustained, especially under conditions of insecurity, scarcity, danger, and loss, *as well as* the ways in which life itself flows through all things, connecting all forms of life in a common web.

This brings us to the relation among ethics, morality, and law. Paul Ricoeur observes, "Before the morality of norms, there is an ethics of the wish to live well." So, he says, "I encounter the word 'life' at the most basic level of ethics." He then adds, "This is also the level on which memory is constituted, beneath discourses, before the stage of predication."[23] Emmanuel Levinas writes of ethics in a similar vein, eschewing the moralistic question "What ought I to do?" and focusing on the concerns of ancient ethics—"How best can we live?"[24] The ethical quest for existential fulfillment therefore entails the

question of whether and to what extent we are justified in moving across class, cultural, national, and discursive borders in our quest for life itself, even though we may infringe moral and legal norms in doing so.

This tension between an ethics embedded in the changing exigencies of life and an abstract discourse of custom, morality, and law preoccupied thinkers as diverse as Socrates, Marx, and Gandhi, all of whom saw that customs and laws tend to favor a select few at the expense of the many, while meting out justice, well-being, wealth, and care in unequal portions. Insofar as migrants cross international borders, becoming global nomads and assuming multiple identities, their ethical concerns often echo those of critical theory, for in seeking an amelioration of their lot, migrants must often turn a blind eye to the values of their natal lifeworlds, as well as to the mores of the countries to which they gravitate in the belief that they are entitled to a better life *simply by virtue of being human.*

On what basis, for instance, does a migrant assume the right to seek his fortune in a place where, strictly speaking, he has no place? What kind of human right is it that leads him to ignore the fact that he may have no legal or constitutional right to live and work in the country on which he has pinned his hopes for a better life? What sense of ethics justifies his claim to a share of the good life in a country where many aver that they owe the migrant nothing and demand to know what gives him the right to come there, take jobs from locals, and benefit from social services that are paid for by the taxes of hardworking citizens?

If migrants often transgress moral norms and act outside the law, then we who seek to understand the migrant must reorient our own thinking and acknowledge the extent to which life interrupts, unsettles, and resists the moral assumptions and logocentric modes of discourse we tend to privilege in our desire to govern the world or render it intelligible.[25] We must go with the broken flow of migrant narratives and migrant imaginaries, working out ways of doing justice to the often paratactic, contradictory, opportunistic, and improvisatory character of transitional experience.

For Heidegger, our being-in-the-world is a "thrownness" *(Geworfenheit)*. We are "thrown" *(geworfen)* into a world that has been made by others at other times and which will outlast us. We choose neither the time nor place of our birth, and our origins are not of our making. Yet we strive to live this givenness as if it were chosen, and the tension between our ethical struggle for well-being and the moral or legal limits on our freedom generates existential dramas that characterize fiction and reality alike. It is not the arbitrariness of

our birth, therefore, that concerns us most, but the contingency of existence itself, in which we are thrown continually off balance, obliged to rethink and reconsider the relationship between what we can and cannot change, comprehend, or endure.[26]

ETHICS AND INTERSUBJECTIVITY

The existential situation of the migrant recalls the situation of the stranger, who, as Simmel observed, suggests a paradoxical mix of mobility and stasis. Unlike the wanderer who comes today and goes tomorrow, the stranger "comes today and stays tomorrow," his ambiguous social position determined by the fact that he has not belonged to the group "from the beginning [and therefore] imports qualities into it which do not and cannot stem from the group itself."[27] In my view, the unsettling quality that the migrant imports into the group is actually a question—the vexed ethical question of whether we see ourselves and others as united by our common humanity or differentiated by our social identities. The migrant brings into sharp relief a discrepancy that is felt, to some degree, by all human beings—between their membership in a specific society and their membership in a single species. The tragedy of the migrant is the tragedy of every marginalized individual, for insofar as his human worth is made a function of his degraded status, he is treated as a nonentity, having no claims on the society to which he has gravitated. In sum, his humanity is wholly determined by his place in a social hierarchy.

Social hierarchies are reinforced by law, morality, and custom. Fortunately, however, though any human life is largely shaped by moral, political, social, and religious regimes, every human life unfolds in ways that only partially realize, replicate, or reinforce these regimes. Indeed, the conversations and stories in this book have persuaded me that it may not be a bad thing that the good cannot be legislated or universalized, for in its surprising randomness we are perennially reminded that our very humanity can never be entirely determined by social orders and their moral rationales, and that this very indeterminacy redeems us.

This sense that virtue cannot be totally prescribed or predetermined means that much ethical activity is best understood as a function of the *relationship* between unpredictable situations and extant moral norms.[28] Because the good, the right, or the true cannot be systematically derived from

any one external measure—be it a social rule, a religious law, or a moral norm—we cannot preemptively declare that any human action is in its very nature absolutely right or wrong, good or bad, true or false. Rather, its worth lies in what we achieve within the limits of what is possible. Accordingly, ethics becomes practically synonymous with freedom, which Sartre understood as a question of what we make of what we are made—"the small movement which makes of a totally conditioned social being someone who does not render back completely what his conditioning has given him."[29]

In what sense, is this struggle for life a social rather than merely personal struggle? And how might we conceptualize the social?

Just as Aristotle observed that "men create the gods after their own image," so Durkheim claimed that "God is only a figurative expression of . . . society."[30] This view that religion and ethics are socially derived was shared by Weber and Marx, and it also informed Geertz's view that religious beliefs are a way in which a social group renders its ethos "intellectually reasonable."[31] The problem with these approaches is that they are at once too abstract and too general. The social is identified with groups and institutions, ethics is confused with moral norms, and religion is made synonymous with belief and meaning.

In many societies—including those in West Africa and Aboriginal Australia, where I have done extensive fieldwork—"religion" and "ethics" are not identified linguistically or conceptually as discrete domains, leading one to ask, as Paul Ricoeur does, whether we would do well to focus neither on a neo-Aristotelian ethics based on the idea of a good life nor on a Kantian approach based on duty and obligation, but rather on questions of "practical wisdom" *(phronesis)* in everyday life, when unprecedented situations arise, problems don't admit of any solution, perfection remains beyond our grasp, and virtue may reside less in achieving the good than in striving for it.[32]

My first suggestion is that we dissolve our conventional concepts of the social and the cultural into the more immediate and dynamic life of intersubjectivity—the everyday interplay of human subjects, coming together and moving apart, giving and taking, communicating and miscommunicating. I take my cues here from Levinas's insistence that ethics begins in our face-to-face encounters with others and our responsiveness to the other,[33] as well as Sartre's late comments that "essentially, ethics is a matter of one person's relationship to another" and that "ethical conscience" arises from one's awareness of always being, to some extent, in the presence of another and conditioned by this sense of being-in-relation with him or her.[34] Sartre notes,

moreover, that classical ethical systems—whether Aristotle's or Kant's—leave unresolved the question of whether one lives ethically all the time. "While having a bite or drinking a glass of wine, does one feel ethical or unethical, or doesn't it matter?" Can we distinguish between an "ethics of everyday life" and an "ethics of exceptional circumstances"?[35]

I share Sartre's view that our sense of the ethical derives only partly from normative maxims, categorical imperatives, or cultural codifications, that it reflects also a deep awareness that our very existence is interwoven with the existence of others and that the reciprocal character of human relations gives rise, from the earliest months of life, to inchoate, conflicted, and diffuse assumptions about fairness, justice, rightness, and goodness. Maurice Merleau-Ponty also espoused this view, speaking of the social as always *there,* existing "obscurely and as a summons"[36]—a "region" where our lives "are prepared."[37] Recent psychological research in the field of primary intersubjectivity supports this view of the ethical as foreshadowed in the infant's initial interactions with the mother. Emphasizing the reciprocity of voice, eye contact, touch, smell, and playful interaction between mother and infant, Ed Tronick speaks of a "collaboration" between infant and parent in regulating interaction and laying down the neurobehavioral foundations of a "dyadic consciousness" that incorporates complex information, experience, and mutual mappings into a relatively coherent whole that functions as a self-regulating system, effectively expanding the consciousness of one person into the consciousness of another.[38] Dyadic consciousness begins in the stage of primary intersubjectivity; should an infant be "deprived of the experience of expanding his or her states of consciousness in collaboration with the other . . . this limits the infant's experience and forces the infant into self-regulatory patterns that eventually compromise the child's development."[39] In brief, the unresponsiveness of a mother or her lack of responsibility for her baby's well-being—contrived experimentally by the mother feigning indifference to her infant and adopting a "still face"—violates reciprocity and has an immediate traumatic effect on the infant.[40]

ETHICS AVANT LA LETTRE

In developing an ethics of the intersubjective, we need a method of study that avoids prejudgments as to what is right and wrong, good and bad, and thus draws us deeply into the complexity of everyday situations. Michael Lambek

has coined the term "ordinary ethics" to signal this departure from the Kantian tradition of Western moral thought—in which a priori assumptions about autonomy, agency, virtue, and community refer to particular situations cursorily, anecdotally, or not at all. For Lambek, ethics is "fundamentally a property or function of action rather than (only) of abstract reason."[41] There are echoes here of Veena Das's argument for a "descent into the ordinary"[42] and David Graeber's claim that "if we really want to understand the moral grounds of economic life, and by extension, human life," we must start not with cosmologies and worldviews but with "the very small things: the everyday details of social existence, the way we treat our friends, enemies, and children—often with gestures so tiny (passing the salt, bumming a cigarette) that we ordinarily never stop to think about them at all."[43]

These gestures toward everyday ethics, and the ways questions of what is right and good figure in almost every human interaction, conversation, and rationalization, effectively reinscribe the role of ethnography as a method for exploring a variety of actual social situations before hazarding generalizations. This is not to say that empirical studies of particular events or lives offer no insights into what may be universal. Rather, by locating the ethical in the field of intersubjective life, we call into question the assumption that existence is a struggle to bring one's life into alignment with given moral norms or a mere enactment of moral scripts, and become more fascinated by our mundane struggles to decide between competing imperatives or deal with impasses, unbearable situations, moral dilemmas, and double binds.

This was the perspective I developed in my 1982 study of ethics in Kuranko storytelling.[44] Almost all Kuranko tales involve journeys between town *(sué)* and bush *(fira)*. As such, the moral customs *(namui* or *bimba kan),* laws *(seriye* or *ton),* and chiefly power *(mansaye)* associated with the town are momentarily placed in abeyance, and the wild ethos of the bush, associated with animals, shape-shifters, djinn, and antinomian possibilities, comes into play. Moreover, Kuranko stories are told at night or in twilight zones that lie on the margins of the workaday waking world. There is a close connection, therefore, between the evocation of antinomian scenarios, states of dream-like or drowsy consciousness, and the narrative suspension of disbelief. Kuranko *tilei* (fables, folktales, fictions) are make-believe; they are framed as occurring outside ordinary time and space *(wo le yan be la—*far-off and long ago)*; they play with reality and entertain possibilities that lie beyond convention and custom. Typically, these tales begin with a dilemma or disturbance in the ideal order of moral relations: three sons of a chief, all born at the same

time and on the same day, all claim the right to succeed their father; an elder brother maltreats his younger brother; a senior cowife exploits a younger cowife; a man betrays the trust of his closest friend; a chief abuses his power or imposes an unjust law on his people; a husband neglects his wife; a love affair jeopardizes a marriage. The ethical quandary lies in how to redress a situation in which there is considerable moral ambiguity, for there are always two sides to every story and several possible ways of restoring order or seeing that justice is done. That is to say, ethical dilemmas are never resolved by simply laying down the law, invoking a moral principle that covers every situation, or passing judgment; the dilemmas require collective *discussion,* in which people attempt to come up with the best solution possible, given the complex circumstances, even though it is understood that any solution may make matters worse and no one is ever in a position to know the repercussions of his or her actions. By not seeking consensus and suspending dogmatic patterns of thinking, Kuranko storytelling creates ethical ambiguity and inspires listeners to think outside the box.[45] Accordingly, virtue is less a matter of achieving or exemplifying goodness than a relative question of doing the best one can, given the limits of the situation and considering the abilities and resources one possesses.

In more recent fieldwork, I have seen how the wider world has become, for young African migrants, a symbolic bush[46]—a place at once of peril and of transformative possibilities, lying beyond the moral and legal space of the "town" and signifying a space of ethical questioning and bargaining, comparable to the space hitherto associated with bush spirits and the ancestral dead. Why should Africans languish in poverty when the Western world enjoys such abundance? Will a young woman's desire to marry for love jeopardize interfamily relations based on arranged marriage? How one can reconcile going abroad in search of one's fortune when this means losing touch with one's homeland and possibly neglecting one's obligations to family back home? By what right do politicians amass wealth for themselves and neglect the welfare of ordinary people?[47]

Methodologically, then, an anthropology of ethics seeks to locate ethics within the social—without, however, reifying society, religion, and morality or regarding them as sui generis phenomena. As Fasching, Dechant, and Lantigua put it, "The study of ethics must be more than an 'objective' survey of abstract theories. . . . The primary and most persuasive ways religious traditions shape ethical behavior are through storytelling and spiritual practices."[48] This implies a focus on *the life stories* of [individuals] who have

wrestled with questions of justice, non-violence, and ecological well-being in an age of racism, sexism, religious prejudice, nationalism, colonialism, terrorism, and nuclear war."[49] Whereas Fasching, Dechant, and Lantigua emphasize the life stories of "extraordinary persons" like Tolstoy, Gandhi, Martin Luther King Jr., and Malcolm X, my focus is on the extraordinary stories of *ordinary people*, all migrants, whose experiences bring into sharp relief the ethical quandaries, qualms, and questions that all human beings encounter in the course of their lives, regardless of their religious, ethnic, cultural, or class identities. To capture this protoethical sense of rightness or goodness, we need to be especially attentive to the ontological metaphors with which people capture a sense of what is ethically at stake for them in any given situation. Such metaphors remind us that an ethical sensibility inheres in our relations with others *(mitwelt)* as well as our relationship to the objective environment *(umwelt)*. Just as the presence of others brings us continually back to ourselves, so the architecture of the world and the things we touch, taste, see, smell, and hear offer a fund of images with which to objectify and articulate our inchoate sense of the right, the true, and the good. People in many societies identify straightness with virtue and crookedness with vice, or invoke images of physical symmetry in expressing the idea of reciprocity (being all square, or fair and square). And commonplace allusions to true lines, fine work, good ideas, upright posture, sweet tastes, or harmonious sound suggest that ethical ideals are never plucked out of thin air but originate in our quotidian, bodily, and practical experience of being-in-the-world.[50]

tropes

Emmanuel

I LIVED AND WORKED IN COPENHAGEN, Denmark, for six years. After moving to the United States in 2005, I returned to Denmark every year to give talks, see old friends, and attend the PhD defenses of my former students.

When Susanne Bregnbaek successfully defended her doctoral thesis in the fall of 2010, I was invited to her apartment in Christianshavn to celebrate the rite of passage with family and friends. Curiously enough, Susanne's thesis, though based on fieldwork in Beijing, resonated with a conversation I would have later that evening with Emmanuel Mulamila, a Ugandan who was married to one of Susanne's closest friends. Susanne had written at length of an ethical dilemma experienced by many tertiary students in Beijing, who were torn between a desire for self-realization and family pressures to take care of elderly parents or government pressures to contribute to the well-being of the nation. This conflict between self-sacrifice and self-actualization weighed so heavily on the minds of many young Chinese students that some chose suicide as the only way of freeing themselves from the double bind.

Susanne's friend Nanna had also been a student of mine at Copenhagen University, and had met Emmanuel in 2002 while doing fieldwork in Uganda. After introducing me to Emmanuel, Nanna explained that he had been reluctant to accompany her to Susanne's graduation party. His situation was depressing, and he did not go out much. Emmanuel was thirty-nine. After marrying and securing a work permit in 2003, he completed an eighteen-month course in Danish language and culture, followed by a second degree, in applied economics and finance, at the Copenhagen Business School. But the only work he had been able to find was as a tour guide in the summer of 2004 and, more recently, a night job sorting mail in the central

post office. It wasn't only the hypercritical rejection letters from potential employers that had worn him down; it was the dispiriting effect of having to negotiate ever-changing state decrees and regulations governing aliens and the unemployed. As Emmanuel described to me the Kafkaesque rigmarole that circumscribed his life, I found it easy to understand his bitterness. "I have given up on ever getting a job that matches my qualifications. I have lost my self-worth. I am at the end of the rope, and there seems to be more pressure now than ever from the government in regard to immigrants getting and staying in jobs. I have become completely demoralized."

I was drawn to Emmanuel and deeply moved by his story. I said I wished I could help in some way. I wanted to suggest that I apply for research funds, offer him a stipend, and publish his story, but I did not wish to seem opportunistic or voyeuristic. I said I would like to keep in touch and left it at that.

Over the next six months, I drafted and submitted an application for a grant to cover the costs of fieldwork among African migrants in three European cities—Copenhagen, Amsterdam, and London. When my application was rejected on the grounds that it was "thinly conceptualized," lacked any "specific research questions," and failed "to engage sufficiently with the extensive existing anthropological literature of migration from Africa," I was thrown, for despite repeated efforts I had not succeeded in getting an anthropological research grant for thirty years. However, I consoled myself that my experiences of negotiating the world of professional anthropology brought me closer to Emmanuel's experiences of trying to find a way through the labyrinth of a society in which he felt himself to be a persona non grata.

In late August 2011, I traveled to Denmark for yet another PhD defense, this time at Aarhus. My modest honorarium allowed me to spend a weekend in Copenhagen, where I was determined to spend as much time as possible with Emmanuel and Nanna.

When I visited their apartment on Smallegade, I found Emmanuel in an upbeat mood. "We hardly recognize him," Nanna said, laughing. "We're only now getting used to the old Emmanuel again." Emmanuel explained that he had recently found work. It was unpaid and probationary, but there was a very real probability that if he did well the position would be made permanent.

I spent that Saturday with Emmanuel, Nanna, and Alice Maria, their three-year-old daughter, enjoying their company and getting acquainted. Emmanuel cooked Ugandan food—rice with vegetables and peanut sauce. Nanna made cinnamon rolls, which we ate with cups of herbal tea. I talked

about my experiences in Sierra Leone and with Kuranko friends in London. And that evening, as I prepared to return to my lodgings, I felt comfortable asking Emmanuel if he had thought more about my suggestion that we record his story and explore ways of publishing it. Emmanuel agreed without hesitation, and when I turned up at his apartment the following morning with a borrowed digital recorder, we began work immediately, sitting at the kitchen table while Nanna and Alice Maria read books, watched TV, or did jigsaw puzzles in the adjacent room.

HISTORY AND BIOGRAPHY

Every biography entails some history. Events that occurred before one was born or in a faraway country may shape one's destiny as much as more immediate events that one had a hand in shaping. This was immediately evident as Emmanuel began recounting his story.

He was born on 23 September 1971, in Mbale, his mother's hometown in eastern Uganda. Had custom determined events, Emmanuel's mother would have been living in her husband's place, and her son would have been born and raised among his father's kin. But Emmanuel's father was living in Tanzania, where he had a job in the Department of Agriculture of the East African Community (EAC), an intergovernmental organization comprising the five East African countries of Burundi, Kenya, Rwanda, Tanzania, and Uganda. After returning to Uganda for the birth of his second-born, Emmanuel's father decided that the family should return with him to Tanzania. When the EAC collapsed in 1977, Emmanuel's father moved his family to Kumi in eastern Uganda, where he thought he might find work with a former employer. When I asked Emmanuel if his father hailed from Kumi and had family there, Emmanuel said his father was originally from the Ruhenjeri Prefecture in Rwanda, a region that bordered Uganda, though he had only learned this recently.

Hutu-Tutsi conflict in Rwanda and Burundi has a long history, though most ethnohistorians agree that it had its origins in the loss of Hutu autonomy as Tutsi pastoralists entered the country from as early as the fourteenth century, imposing, by the mid-sixteenth century, a quasi-feudal state on the autochthonous Hutu majority. Nonetheless, at the time of colonization in the late nineteenth century, there was little to distinguish—culturally, linguistically, or ethically—the people whose "differences" would be played up,

played upon, and racialized under successive colonial administrations and postindependence governments.

As countless oral histories testify, almost everyone in Africa was once a migrant, belonging to an ethnic minority that displaced people already settled in the lands they would come to consider their own. Some arrived as pastoralists (like the Tutsi) in search of greener pastures; others came as conquerors, and still others as refugees from religious persecution or hunters looking for forests replete with game.

In the late 1950s, as the Belgian administration tried to engineer a more equitable balance of power between Hutu and Tutsi, ethnic tensions increased. Following municipal elections in 1960, the Tutsi monarchy was abolished, and many Tutsi fled the country. On 1 July 1962, Belgium, with United Nations oversight, granted full independence to Rwanda and Burundi. As the Hutu revolution gathered momentum, so did Tutsi guerrilla raids from bases in Kivu (Congo) and Uganda. Tens of thousands (mainly Tutsi) were killed in these clashes, and as many as 150,000 were driven into exile, including Emmanuel's father. The Hutu-dominated government of Grégoire Kayibanda now established quotas to increase the number of Hutu in schools and the civil service. This effectively penalized Tutsi, who were allowed only 9 percent of secondary school and university seats, consonant with their proportion of the population. These quotas were also extended to the civil service. The Kayibanda government continued the Belgian colonial government's policy of requiring ethnic identity cards and discouraging "mixed" marriages. Following more violence in 1964, the government suppressed political opposition and executed Tutsi rebels, who were called *inyenzi* (cockroaches), an ominous foretaste of the large-scale genocides that would devastate this region in the 1990s.

The natural symbols are striking: the other as an insect, oneself as autochthonous—born of and belonging to the soil. I was also struck by the tragic ironies in Emmanuel's father's story, for not only does autochthony underpin Hutu claims for ur-belonging; it denies full citizenship to Tutsi, who are alleged to be second-class citizens at best because they were migrants. Driven from his homeland, Emmanuel's father became a cosmopolitan, rootless individual whose tenuous identification with Uganda would shape the destiny of his son, who also wound up in a foreign land where autochthony was invoked to justify the marginalization of foreigners in national life.[1] As a child, Emmanuel was aware of his anomalous situation, raised in his mother's village but with no real relationship with his father's kin—practically an internal exile.

= Jews in Israel

Emmanuel said his father and mother first met in 1969, probably in Kenya. His father returned to Rwanda with his wife and four children in 1974–75, but the mountainous region in the north, with its dire poverty, vertiginous slopes, and difficult living conditions brought them back to Uganda.

"The story is a bit cloudy," Emmanuel explained, "because talking about how you met your husband and the intimacy and so on is something that people don't share, especially the old generation. Maybe they met in a bar. Maybe it was in a restaurant . . ."

"So you are in Kumi . . ."

"We stayed there until 1979. April 11, I think. The Amin regime was breaking up. That same day, we learned that our father had disappeared."

Idi Amin Dada (1925–2003) had come to power in a military coup in January 1971. Amin's regime was characterized by gross human rights abuses, political repression, ethnic persecution, extrajudicial killings, nepotism, corruption, and economic mismanagement. By 1978, Amin's support was eroding, and he faced growing dissent from ordinary Ugandans dismayed at the crumbling infrastructure and ruined economy. Following the murders of Bishop Luwum and ministers Oryema and Oboth Ofumbi in 1977, several of Amin's ministers defected or fled into exile. In November 1978, Amin's vice president, General Mustafa Adrisi, was injured in a car accident, and troops loyal to him mutinied. Amin sent troops to confront the mutineers, some of whom had fled across the Tanzanian border. Amin accused Tanzanian president Julius Nyerere of waging war against Uganda and ordered an invasion to annex a section of Tanzania's Kagera region. In January 1979, Nyerere mobilized the Tanzania People's Defense Force and counterattacked, supported by Ugandan exiles calling themselves the Uganda National Liberation Army (UNLA). Amin's army retreated, and despite military backing from Libya's Muammar al-Gaddafi, Kampala fell and Amin went into exile on 11 April 1979. After a year in Libya, he settled in Saudi Arabia, where the Saudi royal family allowed him sanctuary and provided him with a generous subsidy on the understanding that he would stay out of politics.

Emmanuel's mother was adamant that her husband had not been politically active during the Amin years. But eastern Uganda opposed Amin, and Emmanuel's father was associated with the opposition simply because he lived in that part of the country. He was detained only days before Amin's government collapsed. "After he was picked up, we never saw him again," Emmanuel said. "Apart from a bloody pair of shorts and a shirt they brought

us, indicating that he had been killed, we have never been completely sure what happened to him."

"Who brought the bloody clothes?"

"Strangely enough, it was his friend. They had been traveling together. His friend brought back the clothes and said he'd been given the clothes by the security people. So he brought them to my mum. It was a message that he had been killed. But we never saw the body; we never got any results or any information on where the body was or what happened to the body, so we took it that he had been killed. But in that situation, where we hadn't seen a body and we had no proof that he was actually killed or by whom, we kept hoping that he was in prison and would come out one day, or he was playing a game, leaving the clothes to confuse the security people. But he never came back. Up to now, that hasn't happened."

"Do you have memories of your father?"

"To tell you the truth, no. I don't think I have anything I can remember about what he looked like physically, apart from the stories I was told about him when I was young. He was a massive man, very big, tall. I have never met his relatives, but when I sent them my picture, they told me that I'm a replica of my father. And this brings me back to the issue of why my mum never let me go, never let me visit my father's relatives. Maybe that was the reason, because I looked exactly like him. But no, I don't have a memory of him. Sadly, even pictures, the two or three pictures we had have worn out with time, and now when you look at them you can't actually see many details. There's one picture my brother sent me, but it's not that clear either. So I don't have any visual memory of him, and I can't even remember whether we played together or he carried me, though those who knew him said he had a soft spot for his children. Which was very strange because with most fathers back then, their work was to look for food, to be away working, that kind of thing."

"Did your mother ever talk to you about him, describe what kind of person he was?"

"It was . . . it was, eh . . . what can I say? It was a topic that one wouldn't want to go into, even asking her. Because we tried one time, as children, asking my mum, 'What was our father like?' and 'How were you people?' and she just said, 'Well, I can't say much, he's not there.' It was as if something in her . . . as if we were cutting her heart into two. She seemed to be in pain. Talking about our father by then was horrible for her. My mum is a very hard person. I can tell you, I have seen my mum cry twice in my life, twice. And

that was not the time when my father passed away, no, because I didn't know whether she was crying or not at that time, but the time my grandmother died and the time she had the toothache." Emmanuel gave an embarrassed laugh, then quickly went on. "So when we asked about our father and my mum went inside and came back and her eyes were red, I knew there was something horribly wrong. So we didn't bother asking my mum about our father again. But even though she never sat down and told us intimate things about our father . . . about how he carried us, how he was at home, whether he mistreated us or was sweet to us, or brought us presents or not . . . she did tell us where he came from and who his relatives were. She gave us information about him. That was the only thing that we got from her. Anyway, when my father passed away, or rather, disappeared, it was left to my mum alone to make sure that we safely left that village, because we were not from there. Our presence alone would raise eyebrows, because westerners—especially those from Rwanda, the migrants—were called cowboys."

Emmanuel had touched on one of Africa's oldest problems—the troubled coexistence of pastoralists and sedentary cultivators. It echoes the story of Cain and Abel, post-Neolithic conflicts between townspeople and itinerants, and age-old Asian struggles between valley kingdoms and hill peoples.[2] As settled populations struggled to protect themselves against mobile and marauding outsiders, nomadism became a synonym for barbarism. Seen to belong nowhere and everywhere, the nomad was stigmatized as the antithesis of civilization. As I write (November 2011), a spate of rapes and assaults in northwest Cameroon is being blamed on Akuh cattle herders, with whom Aghem cultivators have long been in dispute over rights to land.[3] In Rwanda, Hutu farmers claimed that their ancestors had generously given land to Tutsi seeking pasture for their herds. But the Tutsi allegedly tricked the Hutu into servitude, and the very word "Hutu" became a synonym for slave.[4] Elsewhere in Africa, pastoralists also tended to be in the minority, supplying cattle (for bridewealth and sacrifices) to farmers in exchange for access to grazing land. But as populations grew and herders migrated from drought-stricken lands, ancient cultural or religious differences were invoked to justify radical separation. In the Kumi district of eastern Uganda, many Tutsi refugees reestablished themselves as cattle herders, though most, including Emmanuel's father, were obliged to work for chiefs or wealthy men on stock contracts.[5] Among the Iteso, cattle were sources of bridewealth, prestige, and political power. It was often said of a heavy-set man that he had grown fat on the milk he had in his home.[6] But owners feared and resented the outsiders to whom

they entrusted their herds. They said, "We can't allow these people to continue keeping our cattle; we have to keep our cattle ourselves." Moreover, Emmanuel explained, "those who had sided with Amin assumed that the cattle keepers were aligned with the rebels." And so, as his mother told him much later, "we had to leave that area because my father's tribe was not accepted there."

"I remember a very big truck. We were put in the truck and covered with banana leaves—literally covered, that's what I remember, because I thought they were covering us from the sun or rain or something. Later on, I told my mum, 'I have a fading memory about how we left Kumi. Why did we leave in a big car?' My mum said, "No, we were hiding. We were being removed from a place where we could be harmed, and there were roadblocks along the road, so we had to be kept under cover.' We went straight to the village where she had been born . . ."

"Mbale?"

"Mbale is a large town. My mum's village is Busiu, which is about thirteen miles south of Mbale on the road to Tororo."

"That is the Bugisu area?"

"Yes, mum is Bagisu."

Mbale is a market town, famous for its arabica coffee. It lies at the foot of Mount Elgon, the oldest and largest solitary volcano in East Africa. The Bagisu occupy a broken landscape of hills and narrow valleys on the western and southern slopes of Mount Elgon. Tradition relates that their ancestor emerged from a hole in the mountain, though they probably arrived in eastern Uganda from the Uasin Gishu plateau in Kenya. In anthropological parlance, the Bagisu reckon descent patrilineally (through one's father and his father and his father ad infinitum), and when a woman marries she customarily resides with or near her husband's family. When the family moved from the area of Uganda where his father had made his home, Emmanuel found himself not only fatherless and without contact with his patrikin; he was now subject to the authority of his matrikin. Ordinarily, Emmanuel would have expected to find affection, care, and freedom among his maternal kin. In fact, the opposite proved to be the case. Moreover, in the absence of a husband to support her, Emmanuel's mother had to become the breadwinner, and Emmanuel was obliged to assume a role that would normally be assigned to an elder sister.

"So when we came to Bugisu, we came to a village where my mum was born and raised, only to face a new set of problems there. I had to grow up fast—not physically, but in understanding that life is not easy. My mum was pregnant

when our father died, and she gave birth to a baby girl in 1980. I was nine years old. Because I was closest in age to Barbara, I had to take care of her."

"But you had other siblings, didn't you?"

"My elder brother Deo had been living with an uncle in the city for many years. My younger brother Peter lived with one of our mum's uncles, three miles from Busiu. And then there was Mariam, my other younger sister, who lived with me and my mum in Busiu."

"You were saying that life was not easy there."

"My mum's sisters and the older women in her family did not concern themselves with our well-being. They were focused on their own survival, and they did not want to sit down with us anyway because we were from a different part of the country. I didn't know any other life. Not like now. But life in that village was not easy for me. It was horrible. Looking back, I would have preferred to be in prison. A prison in Uganda would have been better because you would know you had done something wrong and were being punished for it. But from the word go, people started telling me, mainly because I was so outgoing, so ready to help, 'No, no, you can't do this, you can't come in here, because you are this and this . . .'"

"The fact that you were your mother's son didn't count?"

"No."

"You were considered a stranger, because you were from your father's part of the country?"

"Exactly. I was not welcome, and by the way, what made it worse is that, traditionally, when a girl left a village to go and get married, she's not meant to come back. So you see, my mum coming back with us meant sentencing us to some horrible punishment."

I found it ironic that though Bugisu and Kumi had been equally opposed to the Amin regime, Emmanuel's family was nonetheless regarded as outsiders and ostracized. Emmanuel agreed, pointing out that most members of Milton Obote's Uganda People's Congress (UPC) hailed from Bugisu. But political affiliation counted for much less than customary determinations of identity and belonging.

"They should have protected us, really, but they didn't care that we were on the same side. That was not important. What mattered was that we were from the wrong place, that we came with our mother and lacked a father. I've been avoiding the word 'bastard,' but it is actually used more in our culture than it is here in Denmark. Here it is used as a figure of speech, a way of annoying you. There it is well defined. If you lack a father or if your father

and mother are not married, you are basically a bastard, and so you are not welcome. Worse still, my mum was not staying with any man by then because my father had passed away, and most people didn't even know who my father was. This might sound a bit complicated, but in my culture relations with in-laws are a big deal. A husband doesn't visit his wife's home that often. He has to be invited, or he has to send a message that he is coming, so the in-laws have time to prepare. And he doesn't stay with his parents-in-law, but with a friend or brother-in-law."

"So your mother's people were outraged that you should turn up on their doorstep, because, in effect, it was as if your father had appeared uninvited and unannounced to impose on their hospitality?"

"Yes, we were strangers in that place. We had no right to be there. And what made things worse was that we didn't know the local language—we didn't speak Lugisu; we were speaking Swahili and a bit of English. We knew Swahili because we went to preschool in Tanzania, and we spoke Swahili with our father. In Kumi, in the Teso region, we didn't know the Teso language, and so the only language we spoke was Swahili. So language became an issue for us too. I had a problem learning the local language because I had no one to speak with, and if you spoke with anyone they would actually laugh at you, and so you shut up and gave up. I felt the same way when I came to Denmark. People made no allowance for the fact that I was from another country and could not speak their language. It had the effect of making me feel like a stupid child, just as I felt back then in Uganda.

"The problem was, we had to go to school. With the benefit of hindsight, I think nobody really cared what we were going to experience at school. They just herded us off. 'You are going to that school,' they said. We didn't know Lugisu, we didn't even know much English, but they just put us there. Now came an additional difficulty. From years five to eight, classes are taught in Luganda, because the Baganda, the largest tribe in my country, influenced the education system. Just imagine, you speak Swahili, you know a little English, you don't know your mother's language, and then they go and teach you in yet another language that it is impossible to understand!"

· WHEN KINSHIP IS NOT ENOUGH ·

Emmanuel's story not only underscored the ways in which cultural ascriptions can be radically destabilized by the impact of social violence and

enforced migration; it raised the question of whether any identity is immune to the exigencies of life. Consider kinship, the prevailing idiom in rural Africa for placing people and determining how they should relate to one another. "Kinship is like your buttocks," they say in Bunyole. "You can't cut it off."[7] "Kinship cannot die," say the Bagisu.[8] The consternation among Emmanuel's maternal kin when he and his family turned up in Mbale, effectively as refugees, indicates how inflexible people are when faced with an anomalous situation. But the fact that Emmanuel was fatherless, obliged to follow his mother to her natal country and become a surrogate mother for his little sister, reminds us that even the protocols of kinship can be traumatically disrupted, though they are regarded as immutable and natural. Nor is this necessarily a contemporary aberration, a repercussion of ethnic conflict in a neighboring country (Rwanda) and Idi Amin's despotic government in Uganda. The history of Africa's peoples is a history of upheavals and migrations, every one of which must have entailed the kind of disorientation and suffering that Emmanuel experienced. Under such circumstances, the idea of normativity is more like a consoling illusion, a source of security that people fall back upon when the gap between actuality and ideality becomes intolerably wide.

There is wisdom to be had, therefore, in approaching the social through the biographical. Although the notion of the human subject is construed very differently in different societies and through the history of European thought,[9] it is in the experience of persons—not of groups, animals, or things—that the world makes its appearance, albeit fragmentarily and fleetingly. The whole world does not exist for anyone. It is an idea. What exists are worlds within worlds, and the more we penetrate these microcosms, the more we come to question the generalizations we make concerning the hegemony of the macrocosm, whether this is conceived historically, culturally, or ethnically. It is therefore the indeterminate relationship, the lack of fit, the existential aporias between a person and the world in which he or she exists that become the focus of our anthropological concern.

ALL I COULD DO WAS USE SIGNS

"So they push us to school. To tell you the truth, Michael, my first years of school, probably up to when I was eleven—I have no memory of them. Either I intentionally shut them out or something like that, but I don't remember

anything good or interesting because I didn't understand anything the teachers were saying. All I could do was use signs. I would just sign, 'Oh, where are they going?' and go there. 'What are they doing?' I'd do that. Games—I couldn't play games because I didn't know what anyone was saying. Somebody tells you to run across. I didn't know what he meant. So I'd be excluded from doing that, whatever it was. The worst thing was, I couldn't tell anybody about my problems because, if I did, I'd be punished for trying to get out of going to school. So I kept quiet. It took me a long time to be as talkative as I am now. It wasn't until I was in secondary school that I began to speak a bit, because by then I'd made some friends and learned a bit more English. But even then, I wouldn't say much. I was a bit hesitant about communicating with people because of my fear of making a mistake or saying the wrong thing.

"Those primary school years were also difficult because before going to school in the morning, I had to work in my grandmother's garden, the *shamba*. You had to go dig before you did anything else. You'd wake at five o'clock in the morning, then go with your grandmother and dig, and after tilling the land you'd come back home and go off to school. You didn't have time to clean up or wash off the sweat. The problem was that the school was three kilometers from the place where we were staying, and if you were going to get there on time you'd have to run. If you walked, you'd be late and get punished. And so, you leave the *shamba* and run to school. No time to bathe, and anyway, to bathe you'd have to fetch water from the river, which was four kilometers away—the Manafa, as it is called. So after coming from the *shamba* you only had time to clean your hoe. The rule was simple: you are not supposed to leave sweat on it because it could rust. So you are supposed to clean the hoe and leave the hoe clean. Cleaning yourself didn't matter. So you run to school. And then you are caned. I don't remember any day during that period that I was not caned."

"By the teachers?"

"Yeah, it was like breakfast."

"Because it was a daily occurrence?"

"Truly. Every day. It only stopped when I was sixteen and went to secondary school. Up to then I don't remember a single day that I was not caned. The reason could have been because I was dirty every morning, or I was late (because I was late almost every day), or I was sleeping in class (which also happened every day). Now I know it was because I was tired and hungry, but at the time I didn't understand. And the beating was not like someone

coming along and giving you a rap or a smack. No, no, no. Beating was like an activity on its own. Teachers set aside a time to do it. I mean they could set aside half a period of teaching just for punishment. And I was almost always the first to be beaten because I was late, dirty, or had been caught dozing. Minimum every day I would receive six strokes of the cane. You had to lean over with your hands on the table, and they caned you at the base of your spine. Six for being late, six for being dirty, and six for not answering questions correctly. For me, the problem was that I couldn't even understand what the teacher was saying. I couldn't understand the questions, and I couldn't give the answers. And then there was after school, when you were supposed to run home, meet grandma, get your hoe, and go back to the garden for more work until seven o'clock, when it is too dark to do any more digging."

"Without having eaten anything all day?"

"Not always, because you'd often get the chance to take some leftovers from home, like a piece of sweet potato, cassava, or millet bread. You would hide it in your shorts or in your armpit, because no one would want to eat it if it had been kept in one of those places. Or you could spit on the food when everyone was looking, and so keep it until break or lunchtime without it being taken from you. The problem was that whenever you came to school with food, you reeked of it, and there would be those small, young boys waiting for you, waiting to take it away from you. So I would get used to going without food during the day, from eight in the morning to four or five in the evening. Sometimes I would be able to find some banana peelings and eat the softer part of them. Or you could go for the peelings of sweet potatoes from outside the teachers' homes. They peel their food, so you go and get those peelings and eat them. They were actually very fine and sweet."

"Would you eat in the evening, then, when your work was done?"

"Yeah, but you could never be sure of that meal either, because visitors would often come, and they had priority." ↑

story
analysis ↓

PUNISHMENT, PERSECUTION, AND PERVERSION

Food sharing is at the core of kinship. Providing succor and support to those who are dependent on you for their very existence is the moral basis of family life, and commensality affirms the mutual well-being of the household. However, throughout East Africa, men have migrated from rural villages to

find work in towns, and lives have been lost to HIV/AIDS, leaving countless children orphaned. Grandmothers have had to bear the burden of growing crops and feeding the orphaned grandchildren who now depend on them. Not only is food in short supply and farm labor exhausting; competition for scarce resources breeds resentment and ill will. As Erick Otieno Nyambedha observes in a recent study on western Kenya, "The sharing of food, once a token of warm relations between grandmothers and their grand-children, has now lost its charm and beauty and become a frugal part of day-to-day survival in a grim world."[10] One might also note that denying food was a traditional way of punishing children for being lazy, though deliberate starvation of children would not be tolerated.

It is also worth noting that among the Bagisu, physical punishment was a precondition for the attainment of manhood, and initiation (*imbalu*) was a kind of graduation ceremony for boys who had proven their ability to withstand extreme pain. Each boy had to stand stock still while his foreskin was cut and subcutaneous flesh stripped from around the glans penis. "The degree of pain entailed is never underplayed; the most commonly used descriptive phrases being 'fierce,' 'bitter,' and 'terrifying.' Only those who have faced this fact and overcome their fear can undergo the ordeal successfully."[11] Given the high value placed on male strength (*kamani*) and self-determination in Bagisu society, it is possible that Emmanuel's ordeals were seen as a necessary preparation for manhood. Certainly, his growing ability to endure painful beatings without complaint, achieving complete detachment from the ordeal, resonates with conventional Bagisu ideas about the need to dissociate oneself from emotions of fear and humiliation to attain transcendence. In Bagisu parlance, initiatory ordeals were forms of "punishment,"[12] not for an offense committed but to stir the neophyte into developing metaphysical power. This power consisted in being able to control one's emotions rather than being controlled by them.[13] Manhood was therefore a matter of deciding to submit oneself to the ordeal rather than shrinking from it. As one initiate put it, "No one has asked us to do it. No one is forcing us. We ourselves have overcome our fear. Now it is my heart itself which wants it. No one is forcing me. Father has not ordered me. It comes from my heart alone. Let me explain it this way, even though I am here talking with my friends I feel like a [disembodied] spirit-shadow (*cisimu*)."[14]

Clearly, Emmanuel achieved this dissociation and disembodiment. But where Bagisu initiates gained metaphysical power from mastering their emotions, Emmanuel gained nothing. His personal fortitude was not recognized

by others, and therefore gave him no social advantage. Proving himself capable of withstanding hardship entailed no redeeming transfiguration, no new social status, no right to assert himself. He remained like a child, unable to act and without a voice. He could do nothing except bow to the will of others, following their orders, doing what he was told, enduring their punishments. Reduced to the status of an object, he gradually became desensitized to life as if he was, indeed, a mere thing—without will, without consciousness, without feeling. In a sense, he was already a migrant, adrift and disoriented in a foreign environment, ignorant of the local language, lacking a place he could call his own.

Dismayed that there seemed to have been no one he could turn to, no place of refuge, I asked Emmanuel if any of his mother's brothers showed concern for his plight.[15] "No. In fact, they were avoiding us. And that's another problem I have with my uncles, by the way. I don't like my uncles because of that. By that time, my mum had got a job as a cleaner in the municipal offices in Mbale. She was living in town, and I was left behind in the village with my younger sisters. There was no one to protect me from my uncles and aunties. I was living with them, but they never liked us, no, no, no."

"So you were staying in your grandmother's house?"

"Yes."

"And your grandmother was the person taking care of you?"

"Yes."

"And your mother was how far away?"

"Uh, let me see. Thirteen miles."

"How often did you get to see her?"

"At first, she went early in the morning and came back in the evening. But it was expensive, transportwise, so she rented a room in the city center. We used to see her over the weekend, when she came back. But she was away most of the time. The problem for me was that I was stuck in my grandmother's house, and her sons and daughters were coming there regularly. You couldn't avoid them, even if you wanted to. They would come and eat supper with us. It was a kind of millet porridge, halfway between porridge and bread. My grandmother would break a big piece off behind her hand and hide it in a cloth. She would give my sister and me that piece later, because she knew we had not got enough to eat, because my uncles and those relatives would just grab food very fast, and we were very slow and young. So she used to give us that food afterward when we were alone, when we were sitting somewhere. We didn't have electricity in the village, and the only source of light was a

candle that was actually powered by kerosene, and kerosene is very expensive, so she used to blow it out and say, 'Eat, eat this fast before they come, eat.' So that's how we used to survive. And then there were days, of course, when we used to sit at home and she would prepare lunch. The problem is that when she prepared food, we had to eat it alone, because as soon as my uncles and the others came, that was it, you weren't going to have food. These big people wanted to eat, and they didn't care much about the rest of us. My mum was not told about any of this. And we did not dare tell her because the problem was, if we told her she would ask my grandmother, and if she asked my grandmother, my grandmother would ask the brothers and the sisters, and we would end up having even more problems."

Emmanuel tended to move between past and present tense, as if the events he recalled from twenty-five years ago had the force of something that had occurred only yesterday. There was a similar slippage between "I" and "we," as if he was mindful, as he spoke of his own tribulations, that they were shared by his younger brother Peter—when he returned home on visits—and his younger sisters, Mariam and Barbara.

"Yet they punished us, and when I talk about punishment it was not just a matter of refusing to give us food, no, these relatives would go drinking, come back drunk, and then unloose their sorrows on us. They'd just call us, saying, 'Line up and lie down.' Being beaten was not a problem for me, but my sister Mariam and my brother Peter, that was too much for me, so—I don't want to use the word, but I hated them from that point. These are kids, you know, I was ten years old, eleven. I could take it, but the two kids could not."

"What kind of abuse was it?"

"Actually, the name they called us was a name they called the cattle keepers. They called them 'bararo.' It was a term of abuse, like the word 'nigger.' The way I understand the word 'bararo' is the same way I understand the word 'nigger.' Originally, it was negro, meaning black, and not really a term of abuse at all. It was like calling someone 'Asian.' The same with 'mulalo.' It defined a people who came from a particular place, people who herded cattle for survival, but then 'mulalo' became a term of abuse."

"You say you were beaten as well as abused verbally."

"I got used to the word 'mulalo.' I didn't really understand what it meant anyway. But being told to lie down on the ground was actually preparing you to be caned. When they come back in the evening they are drunk, or if it's the weekend they start drinking in the morning and come back in the middle

of the day. They call you from the house, where you are probably in the shade because it is very hot. We're talking about a heat of about thirty to thirty-two degrees Celsius, but they tell you to lie down. So you lie down. There was the grave of my great-grandfather in the middle of the courtyard, and so they tell you to put your feet up on the grave and then you lie down in that slanting kind of position, me first, then my young sister and my young brother. And these guys are celebrating beating us, caning us. Whether they gave excuses I don't remember. I just remember the beatings and how I could just control the pain. What was really painful for me was watching my younger siblings get punished for no reason. It still pains me to remember. Even today, I would rather somebody beat me than beat the next guy. I always knew that I could take more beatings than the guy next to me, and until now I still have the same feeling. Even with Nanna, whenever she is sick, I say, 'I would prefer being sick because I can take it.' Of course I can't really take the sickness away from her, but that's the feeling I have. That's how I developed it and how I became protective of other people, especially Barbara, my youngest sister. She was never caned. Yet she ended up being the loser because we could not care for her properly. She wasn't getting fed regularly or being bathed, because they were either caning us or sending us on funny errands or taking us to the gardens or something like that."

"In one of your letters to me last year, you described how demoralized you had become in Denmark. Did you feel as demoralized as a child, suffering these beatings and unable to help your more vulnerable younger siblings?"

"There was one time I felt like that. This is a bit tricky. It was the lowest point. My auntie—"

"Your mother's sister?"

"Yes, her blood sister. What she did probably prepared me for everything that I could stand. I woke up one morning when my grandmother wasn't there. I didn't know she had gone, but she wasn't there. My auntie had been doing bad things to us for some time, but this morning she wakes up and tells me to undress and tells my young sister Mariam to undress as well, and then she calls her brother—she had a young brother called William—called him to come. And we are all in the same room, and then she is telling me basically to lie together with my sister and telling her young brother to lie with her in the same room. When we resisted, she throws me and my sister out of the room. We're basically naked, and I didn't care about that as much, but then she, she, she goes—how do you call that, how do I put that politely? She goes to the toilet, she excretes in the room, in the house itself. In the village we

don't have toilets in the house, we're supposed to walk and go to a latrine, but she really does it in the room, and then she calls me and my sister to clean it up."

"When you say that she made you and Mariam lie down together, you mean—"

"Yeah, she wanted us to have intercourse."

"Seriously!"

"Yeah, it was very serious. And when I say, 'Your aunt cannot ask you to do something like that,' she punishes me and my sister by telling us to clean up her excrement. And by the way, we're not supposed to come with a hoe or anything, we're supposed to collect it with our hands—yeah—literally wipe it up like cow dung and then take it out. So as I was hesitating, not wanting to do what she says, she says, 'Now, Emma, you go and get leaves and come clean me up.' And by the way, I'm talking about an auntie who is over eighteen years old—she was a big woman, she had boyfriends, we used to take messages to them, so she was an adult, she was not a young kid. So she tells me to clean her, and I think that was the point when I started to think of running away from that place. But what kept me going was the thought of my siblings. The problem was that there was no one I could ask to help. If I told someone, my auntie would get to hear of it, and there would be another war. Anyway, I think she was very good at convincing each and everybody that everything was okay. The problem was that she was almost always the one left to take care of us whenever the others went away. So that was how I got to the point where I could take anything. I didn't care, didn't blink. Even today, anything you told me to do, even walk around naked, I would do it without a second thought and come back here, pick up my coffee cup again and be okay."

"Did your auntie resent having to look after you and your sister?

"Probably."

"And she had to express that resentment by being unkind to you."

"I wouldn't think so, because, first of all, this is the most strange part of it—when my grandmother wanted to rest or have a free day at home, my aunt actually offered to look after us. If my grandmother was going for a burial or some other event, my aunt would offer to stay behind and keep us. She was never forced to do this. The problem was that no one ever questioned her. She was like a queen in that village. Everyone knew her. No one would believe our word against hers. And so we went on being punished, receiving the same treatment over and over again. She didn't resent keeping us, no. I think she

had this funny feeling of wanting to bully us, and probably because everybody was doing the same thing, she did it too. Ironically, she got pregnant, and then she died eight months into the pregnancy. There was a complication, and she passed away. Even at that moment, I refused to go for the burial. I said, 'No, I can't,' even though it was really bad in our village not to go to a burial. But I didn't, I didn't go. And when I left that village in 1984 to stay with my mum, I did not return until 1990, when my grandmother passed away. She was the only person I would go there for, the only reason that would take me back there. Her death was the last time I went to that village, until 2007, when Nanna wanted to see the village. I went with her. Even then, they did not want us there, and I have extremely bad feelings whenever I go down there. Extremely bad feelings." Emmanuel interrupted his narrative and called to Alice Maria, "Are you okay?" Maria responded in Danish. She was fine. But I couldn't help remarking the connection between his sudden concern for Maria and his painful recollections of Peter and Mariam. And for a fleeting moment I asked myself whether Emmanuel's spontaneous responsiveness to the ordeal of his siblings—answering the summons of their suffering, as it were, and suffering the eclipse of himself on their behalf—exemplified the ethical responsiveness of which Levinas spoke.

"So the punishment went on, and the worst of it was not what happened to me but what happened to my young siblings. I didn't want anybody to touch them. Even when we went to school, the worst part was that we got separated. I went to one school and they went to another, and that almost killed me. I did not want to go to a different school, I wanted to stay with my younger siblings. I was not strong. I almost gave up. I ran away from home, from my grandmother's place. I took off. I walked and walked and ended up in somebody's home, where I started cleaning the house. I didn't know them, but I cleaned their home anyway. They asked me where I'm from. I didn't want to tell them, because I was scared they would send me back, just like that.

"It was from that period that I stopped being immobile, I stopped being home. That's the time I realized that if life got too hard for me, I had the alternative to leave."

When Emmanuel got up from the table to talk to Maria again, I asked myself whether this was what people do in an impasse, with all passages blocked. Desperate to recover some sense of freedom in mobility, they hit the road. Had the seeds of this solution been planted in Emmanuel's mind when, as a small child, he learned of his father's flight from Rwanda, and later, when

his family fled the Iteso region where they had no right to be, no way of making a viable life?

Emmanuel returned to the table and apologized for the interruption.

"Were you in school during that period?" I asked. "That period when you were moving from place to place?"

"No, no, I wasn't in school."

"When you said before that you were not strong, what did you mean?"

"I was not strong enough to protect Peter and Mariam."

"From what?"

"From the bullying at their school. But I developed a sense, a trick or ability to make friends, and I started making friends that I thought could help protect my brother and sister. I started finding ways of getting friendly with the bullies, so they could actually save my brother and sister, or let them be. And I also developed a trick of making friends at the school where I went, because it was the only way."

"What was the trick?"

"The trick was complicated, rough, but to me it was very simple. I stole some of the things that we came with from Tanzania, things we came with that were very rare in the village. I stole them from home. My trousers, the shirts we were not allowed to wear because we would look strange in the village. I would carry them, hide them, and take them to the bullies so I could buy them off."

"Wow."

"Yeah, I literally bought them off, you know. Things like spoons, the things we had before we came to Bugisu. I gave them out, and mum has never recovered them, even now."

"But she must have known they were disappearing."

"In the beginning, no, because they were locked away, and she was never there. So I had a way of breaking the box on the side. I could pull out one thing at a time and take it to buy off those people. It was the only way I could survive the bullying. I bought them off with those small things we got when we left the village where my father disappeared. And I did the same thing to help protect my brother and sister, right up to the time we all left my mum's village and went to the same primary school."

"When was that?"

"Around 1984. My mum was still working as a cleaner in Mbale, and she had met our stepfather, who was a primary school teacher in that area. We all moved to where he lived, and he encouraged me to go back to school,

even though I had to begin again at primary five. Most kids were starting secondary school at my age, but I was far behind. The prime of my life, I lost it. But my stepfather helped me with my English, so now I began to understand most of the things the teachers were saying. Although he is my stepfather, we have always called him father—so my father got me tutoring with other teachers, for other courses, and I ended up performing quite well with that assistance, so when I reached primary seven, I was under his wing and he tutored me, trained me, and we became very close. It is in that period that my mum got pregnant and had twins, though one of the twins passed away. He had a hole in his heart, and at that time, of course . . . money, issues of knowledge, and so on . . . we didn't know that could actually be repaired. So David passed away, though Paul is still there, our sixth in the family. That is why we say we are six. So I became a babysitter for Paul as well as the others. I was very good at looking after children, and Barbara and Paul grew up without much age difference between them. They became my kids, and I paid their school fees right up to the time they finished their schooling. Even when I started working and came to Denmark, I continued paying their fees."

"Can I backtrack a little and ask you to talk more about the changes you experienced when you moved from your mother's village to live with your stepfather in Mbale?"

"For two years, from primary five to primary seven, I hardly ever got punished for anything. I mean, I could get punishment if I got a lower mark than I was expected to. I accepted caning as part of the system. I didn't care so much about caning. I developed a mechanism in me whenever I was going to be caned. You could actually tell me to lie down and you could cane me, but I would just allow very little pain to go in. I learned how to do that because there is no way that I could take being caned every day. Basically, some teachers make it a point that if you cry out, they add to the punishment. If you talked or said 'Ow,' you'd get two more strokes. So you learned to be a corpse as a way of dodging the pain. I also learned to accept caning as a punishment for low marks or laziness. I used it as a way of pushing myself to do better."

"Did you ever see your mother's people during those years?"

"By the time I finished primary seven, the relationship between me and my relatives, my aunties and uncles, was at zero—I had nothing to do with them. In fact, whenever they would come visiting, I would go away for a day or two, stay with my friends or something, and that has continued until now."

BUILDING SMOKE

There were moments, as Emmanuel recounted his life story, when I felt as if I was listening to a tale from the Brothers Grimm or the corpus of Kuranko oral narratives that I recorded in northern Sierra Leone forty years ago. Emmanuel's story was as stark as the experiential ground it covered. First, there were the dramatic contrasts between an absent father or lost paternal heritage and the harsh realities of everyday life in his maternal village. Then there were the Manichean contrasts between innocence and malevolence: the famished and persecuted child whose plight was only momentarily relieved by running away, bribing bullies, and preparing to be beaten by turning himself to stone.

In his recourse to what he called "tricks," Emmanuel calls to my mind the trickster figures in African folktales who reclaim by fair means or foul what has been unjustly withheld or taken from them. Many years ago, Kuranko informants helped me understand the ethical reasoning that governed the structure of these tales.[16] The initial situation is one in which a person in a vulnerable and relatively powerless position is treated unjustly by someone in a position of authority. The paradigmatic relationship is between younger brother and elder brother, though other relationships of inequality are also implied: between junior cowife and senior cowife, between husband and wife, between father and child, between chief and commoner. Crucial to the story that unfolds is the characterization of the authority figure as a slow-witted dolt, by contrast with the quick-witted underling. It is the underling's superior intelligence that enables him to turn the tables on his oppressor and thus prevent the latter's continued abuse of his authority. Indeed, the denouement of the story often involves the clever, small, and agile status inferior actually displacing the status superior, effectively combining the virtue of moral intelligence and the social position with which it is ideally associated.

If one can reduce the ethics of the trickster story to a single principle, it is this: that trickery and deceit are justified when they help redress a social wrong, but not when used to secure a personal advantage. Paradoxically, therefore, the restoration of moral order depends on actions that are, strictly speaking, amoral. This implies that the difference between ethical and unethical action is determined not by measuring an action against some abstract norm but by considering its context and social *consequences*.

This pragmatic perspective helps us understand Emmanuel's ethical stratagems for surviving an oppressive and nonnegotiable childhood situation.

When he steals clothing from the trunk in his grandmother's house, he is acting like Jack in *The History of Jack and the Bean-Stalk.* Just as Jack steals from the ogre articles that once belonged to his father (whom the ogre dispossessed and murdered),[17] so Emmanuel lays claim to his inheritance as a way of transforming a situation he has, up to then, been powerless to act upon. He is, indeed, playing the role of a trickster or daemon, redistributing possessions to create a more equitable and endurable situation, not only for himself but for those who are dependent on him. As for Emmanuel's action of running away, he suffers remorse for having abandoned his siblings but achieves a sense of freedom to move in a world that had previously been constrictive and closed. However, the absolute deprivation he has suffered in his mother's village now translates into an assumption that he has the right to a life elsewhere. The ethics of reciprocity informs his every move. In cleaning the homes of strangers, he justifies a claim on their hospitality and help. He is already a migrant. Rather than suffering the degradation of being in a place where he has no voice and no freedom of movement, he chooses degradation in the place of a stranger, in the hope that the natural home of which he was deprived through no fault of his own will be found elsewhere. Choice is the operative word. For even though he continues to be abused, he embraces the abuse, even boasting of his ability to withstand what others could not possibly endure. Sartre perceptively refers to this tactic as "provocative impotence," since the disempowered individual "reacts with an aggressive show of the passivity to which he has been reduced, and arrogantly takes on himself what the other did to him." Sartre goes on to say that this attitude "in its pure form" is found "among colonized peoples at a certain stage of their struggle . . . when they become conscious of their oppression yet still lack the means to drive out the oppressor; in this case, the challenge, an ineffectual ideal, demonstrates at once the impossibility and the necessity of revolt."[18]

In every folktale there is also a supernatural helper, a powerful intercessory without whom the questing hero could not survive the vicissitudes he encounters or the obstacles thrown in his path. Throughout Emmanuel's narrative, the figures that would customarily provide support fail to do so (his maternal uncles), while the figure of a stepparent, the embodiment of evil in so many folktales, becomes the means by which his dreams are realized.

Emmanuel did so well at school that he won a scholarship to one of Uganda's top secondary schools, renowned for the political leaders who had gone there, including Milton Obote. It was a boarding school, and Emmanuel

described it as "the Eton of Uganda." But even though he drew increasing satisfaction from his studies, Emmanuel continued to find himself marginalized because of his impoverished, rural background and stigmatized by the wealthier kids. "I had the smallest mattress in thickness, the smallest blanket in width and length, and the smallest pair of sheets on my bed. I had no pillow. The bed was one of those you can fold up and go traveling with. A safari bed, we called it. I was the only student with such a bed. All this was another big problem for me. I had to work out how best to survive this new situation. So I developed a sense of making fun. I became the funny guy, making fun of everything and making friends that way."

To his repertoire of "tricks," Emmanuel now added an existential strategy common to the oppressed in every human society—the strategy of currying favor with one's oppressors by acting the clown, subverting an oppressive situation through ridicule, mockery, and gallows humor.

"Did you ever make fun of yourself? Put yourself down?"

"No, no, no, I avoided that totally. The fun I used to make was related to experiences I met along the way. Telling stories but in a funny way. Whenever I could make people laugh, I was the happiest person around. I did the same with Nanna. In the beginning I had to really make sure Nanna was happy, but of course I sensed later that the mode of our storytelling is cultural, based on Ugandan experience. Nanna is Danish and could not understand it, so there are times when my jokes or the funny things I say get lost in translation, and Nanna no longer responds—"

"Can you give me an example of this style of storytelling?"

"Yeah, like an example could be . . . it's a long time since I've done this, but I could tell a story, for example . . . there was an old man, and the old man had a daughter, and this daughter had a problem because she could not get pregnant. She was married but she could not conceive a child, so she had to seek the medicine man's help. So the witch doctor advises the girl or the woman to wake up one morning when it is still dark and go to an anthill. On the anthill she will see a mushroom that has not yet widened and resembles a penis. She will go and sit on it. [Emmanuel laughed, and so did I, recalling an identical Kuranko tale.] She will sit on that and get pregnant. So whenever I would tell this story, I would tell it quickly up to that point, and then everyone would burst out laughing, knowing exactly what I was talking about."

"Did you make the stories up?"

"In most cases, yes."

"But these are so typically African, you must have learned to tell such stories—you must have known this style of storytelling."

"Yes, the style of telling and the creation of suspense and mystery—that was what I learned as a child."

"And the exaggeration!"

"I was very good at building smoke, as we used to call it. I would build smoke on the story, even if the story was sad. I didn't want to tell sad stories. I used to turn even the folklore stories that were very sad into something funny, because I didn't want people to be sad. I wanted people to be laughing, because I grew up not laughing. If you laughed, you'd be asked, 'Why you are laughing?' you see, so I wanted people to laugh. People would laugh, and sometimes they would come and push me and tap me, and that felt good to me. And that is how I could survive most of the bullying and the pressure on me. Whenever you make fun and people laugh, they'll share bites to eat. So I could get my basic necessities that way. It was a survival thing I developed. I started it with my brothers and sisters. Creating stories from what I heard from the older people, making them into funny stories. If I met a person on the way, I might notice his clothes or his way of walking and turn that into something interesting and funny. Instead of abusing someone or describing something that was wrong, I would work out how to tell it in a funny way. But when I started telling stories like that to Nanna, it was lost in translation—she couldn't get it. She would ask, 'What do you mean?' But when you are telling something funny and somebody asks you about a detail, you lose the story. Yeah, you lose the whole trail and it is no longer funny. And Nanna and I began to lose that ability to make fun of the hard things we were up against in our life."

Comedy is a common antidote to tragedy. In Paul Auster's novel *The Book of Illusions,* his main character, David Zimmer, loses his wife and two sons in a plane crash just one week short of his tenth wedding anniversary. Many months later, Zimmer is surprised to find himself laughing at the antics of a Chaplinesque figure in a silent movie. He searches out more movies by this long-forgotten slapstick star and gradually begins writing a book about him. "Writing about comedy had been no more than a pretext, an odd form of medicine that I had swallowed every day for over a year on the off chance that it would dull the pain inside me."[19]

It is often said that comedians come from unhappy childhoods. Speaking of the defensive power of humor, Art Buchwald commented, "When you make the bullies laugh, they don't beat you up," and John Dryden claimed

that "the true end of satire is the amendment of vices." But it is to Henri Bergson that we owe one of the most compelling analyses of the comedic power of exaggeration.[20] An event or experience is <u>tragic</u> because it utterly overwhelms us. We cannot rest for thinking of what has befallen us, rehearsing it in our minds, unable to shake it off. We are, in effect<u>, possessed</u>. We are at the mercy of our situation. Our power to act or speak is nullified, and we are rendered immobile and mute. But by telling a story about the events that devastated us, we reclaim a sense of agency. Not only do we now call the shots, but we separate ourselves from the events as they were originally experienced. However, this dissociation or detachment requires that the events we ourselves suffered be recast as events that befell a depersonalized character. A woman who cannot conceive a child is a potentially tragic figure, but in the tall tale she becomes a figure of fun, a stereotype. We laugh at a situation that in reality is too close, too real, too tragic to entertain. To use Emmanuel's own words, we "buy off" the situation by rendering it ridiculous. We separate ourselves from the hapless victim and recover our power to determine events as retrospective commentators on the human condition. The comic is not the opposite of the tragic so much as a strategy for <u>counter-manding the tragic with distance and indirection</u>. Tragedy befalls us like a bolt from the blue, a natural disaster, a physical accident, a random act of violence. Such traumatic events eclipse and diminish us, and we withdraw into ourselves, feeling singled out, silenced, and powerless in the face of forces we can neither comprehend nor control. Though tragedy is suffered in solitude and silence, comedy opens up the possibility of transfiguring the original event by replaying it in such dramatically altered and exaggerated form that it is experienced as "other." It is often said of tragedy that healing takes time. With distance comes release. The comedic is the ultimate expression of this kind of distancing and release, and it entails three critical transformations in our experience. <u>First, the comedic restores a sense of</u> agency. Second, it fosters emotio<u>nal detachmen</u>t. Third, i<u>t entails shared laughter</u>, thus <u>returning us to a community of others</u>. In taking us out of ourselves and eclipsing our emotions, comedy returns us to the world, allowing us to see that we are a part of *la comédie humaine* rather than a victim of it. In this sense we are able to review the human condition from a general rather than exclusively personal standpoint. This is why comic characters are always stereotypes—"the mother," "the daughter," "the senior cowife," "the wicked stepmother"—rather than particular individuals, why they are often depicted as animals rather than persons, why they have one-track minds rather than

[margin note: the ethics and power of humor.]

complex sensibilities, why their personalities are one-dimensional, and why what they have in common is given more weight than their idiosyncratic features. Moreover, insofar as they transcend private and particular identifications, funny stories can be more widely shared than tragic ones.

But there must be events that defy such imaginative reworking, that cannot be escaped, disguised, or bought off. And so I asked Emmanuel if we could go back to the time when his aunt tried to force him into an incestuous relationship with his sister.

"Actually," Emmanuel said, "I think you are, if I'm not mistaken, only the fourth or the fifth person I've told about that. The reason is that one of the main taboos where I come from is against seeing the private parts of your auntie. It is a very big taboo, because aunties have a very serious and strong role in your upbringing, in your mannerisms, in your life, in your future marriage, and so on. So having seen what I should not have seen became something I had to put aside, something I could never tell anybody, because if I told it to someone, especially in Uganda, I would be the person, not the auntie, who would be in trouble. Now, having seen my auntie in that condition and having been made to do what I did became a no-go zone in my life. I never even told my mother. The only people who know of it are Nanna, my sister, and my brother-in-law, because he had to know where his wife was coming from."

"So there are things a person simply does not joke about, that are too serious to—".

"Precisely. You couldn't make any fun out of it. You cannot make fun out of your aunt telling you to have intimate relations with your sister. It is beyond belief."

"It would have been breaking an absolute taboo."

"The worst taboo. Nothing rivals it. Even seeing your sister naked is a taboo, or thinking sexual thoughts about your sister. Until I grew up and started dating or having girlfriends, I could never speak of it."

"It seems unforgivable."

"Yes. If a person was a serial killer, that would be a different issue altogether. You could explain that in many ways. Even though killing is wrong, you could understand why that person might be driven to kill. But if a person tells you to have intimacy with your sister, or with your brother, and they do that—well, until recently, I couldn't put words on that. It's what sent me out of the village, it's what made me dislike or hate everybody related to my auntie, apart from my mum. I excused my mum, but I don't know whether it is a

biological reason or if I had justification for it because she was busy or something like that, but I never really told her."

"Did your mother ever find out from others or ever have any idea?"

"I think she did, or maybe my grandmother told her, because I think my uncle, my young uncle who was also in the same village, must have told my grandmother, yeah. She could have been told. Because I realized later that whenever my mum talked about going to the village, she would make sure my aunt was not there before we went. And whenever my aunt came to visit, my mum was very prickly, you know. But being sisters, that close relationship, I think she had no choice but to avoid the whole topic. But I don't think she knew about this issue of us being naked in the room. She knew about the punishment my aunt was subjecting us to, but I don't think—"

"It would have been devastating if she knew the full story."

"Yes, it would, for her. Until recently we didn't talk about it, but then I had a talk with my sister when I was back in Uganda this January. It was the first time we ever talked openly together about what happened. I call her Mama Ali, because her firstborn is called Ali. I said to her, 'Mama Ali, do you remember our auntie Namibia?' She said, 'Yeah, our witch auntie?' I said, 'Yeah.' I said, 'Do you remember what she did to us?' She said, 'Yeah, I do. I wanted to tell Dada Ali [her husband], but I haven't.' I said, 'Okay, no problem, you tell him.' You see, she was thinking of my position if she told him the whole story. I told her, 'No, tell him what you think.' Because there were times when my sister would get angry over some small thing, and my brother-in-law would call me and say, 'Your sister is angry, and I don't know why; I don't know what has happened.' So I told Mama Ali, 'You'd better tell your husband about the way you feel sometimes and about what is affecting you.' There were two things affecting her: that experience with our auntie was one, and the other was not knowing where our father came from, not knowing any of his family. So first we solved the issue of our experiences. We talked about everything—we had a very long day that day talking about everything, and I can tell you I've never seen my sister so happy. After that day, she was really a very excited woman. A weight had been lifted from her head. I think she had been carrying it—maybe she thought she had imagined it, maybe she was not really sure it had happened at all. So then, the next thing was to solve the issue of where our father came from. Luckily, we did that as well. We dealt with the two things that had been weighing so much on her. In my case, I dealt with these things by learning to hold them in and thinking of only one small bit at a time, never wanting them to affect me. My biggest fear was

that those experiences would make me have a negative reaction or relationship to other people. But luckily, I think that by and large I turned that experience into something positive. But I never told anybody the story about my auntie and the issue of cleaning her and so on, and that picture has remained in me up until now. It is a very bad picture, and I didn't want anybody else to experience it."

Once again, I was struck by the ethical emphasis that Emmanuel placed on relationships. He appeared to be less mindful of how the infringement of a moral law affected him—a trauma suffered or a shame endured—than on how it had damaged relations among the six individuals closest to him. In having recourse to silence and forgetting, Emmanuel might be accused of avoiding an issue that required a talking cure, a confession, an expiation. But, as a Ugandan, the ethical priority was not revisiting the past but looking toward the future. Moving on, as we say. Finding a way around an obstacle rather than confronting it head on.[21]

And so, after reminding Emmanuel of how he dealt with bullying by becoming an entertainer, a comedian, I asked, "How did you deal with this other issue, concerning your aunt?"

"By not thinking about it. By trying to forget it. I literally closed it down. I mean I never spoke of it before the day I talked about it with my sister. I could never bring it up in any situation, never. I totally killed it off. I continued to have a very good relationship with my sisters, my brothers, and so on, but I closed that memory totally and never told anyone about it. It was simple, really. I pretended it never happened. The bullying was a daily thing, a daily activity, so I had to find ways of dealing with that. There is only so much you can take. I could take any verbal abuse—anyone could start abusing me from morning to evening, from now to next year, and I wouldn't care. But physical abuse—there is a limit to what I can take. Especially, I hate being punished for something I have not done. If you saw me being punished for something I didn't do, you would soon see how those old memories come back, how everything will come up again, and I will be remembering how they punished me when I was a child even though I had done nothing to deserve it. You would see me change. I would be very different."

"I think I'm beginning to understand your experience in Denmark, because, in a sense, when you were telling me yesterday about your experiences here, it was as if you were being punished every day for something you hadn't done."

"Precisely, yeah."

"You had done everything right—you had done everything that was expected of you here in Denmark—yet you were still not finding work. You were still being punished, as it were. So this was the limit for you? This is what you could not take?"

"Yes. After six, seven years, it was really pushing it, and the reason was that Nanna and I had chosen to have this relationship. I was part and parcel of it. I was there, half-half, so there was no way I could just back out of it. But even so, it reached the point where I said, no, I cannot live in a place where there is nothing I can do. There's no way you can tell me that in the whole country there is literally nothing for me to do."

"You said that when you were a child, in Uganda, and the situation become unbearable, you could always move. You could always find some other household—"

"Yes, or some other place."

"But here you were totally stuck."

"Yes, totally, between two places, here and Nanna's parents' place. And I tell you, Michael, I got tired of it. I never get tired of anything, but I tried *everything* I learned in my life, in all the books I read, to survive this situation—avoiding going to Nanna's parents' home for a period, maybe for three months at a time, giving excuses for why I wasn't working or why I wasn't visiting them. Or I would lie to my friends. Even to Nanna I would lie. Nanna, this weekend I'm going to see so and so. So and so has called me, so I'm going there."

"You were ashamed to be seen without work, without prospects?"

"Yes. I was ashamed. What kind of person am I, who cannot find work, who cannot support his family? I would stay here, lock the door, and watch TV, or browse the Internet or sometimes read a book, though not much. I became very selective of what I would read, you know. I'd say, 'What can I reread now.' I'd say, 'Ah, let me look at the atlas.' So I would start studying geography again. But why? Because I did not want to sit and think, 'Should I take a beer?' Or, 'Should I go and smoke?' Or, 'What should I do now? What can I do now?' So this was basically me, here. To tell you the truth, for six years [Emmanuel chuckled], I was never stuck for something to do!"

"Like you said earlier, it was like being in prison."

"Yes, and as I told Nanna, it is a wall-less prison.[22] You're in prison, there are no walls, but where to go? Traveling to Uganda, you need money. If I left Denmark for a certain period, I would not be able to get back into the country. How do you call that? Status, your residential status is reviewed

immediately, so coming back becomes very hard. The excuse that you are coming to see your family might not work again. And going to Uganda without money is worse than being in Denmark without a job. Because how are you going to start again? Even those who might be sympathizing with you say, 'You left us here and went to Denmark—what happened?' Even if they are not laughing at you, you definitely know that everybody is going to be cynical. 'Welcome back, Emma, how are you doing? How did you do in Denmark?' I mean, such questions kill you because in your small world you say, 'Why did I even come back?' Going to stay with my mum would be very difficult, too, so I was driven to stay on here. And not only that, I was thinking of the money I had spent on my education in Denmark, so much money. Two years of education in Denmark is a horrendous amount of money—it's too much—and then you sit at home and they start telling you what to do. You are literally told everything. Come here, do this, send this application, go here, go there. When I tried to be proactive, like going to the municipal office here that finds people to fill vacancies in Danish companies, I would say, 'Ma'am, can you help me? Do you have companies that need anybody, from a cleaner to anything?' She says, 'No, sir.' They send me away, this office that is supposed to help me. Michael, I didn't need to go walking around looking for jobs. That office could tell me, 'Here's a company that wants this and this. The official language is English. You speak both Danish and English. You might apply there.' But no, I am told there is nothing, over and over again."

"How did you explain this to yourself?"

"Simple, my rationalization was simple. I used to think, yeah, the economy is not good, so they are not hiring. Or they probably need somebody with longer work experience in Denmark. Or they need someone with a different qualification."

"So you were giving them the benefit of the doubt."

"Precisely. And that is probably what kept me sane. If I admitted that I was not getting the job because I'm black, that would have killed me. I would have probably given up a long time ago. But I kept on telling myself that with the qualifications I had, including a master's in applied economy and finance, there must be somebody out there, and I would find that somebody. But by 2009, 2010, there was no longer that hope, no longer any explanation I could come up with."

"At that point, did you come to the conclusion—you were honest with yourself and said, it's because I'm Ugandan that—"

"Yes, I started even telling Nanna now, openly I told her, 'Nanna, these are the real problems. First, my age. Second, where I come from. Third, the way I look. I don't think it is qualifications, I don't think it is a lack of positions to be filled, not at all. It's those three things. This was in 2009, 2010. By this time, Nanna would ask me something and I would not answer. It was too painful to respond to her questions, even when she greeted me. She might ask, 'Emma, today you sent an application, where did you send it?' I wouldn't answer, because it had reached a point where I told myself I would never get a job in Denmark ever. I even went looking for a job as a sweeper or cleaner, but they told me I was overqualified. I looked for jobs that suited my education, and they told me, 'Ah, there are many who have applied for this position who are more qualified than you.' Those were the answers I was getting from almost everybody. Either I was overqualified or there were people more qualified to take the job."

CHEAP PLASTIC SANDALS

By the time Nanna suggested we break for lunch, I had lost track of time. Emmanuel's story had, by turns, absorbed, amused, and perturbed me. It had also made me angry, despite my conviction that decrying the injustices of this world is seldom the best method for dealing with them, for the perpetrators of social violence are often immune to our outrage and indifferent to the consequences of their own actions, while the causes of social injustice all too often remain beyond our power to change. It was for this reason that, over lunch, I turned the talk to the ingenious ways in which Emmanuel had come to terms with his situation and the uncanny similarity of coping strategies in cultures across the world. One of these strategies is to rework our experiences of adversity as stories, thus sharing with others the ordeals we have undergone. Not only does confession free us from thralldom to what has been repressed; it clears the way for a fresh start in relationships that have been lived under a cloud of ambiguity and shame. There is no more moving example of this transformation than Emmanuel's trip to Uganda and his decision to recall with his sister Mariam the abuse they had suffered at the hands of their maternal aunt and to clarify exactly what had happened. I remembered an e-mail I received from Emmanuel in October 2010 in which he expressed gratitude for my willingness to remunerate him if I published his story and for providing a "breath of hope and an eye opener." Just as Mariam had been

liberated by Emmanuel's recounting of events that she had, for many years, scarcely believed to have actually occurred, so Emmanuel, inspired by Mariam's desire to know more about their father, seemed to have come to his own reckoning with the past. I had been so troubled, however, by the echoes in Emmanuel's humiliations in Denmark of his maltreatment and marginalization in his mother's village, that I had interrupted his story about his schooling in Uganda and now suggested we go back to his boarding school years.

"Initially," Emmanuel said, "I didn't perform very well. Too much of my time was taken up with appeasing my classmates and catching up with the schooling I had missed.

"I was much older than the average student. At least two to three years older. So by the time I began secondary school, I had to deal with the pressure of meeting my basic needs and the pressure of being older but not yet able to convert that into being better or the best in class. I failed to do that. Why? Because I was spending more time solving the basic needs thing, getting something to eat from others, appeasing them. And though I passed my O-levels with a poor performance, considering my abilities, I now faced new pressures because of the opposite sex. There was an understanding in the school that every boy should have a girlfriend. Those who had girlfriends were good at sports or studies, or they had money or were popular. I didn't know how I was going to survive this new experience. I was the oldest in the class, every class I was going to, and all the boys had girlfriends except me. The girls communicated with me. But I was afraid of them. I had no money to buy them presents. And I was spending all my time amusing and appeasing the other boys. So there it was, silently killing me, and since I really wanted to be like the other boys, I also wanted to have a girlfriend. And that brings me to my second most memorable situation in secondary school. When I reached the third year, I was suspended from school—for a full month. I was sent home because I had been working so hard to get a girlfriend that I ended up being caught sitting with a girl."

"How did everyone else get away with having a girlfriend?"

"That's the point—they knew the system. Me, I was a newcomer, and you know, I had never developed a sense of having relationships with the opposite sex. I learned later that the others did it by avoiding being seen, because even touching a girl's shoulder warranted expulsion. They would hide at night, get out of the dormitories through windows or whatever, and go and meet their girlfriends in the bushes. I thought it was, you know, okay if I did that too, so

one evening I was sitting with a girl, and I got arrested and suspended. The problem was, how do I go and explain to my mum that I had been suspended from school because of a girl? She's struggling to pay fees and everything, so I didn't tell her, I didn't even go home, I went and hid at my friend's place. The problem is that my mum got a letter. The school was very wise. They give you a letter of suspension, and they also send one to your mum [Emmanuel laughed]. So when you go back to school after the full month, you are required to come with your parent. So how do I convince my mum? I went around and found a friend. I had become so good at making friends, amusing them with stories, entertaining them; I had made friends with a full colonel in the military, and by then, in the '80s, having a friend who was a soldier, a colonel—[Emmanuel whistled to emphasize this value of this connection]. So we had become friends, and he is the one I took to school as a 'parent.' But they didn't allow it. They said, 'Emma, I thought you said your father was dead? So who is this?' Of course they caught me in the lie. I couldn't explain—"

"You really are a trickster!"

"That was the problem. When I started secondary school, I didn't tell anybody that my father was dead. Nobody knew. Because being an orphan was a very negative thing.

"A stigma?"

"Yes, indeed. And so I had told lots of stories about my father."

"And you had to turn up with someone?"

"Yes, I had to come with someone. But I was so occupied with trying to convince my friends that my father was alive and was a soldier or something, that I forgot that when I registered for school I had actually registered as an orphan [Emmanuel laughed at his entanglement], so I was caught in the lie. So they told me, 'Go back and bring your parent.' I had to go to my mum. That was the first time that I had approached my mum with a problem. What has helped me a lot in life is knowing that when you have no alternative but to do or say the wrong thing, things will only get worse unless you go back and correct your mistake. So if I lied about something, I would immediately start thinking, 'Oh, what lie will I have to use next?' So I usually went back and corrected my mistake. I went straight to my mum and told her, 'Mum, for the last month I have been away, suspended, and I've been living with so and so. When I went back to school, I went with somebody that was not really my parent. I didn't want to bother you, but the school knew I didn't have a father, and they sent me away to collect a parent. I told them I would

go and collect you.' I didn't know what to expect from my mum. My mum just kept quiet for a while. Then she said, 'Okay, when do they want me?' I said, 'They want you tomorrow.' So my mum never reacted. And Michael, that was new to me, because one thing my mum was good at was appeasing, but another thing she was good at was punishing, though my mum would never punish you for what you had not done. I think that is why I love my mum. By the way, when I talk about punishment, where I come from it is part and parcel of growing up—being caned and being punished for what you have done. So my mum did not punish me—she just asked me, 'So when do you want me to go?' That almost killed me. It was something I did not expect from her. She just told me, 'Okay, they want to see me tomorrow? Now go home, go eat, something is there for you to cook. Then bathe and prepare for tomorrow. I will be coming later in the evening.' She gave me transport money to get from town to where we stayed. I went home, but I can tell you, I was unsettled. I was home, I bathed, I cut my nails, I made sure I didn't give her an excuse to punish me for anything but being suspended from school for a month. I was waiting for my mum, but by the time she came home in the evening I was sweating, I was panicking, everything I touched was falling, and she comes back home and says, 'So have you eaten?' I said, 'Yeah, I had lunch.' Then she asks the girl who used to help us cook. 'What are we having for supper?' Then she says, 'Emma, come, we'll go and buy sauce.' To tell you the truth, I thought Mum was planning to bury me alive. I don't know [Emmanuel laughed], it was so unlike her. So we went to the butcher, came back, prepared the sauce, and ate. In the morning we woke, prepared, and went to the bus stop and on to school with all my things. She went to the office and talked. When she came out, she gave me some pocket money, two hundred shillings. Most of my friends spent two hundred shillings in a day, but that two hundred shillings was supposed to last me for half a term. You see [Emmanuel laughed again], it was a bit tricky to survive on that. So she gave me money and then said, 'Okay, I hope you don't get suspended again!' Then she left."

"Seems like your mother had a sense of humor too!"

"Yes."

"Could your stepfather have helped out in any way, when you got into that jam?"

"He could and he did. He was probably the one who told my mum, when they got the letter. My father has always raised us from a teacher's view on child development. He's always been like that with us. At home, my father

has been like an angel. And this is strange, to have a stepfather who basically does not behave like a stepfather. I grew up in situations where my friends had stepfathers who punished them on a daily basis, but with us, no, it was our mum who punished us, not our father, though he had the authority to do so. At school, he also had the authority to cane us, and he used to cane us when we failed or did something wrong, but if we got caught doing something wrong somewhere else, he would not let anyone else cane us. He'd say, 'You call me. I don't want anyone to touch my kids.' So he was the only one to cane us, and immediately he was finished, he'd say, 'Go to class,' and then he'd come after maybe an hour and say, 'Emma, come,' and also my brother if he was there, and he'd take us to a stall where they sell bananas, ripe yellow bananas, mangoes, and, oh, it was heavenly to be bought a full cluster of yellow bananas—it was like being a king, you know. So he buys us each a cluster of bananas and says, 'Eat, you have to eat before you go back to class.' Then we would sit and eat. In the evening, when we got home, the first thing he would tell our mum was the punishment he gave us. He had this policy, he never wanted to punish us and mum knew this. So he would come home and say, "Uh, by the way, Jen, Emma and Deo did this and this today, but I punished them and everything is okay.' My mum knew of it. At home the coolant was our father. Whenever our mum was burning up, he would say, 'No, no, Jen, take it slow, there could be a reason why he did this, can we ask him why he did this?' And then they'd ask us, and we would explain. My father would say, 'You see, Jen, even if he's lying, at least he has an explanation for it.' So that's how they raised us. Even though they are no longer together, my stepfather and my mum, he is the closest thing I've had to a father, and he is the closest adult friend I have had. So I usually go to him, and we talk, we argue, we discuss. Our behaviors are mostly copied from him, because he has never drunk, he has never smoked, he was always a hundred percent sober at home. If he punished you, it was because he was sober and able to understand your problem, not because he wanted to vent his anger or frustration on you. That was only at school. Never at home. He would always ask you to explain why you were doing wrong. And my father could convince my mum not to react immediately. He would always talk to her."

By the time Emmanuel left secondary school, he was at the top of his class. "I did nothing but study," he said. "I didn't care what anybody else was saying, I didn't care about food, I didn't care about anything, I just read books."

"You stopped being the joker?"

"I'm telling you, I stopped totally making fun. People began to be afraid for me. They said, 'Eh, Emma, what's wrong?' I said, 'Be quiet, I'm reading. There were four streams, and I was the best student in stream three."

"What drove you to work so hard at academic success?"

"What pushed me is the way my mum reacted. My mum never abused me, never pushed me. Instead, she was very positive."

"So you felt you owed her a positive result at school?"

"Exactly, a good report card. And when I brought it home, my mum was so happy she bought me my first pair of shoes, yeah. By the way, Michael, I didn't tell you, but that was the first time I put on a pair of shoes."

"You wore sandals until then?"

"Yeah, plastic ones, like these." Emmanuel got up from the table, went to the front door, and returned with a pair of cheap plastic shoes. "See, they were made like this. Open here, on the sides. But I can tell you one thing, believe me when I say that you would rather put your feet in the fire than wear these plastic shoes in Uganda. We had to wear them from seven o'clock in the morning up to six in the evening. The problem was, at six you were supposed to remove those shoes and go to sleep, but you couldn't remove them in the dormitory—you had to go and sit outside because the smell was worse than a dead cat. You literally got rotten feet in a day, and when I say rotten, we Africans are good at handling awful smells, but this you couldn't stomach—your feet stank like a dead cat, so bad that you had to sit out there for two or three hours."

"And the other kids? They had leather shoes?"

"Yes, they had good shoes. Some of them had normal sandals like the ones I'm wearing now, but me, I was in those ones. They were plastic *and* too small for my feet. So my feet really got burned. The signs disappeared as I grew older, but my heels used to be white and my toes . . . here, some of the scars are still here . . . after twenty years. Yeah, my feet were totally burned. And whenever you remove them at night, the smell comes off them and you have to take them outside, then put your feet inside your blanket because of the smell. I used my sheet and blanket to cover my feet. The top part of me had no cover. And then I had only one pair of socks. That is, until my mum bought me a pair of shoes from Bata—"

"I remember Bata shoes from Freetown—"

"Shoes from Bata were not real leather, but at least they were better than those plastics. They were made by a company, a foreign company that came in from Europe, I think. So these guys from Europe were making these

shoes, and we bought them because they were cheap and well shaped, but I don't think our parents knew how bad these things were. My feet almost got deformed, because even though your feet were paining you, and you are dying in your heart and your brain is burning, in the compound you had to pretend to walk normally. So when I got my shoes, I was very happy, and I finished senior three and went on to senior four. Then, three months into the second term, I messed up again. I left school without permission to escort a friend who was leaving for America. I didn't know we were supposed to get permission. We got caught up in the emotions of Teba Henry going to America. Anyway, we got caught off the school premises, and I was expelled for a term. I went straight home. I thought they had expelled me for a reason that was so flimsy. I thought they would be more kind and understanding, with our friend leaving us in the middle of the term to go to America. So I went home, knowing my mum would understand, which she did. I did most of my schooling at home, then, right up to my O-levels at the end of senior four.

"Next year, my mum took me to a new school. Maybe she was angry with me or had given up on me, but she took me to a school where no one in his right mind would take a child. The school had no toilets, no latrines. There are some tribes in Uganda where latrines are not allowed. It is not allowed to shit in a latrine or toilet. It's not that they don't have toilets; they just don't use them, that's their culture."

"They go in the bush?"

"Yeah."

"But they must designate areas in the bush, otherwise—"

"I think so, yeah. Some of them don't really care. They consider shit to be part of nature, manure for the land. And this part of their culture—I don't know whether I'm using the word 'culture' properly here—this was part of the school's culture too. It was a boy's school. I was put in there. I didn't understand anything. So when I woke up in the morning and said I needed to use the latrine, people were laughing. I said, 'Why are you laughing?' They said, 'Ah, Emma, you don't know? You're supposed to go to Beirut' [Emmanuel laughed]. Yeah, the place they went to shit they called Beirut! So they said, 'Ah, everybody goes to Beirut, man, you'd better go there.' So I went with a group of people in the morning. We walked, we walked, we walked across the school, and I asked, 'Excuse me, where is Beirut?' So they say, 'You'll find it.' And sure enough, just as I step outside the main compound of the school I step into a minefield of shit. That's what they called

it—mines. Everyone was using military language. The shape of a shit indicated whether it was a machine gun, a certain caliber bullet, a missile, or—how do you call it, that gas, that chemical they spread in war zones? They used to name everything according to how it looked. Now they told me, 'Yeah, you're a new fellow, you're going into the minefield, and the rest of us are going to the gun ships.' These were places where the ground was still clear, and you could squat down all right. But where I was, there was nothing but mines. First you had to place your leg, and then—"

By now, Emmanuel was in stitches, and I was laughing too. I did not need to be convinced of his ability to transform a potentially degrading situation into slapstick comedy.

"Well, you get the picture! You had to be careful not to bring more shit back from that place than you took there! And then it would rain! You know what tropical rain is like? Ah, you leave that place in the morning, and you've completely lost your appetite. You're hungry—food is hard to come by, but you can't bring yourself to eat. And then later in the day, you have to go back. Nature is calling!"

"I'm laughing, Emmanuel, but I'm sure it wasn't funny at the time."

"When I tell this story, everyone laughs, even Nanna. But let me tell you, being in that situation was no joke. No, no, no. When I told my brother-in-law, who is actually Ugandan and has been to secondary school, he could not believe it. I even told my brother, Deo. He couldn't believe it. A secondary school, senior five, A-levels, where you are preparing yourself to go the university, and you don't have a latrine!"

"What was the quality of the teaching there?"

"Actually the reason I was sent there was historical. Like a prince going to Eton, then twenty years down the road sending his son there. My school was called Katchonga Senior Secondary School, and my father remembered his older brother having gone there and later getting a very big position in government. Also, Charles Onyango-Obbo went there.[23] By the way, that is what mostly influences people. They look at who has been at a certain school, then say, 'Ah, that's the school you should go to.' But the school I went to was not the school they thought it would be, and I stayed only a year and a half before leaving.

"Did you finish your A-levels there?"

"No, I decided to go to a day school, even though my mum wasn't keen on it."

"How old were you when you finally finished your A-levels?"

"I finished them in 1994. I was twenty-three years old, four or five years older than anyone else in my class."

"Yet considering your circumstances, that was quite an achievement."

"I had to work terribly hard. I didn't want to repeat or fail a class. With my very poor primary education, I had a lot of catching up to do. I had to work out a system for studying. Coaching and extra tutoring became central. Some of the teachers who helped me have remained friends to this day. One of my main helpers was also called Emma. I could not have passed without his help and advice. I was very good at some subjects, like mathematics, and so I took mathematics, economics, and geography as my specialized subjects for A-levels. But I still didn't have enough points to go straight to university, and I had to find a college in Kampala. I spent two years there doing a commercial course and paid for my education by doing odd jobs. I was thinking I would become a teacher like my father, so when I finished the courses I got a teaching assistant's job at my brother-in-law's school. I used to help in accounting and commercial courses, marking and helping students who were not understanding in class. It was actually my brother-in-law who suggested I go to university."

"This was Mariam's husband?"

"Yes. Mr. Kitez. He's the one who actually said to me, 'Emma, you have this certificate, why don't you use it to enroll at university?' I said, 'Yeah, that would be okay.' He said, 'I can help you get in contact with a university. Would you go there if they offered you a place?' I said, 'Yeah, I'm willing.' I went to my mum and presented my suggestions to her. My mum was excited, but the university was private and funded by an Islamic organization based in ... I think ... the United Arab Emirates. It sponsors Islamic universities in many African countries. This one was in Mbale, where I came from. The dream of most people in Uganda is to go to Makerere. Makerere is like Oxford in the U.K., or Harvard in America. But even though it would have cost no more to go to Makerere, I really wanted to go to IUIU."

"Can you explain why?"

"Commitment of the teaching staff. Let me say they are not drunkards—there are no unserious people there ... no professors and lecturers who look at you and want to give you less marks because you may have shorter hair than someone else. The standards at Makerere University have fallen, because politicians got involved and academics became corrupted. I wanted to go to an institution that was seriously concentrated on helping students, an institution that allowed students to develop their own understanding of things

rather than being forced to think in only one way. It was there that I was brought out of limbo. I was happy to be there. If professors gave you 20 it was because you had earned 20; it wasn't because you were a Christian or a Muslim. And the girls didn't have to show their breasts to get more marks, like at Makerere. Also, I didn't want to get distracted. There were no bars, no dance halls at IUIU, so you could focus on your academic work."

"And no expectation that you should be Muslim?"

"No, no one ever came to me in the three and a half years I was there, no one asked me, 'Emma, are you becoming Muslim?' In fact, Muslims don't do that. They want you to actually admire what they are doing, so you become a Muslim because of their deeds. We mistakenly think that Muslims are like Pentecostals. But they don't try to convert you at all. I almost married a Muslim girl, but she never once asked me about becoming Muslim. She was willing to accept me the way I was, though probably her family could not have done so. But this is the thing, I was comfortable at the Islamic University because they let you be who you are. You have only to follow the rules: don't come drunk to school, don't smoke in class, don't kiss or fondle females or do anything that makes people lose their concentration. These are rules that would apply anywhere. Anyway, I liked Islamic University because there was nothing to drag me from my goal, and so I succeeded in performing quite well. When I finished my bachelor's, they actually wanted me to continue with a master's there, but then I came to Denmark."

THE SCAPEGOAT

Emmanuel's story brought to mind René Girard's work on the scapegoat. I had already noticed the close kinship between Emmanuel's narrative and the folktale, for despite the deeply personal nature of what was being recounted, the minimalist and austere style of the folktale prevailed, as if Emmanuel were recounting his experiences from afar or through a lens that lent objectivity to what might otherwise have been an unbearably intimate and abject catalogue of misfortunes. It was perhaps this paradoxical juxtaposition of the idiosyncratic and the stereotypical that gave his story a quasi-mythical dimension, as if it were an allegory of Everyman.

In calling a story mythic, Girard means that private, historical, or geographical details play a secondary role in what is essentially an archetypal form, in this instance "a persecution text," examples of which can be found

in all human societies. Girard's insights into the conditions under which such persecution texts are born and his argument for why certain elements recur in them are directly relevant to Emmanuel's story. First, Girard notes, stereotypes of persecution tend to draw on a cluster of closely related words that suggest deep affinities linking critical events to criminality and condemnation. Thus the Greek verb *krino*, meaning "to judge, differentiate, and condemn a victim," is the etymological root of our words *crisis, crime, criteria,* and *critique*.[24] It is worth observing, therefore, that during the critical period in Emmanuel's childhood, when, following the death of his father and the family's exodus from central Uganda and migration to Bugisu, Uganda was suffering civil unrest, widespread famine, and the impact of the HIV/Aids epidemic. Moreover, from as long ago as the mid-twentieth century, Bugisu had the highest density of population per square mile in Uganda, and in the 1960s increasing pressure on scarce land meant a growing intolerance of the landless poor, who were not only resented but often accused of witchcraft and thievery.[25]

In 1980, despite post-Amin turmoil, the first elections for eighteen years were held. But in many parts of the country, only half the population was self-sufficient in food, and infant mortality rates had increased tenfold.[26] To keep his baby sister alive, Emmanuel fed her small balls of moist clay, while he survived by drinking cattle urine and eating leaves from bushes. His mother, who had traveled far and wide in search of work or money, returned to the village on one occasion to find Emmanuel so weakened by starvation that he was hospitalized, unable to walk, and for two long weeks it was not known if he would live.

When the world falls apart, people are typically thrown into panic, despair, and rage. These emotions tend to be projected onto the cosmos or polis, which is described as corrupt, rotten, or awry, as well as onto members of the community who are seen as outside the pale, anomalous, or abnormal.[27] That is to say, in crisis the moral order is suspended, and it is this very suspension of normal moral constraints that opens up a space for both aberrant and exemplary behavior. On the positive side, one might cite the risks that Emmanuel's grandmother ran in feeding her grandchildren. For the philosophical ethicist, K. E. Løgstrup, this is an example of what he calls "the sovereign expressions of life"—spontaneous and unconditional acts of compassion toward another that eclipse any consideration of the cost to oneself. Such actions are both free and ethical, Løgstrup argues, because they are not wholly determined by moral rules. Nor can they be instrumentalized and

generalized after the fact as moral norms.[28] What Løgstrup fails to mention, however, is that the very crises that often bring out the best in people also bring out the worst in them, and immorality is part of the fallout from this state of moral anarchy.

Individual or social differences that were tolerated in times of plenty may be dramatically exaggerated and seen to be implicated in the misfortune that has befallen the community. But the person or persons to be blamed are not simply marked as different by virtue of appearance, personality, age, or gender. They are strangers within, outsiders masquerading as insiders, bent on mischief or worse. Emmanuel was therefore already a *potential* victim when he arrived in his mother's village in 1979. His mother had forfeited all rights in her natal village when she married and moved away several years before. That she was widowed and did not have her late husband's brothers to take care of her made no difference. As for her children, they had no claims on their mother's kin, who were within their rights to treat these refugees with kindness or drive them away. Given the terrible conditions of food scarcity and political uncertainty, the die was cast against the strangers. Not only was their social status considered anomalous, but the older children spoke neither Lugisu nor English, were bereft of any adult male guardian, and came from elsewhere. Whatever they did and whatever they said only reinforced the impression that they were outsiders. It was but a short, logical step to seeing them as threats and imagining them as monsters. If they were bullied at school and persecuted by their aunt, it was not necessarily because their oppressors were motivated by malice; rather it was because the oppressors fell prey to the pressures they were under in a critical situation where, morally, politically, and economically, the world seemed not only disordered but perverted. Under these extreme conditions in which the moral order is in abeyance, it is not inconceivable that incest and bestiality should make their appearance as signs of the times. But there is another logic at play here, for the victim is not only persecuted for not belonging to the place where he or she had hoped for asylum; he is persecuted because he is made morally responsible for the misfortunes that have befallen that place. To save themselves, the local populace drive the foreigner from their midst, believing that he will carry their affliction out into the wilderness and free them from it.

Persecution becomes a double-edged sign. For the victim, it sets in motion a fantasy of being owed recompense for the pain and deprivation he has suffered. If he is guilty of no wrong and has been the victim of a series of gross injustices, then he has earned the right to one day reclaim his lost dignity, his

[handwritten margin note: How immigrants become perceived as monsters]

lost life, and this sense of possessing a natural right to redemption will hence-forth govern his thinking. For the persecutor, a very different transformation occurs, since no one robs another person of his or her humanity without losing something of his or her own humanity. The persecutor has only two options in dealing with this loss. He can attempt to erase from his mind and conscience all memory of his victim. To achieve this, he hopes the victim will disappear (dying of starvation or driven to flee), or he actively drives the vic-tim from his sight and his community. Alternatively, he may beg the victim for forgiveness, thus erasing the moral difference between persecutor and persecuted, as the virtue of a humble apology cancels out the hurt the former visited on the latter, who, in accepting the apology, grows in moral stature.

Long before Emmanuel's story was finished, I was aware of the symmetry between its two chapters—the first located in Uganda, the second in Denmark. Both chapters were persecution texts, though their background situations were very different.

Emmanuel's arrival in Denmark in 2002 coincided with the adoption, by the recently elected Liberal-Conservative *(Venstre-Konservative)* govern-ment, of immigration legislation that made it difficult for foreigners, as well as Danish citizens with immigrant backgrounds, to obtain family reunifica-tion with non-European spouses. This legislation reflected post-9/11 anxieties about Muslim immigrants in Europe, as well as a growing concern in Denmark over the depth and sincerity of migrants' attachment to Danish culture and their ability or willingness to integrate. Underlying this concern was an implicit distinction between "real" and "not-quite-real" Danes.[29] As Bertel Haarder, the former minister of integration, put it in a newspaper article published in September 2003: "We [the Danes] have a job, because we care about what our family and neighbors think about us, and because we want to set a good example for our children. But foreigners do not feel these inhibitions in the same way. They live in a subculture outside the Danish tribe. That is why they so quickly learn about the possibilities of getting money [out of the welfare system] without making an effort."[30]

It was against this background of xenophobia and cultural fundamental-ism that Emmanuel experienced his first inklings of what it would mean to live in Denmark, married to a Dane, and of what he might stand to lose by leaving Uganda. "It was during that period when I was in university that I met Nanna. I was beginning my thesis at the time, and we first came to Denmark the day after I handed it in. It was supposed to be a very brief trip to meet Nanna's parents, because I had to return to university to complete

my second and final year. But with the new Conservative government in power, and the new immigration laws, we decided to get married immediately. Ordinarily, we would have waited so my family from Uganda could attend the wedding, but we felt pressured because 'family reunion'—which is the official name for applying for permission to come and live with your spouse in Denmark—would only be possible if we were married. This was my first dramatic encounter with the Danish system, a system I have come to know extremely well.

"So I didn't have time to think about the offer the Islamic University had made to sponsor my master's there, and I didn't even respond to offers of work from companies and friends. I didn't even consider them, because I thought that I would also find openings in Denmark."

"You felt sure you'd find work here?"

"Yeah, I sincerely did. I knew people were more organized here, the system was more open, more efficient than back home, and I knew that I had an education I could use. I was also willing to work. I didn't want to just come here and sit back—I never wanted that—so when I came and found that things were very different from what I'd imagined, it became a bit of a disappointment to me. Nanna will also tell you that I have always considered Denmark one of the best places to live."

"Did you speak any Danish at that time?"

"Oh no, I didn't even understand 'good morning.'"

"What kind of work did you think you would find here?"

"Firstly, I knew that people in Denmark spoke English. Secondly, I had read a lot about Denmark in my university courses, and so I knew about the big international companies that are located here. Maersk, for example, has very big operations in Uganda. Thirdly, I knew of another company called Schmidt, a transportation company, so I knew there would be something I could do. Even if there was no work with these big international companies, I could do office work, or deskwork as they say, or drive, or do cleaning work. What I didn't know was that even cleaners in this country have to have a special education. So when I came, I thought cleaning was simply a matter of getting a broom and, you know, dusting things and carrying dirty things. But no, cleaners have an education; there are institutions that train them. So that was the first blow, because the first job application I sent off was for a lowly job. I've always had this view that to get satisfaction in your career you should start from a lower level and feel that you're actually growing with an organization, so I thought that entering an organization as a messenger or a

cleaner would help me get a better understanding of the organization, help me learn the language faster, become socialized, and probably make friends. What I didn't know was that even if you wanted to be a messenger there was a proper administration for that."

"Did you have a work permit at this time?"

"After I went back to Uganda to finish my degree, I had to wait more than six months before I was permitted to return to Denmark and start a new life there with Nanna."

Emmanuel called to Nanna, who was in the bedroom with Maria, reading a story. Emmanuel asked Nanna to explain the bureaucratic obstacle course she had had to run.

"First," Nanna said, "I had to prove that I earned enough to support us both. I had to show the Danish authorities my pay slips, because it was not permitted for my parents to help with our living expenses. I was still a student, writing up my thesis. So I had to postpone finishing the thesis and find work. Then I had to put up a guarantee of fifty thousand Danish kroner, which was roughly equivalent to ten thousand American dollars. This money had to be available to the state in case Emma and I became a burden on Danish society. The money had to be available for seven years but would be reduced gradually as Emma acquired skills in Danish language and knowledge of local customs. Even so, I had to relinquish my rights to Danish social security, even though every Danish citizen is entitled to it. For as long as our marriage lasted, I would not be permitted to receive anything from the state. These were the financial obstacles. But an evaluation would have to be made to see whether our attachment to Denmark was stronger than our attachment to Uganda. How could Emma show attachment to Denmark, when he had never lived here? Then we had to have our apartment evaluated to see if it was big enough for both of us and that it was not rented. We had to actually own it. Finally, we both had to sign papers where we agreed to follow all the new government initiatives for integrating migrants into Danish society—learning Danish language and customs in a relatively short time and agreeing to DNA testing in case we were genetically related. All these requirements had to be satisfied; otherwise the state had every right to send Emma back to Uganda. Michael, I cannot tell you what it is like living under this pressure. And in a country, my country, internationally know for its humanism."

"So I returned here in the summer of 2003," Emmanuel said. "I had only just arrived when I received a letter from the municipality stating all the necessary steps to be taken for becoming integrated into Danish society,

which of course we had to agree to. I was required to attend a cultural and language institution, where I spent the next one and a half years learning Danish and learning about Danish culture. The process included meeting and making new friends, learning about life in Denmark, the Danish kitchen, the school system, the legal and political systems. Showing I was not here to suck the state coffers dry."

In the summer of 2004, Nanna helped Emmanuel find seasonal employment as a guide for a tourist company, welcoming people off cruise ships, advising them on sightseeing, and escorting them to the airport. In 2005, Emmanuel discovered that he could enroll at the Copenhagen Business School, where courses were in English and required no fees.

During this time, he continued to network, send out job applications, and attend four-week training programs organized by the municipality. But even after completing his master's at CBS, Emmanuel could not find a job.

"I would provide every kind of information, describe my abilities, say what I was willing and able to do, but nothing happened. I wanted to work in Denmark and pay Danish taxes as a thank-you for having received a free education at CBS. This was my genuine desire, to work and pay back taxes. Why? Because I come from a country where schooling is not free. There is no way you can wake up one morning and get such a very high standard of education free of charge. This only happens in some of the wealthier countries of the world. At first, I wasn't so pressured. I said to myself, 'Well, it's just the beginning. I've only been here for two years, three years, four years, five years, so it's okay.' Then I began giving myself excuses: the jobs are going to people who have been here longer than me; I need better qualifications. But then it dawned on me that this had become a permanent problem. It was a little easier in the summer, because I had that part-time job to look forward to. But there was a catch. You're not allowed to work beyond a certain number of hours per week. If you go over the limit, you miss out on your right to receive unemployment benefits. But even if you work as many hours as you're allowed, you still may not earn as much as the unemployment benefit. So staying home and doing nothing often earns you more money than going out and working in these part-time jobs. I was not used to sitting at home and receiving cash payments for doing nothing. I don't want to be a man who sits at home while his wife goes out and works. I'm not lame, I'm not blind, I'm not deaf. Even people with those disabilities find work, so what's wrong with me? I have an education, two degrees. I didn't care where I found work, even if it was in Jylland. Because Nanna was an anthropologist, we had agreed that

she might end up getting a job anywhere in the world. We had agreed to go where the work took us, to Indonesia, to Greenland, to Brazil. But it was trickier for me, because I could easily find work in Kenya or Uganda, and Nanna had a problem with that. I couldn't understand her. I asked myself, 'Why is it that Nanna prefers me sitting here, being upset, being demoralized, to letting me go where I can find a job?' This compounded my frustrations, because Nanna seemed unwilling to go to places where I could find work, even though I was willing to go anywhere her work took us.

"At the same time, I was struggling inside myself with the fact that even when I tried to explain why I was not working, I wasn't sure whether I had the right explanation, whether it was because I was Ugandan, whether it was because I had studied the wrong things and was unemployable, or whether it was because I was going to the wrong companies or something like that. But then I would contradict myself by saying, 'Well, there's no company without a finance department, and this is what I am qualified to do, so why can't they just give me a job or at least try me out, put me on probation?' My complaint was that the government was trying to help people find work, but it had created so many rules and regulations that life had become unlivable. They want to make sure you're not here under false pretenses, but they make life impossible for you. I don't want to get handouts from the government. I want to work and earn money and keep my family. I don't want to get money from a government that I'm not working for. So the war within myself has been over whether to sacrifice my relationship with Nanna and Maria by going to Uganda and finding work, or to stay here as a homebound father who has everything but nothing. Already, my daughter has begun to understand the concept of going out to work, so I can't just sit here every morning with her knowing that Mummy is going to work and asking me, 'Dad, where do you work?' or 'Dad, when are you going to work?' Sometimes I tell her I am going to work, pretending I will see her in the evening. And even Maria likes to say that she's going to work when she leaves for kindergarten in the morning. She says that kindergarten is her workplace, and she says, 'Come and visit me there.' So how could I tell her, 'No, I am not going to work, I am just going to sit here the whole day.' That would not make sense to her. So even though this might seem trivial to you, it killed me basically, it cut off my feet. I was growing older but not doing anything. Changes were happening to me, but I was changing nothing."

"How did you pass the time when you were here on your own?"

"I hate to admit it, but I watched television. Can you imagine yourself watching television and not even bothering to check the mail for responses

from companies you've written to. You are even too lazy to do that; you don't want to think anything outside of what you're seeing there; you don't want to think about the job situation and the frustrations associated with it. You concentrate only on the television."

"Did you ever go out?"

"Well, I took up running. I ran. This became my focus. One kilometer, fifteen, but not because I wanted to get fit or feel fit. It was to avoid the apartment, to get away, to do something rather than nothing."

I told Emmanuel about a Sierra Leonean friend of mine who had spent more than a year in prison as a political detainee, expecting every day to be led from his cell to be executed. Even though S. B. Marah was in solitary confinement, he would spend time every day running on the spot, imagining that he was running through the streets of Freetown. At every place he passed, he would say aloud where he was. "I am approaching my house now, I am getting close to home, I am coming to the compound, I am saying to Rose, 'How are you? How are the children?'"[31] S.B. called this routine his "exercise," but it was not simply a physical exercise; it was a technique of existential survival.

Later, I would return to Emmanuel's comment on the need "to do something rather than nothing," as well as S.B.'s account of how he endured solitary confinement. Both brought into sharp relief the connection between movement and agency and suggested that hope is grounded in a sense of moving forward rather than being stuck or slipping backward. Everyday forms of greeting also disclose this link between well-being and being on the move: "How's it going?" "How are you getting on?" "Ça va?" "Ça marche?" "Ça bouge?" In countries in crisis, existential anxieties are often expressed in images of the flow of life being blocked or grinding to a standstill. Writing of life in the eastern Congo, Stephen Jackson observes, "Kivutiens would seldom provide a straight answer to the regular French greeting 'Ça va?' (how's it going?). Among the defiantly humorous responses were: 'Ça ira un jour!' (one day it will go!); 'Ça peut aller' (it might be going/it could go); or 'Ça va au rythme du pays!' (it goes to the rhythm of the country!)."[32] Even more frequent was the resigned yet ironic response, "Ça semble aller" (it seems to be going). "The ambiguity was deliberate," Jackson writes. "Things give the appearance of progressing or 'simulate' progress; maybe things are going, maybe they aren't, I really don't know, I really couldn't commit."

Emmanuel resumed his narrative by describing the thankless routine of sending out job applications only to receive formal letters of rejection. "I was

avoiding even opening some of them, because they always say the same thing: 'We have read your CV and your application, you seem to be qualified, but we are sorry to inform you that at this moment we've had many applications from very qualified people. We hope that you will continue to take an interest in our company and check for new openings and that you will send us an application again.' I'm telling you, this is a direct translation from the Danish. No matter what the company, the letters were always the same."

"Did you keep count of the number of letters you wrote?"

"Yes, I was sending approximately four a week."

"And these were responses to advertised positions, or—?"

"About half were. The others were proactive."

"You were identifying multinational companies?"

"Yes, they were my best chance. I would identify well-established international companies and explain how my qualifications and abilities were relevant to specific operations they were involved in."

"During this period, did you meet other people in the same situation as yourself?"

"Yes, in those four-week courses. Some of these people had been employed but laid off. Some had come to Denmark and were trying to find jobs. Some of them were like me, but not married and with a different residential status than mine. Surprisingly, almost always in these courses I was put in with groups of people who were basically Danish and had ten or fifteen years' work experience. People who were in the process of changing from one job to another, who had been laid off or had laid themselves off, hoping to find a better job."

"Why were you placed with that group?"

"I often asked myself that question. I think it was because I was using Nanna's name, Olsen. I thought it would help, but it only caused more problems."

"People assumed you were Danish?"

"Probably, yes, because they hadn't seen me before I turned up in one of their courses. I would sense that they were surprised to see me. They were probably thinking, 'Ah, no, this is not Emmanuel Olsen,' because they were not expecting an African."

"Why did you choose the name Olsen?"

"That is another issue. My full name is quite long and hard to spell out on the phone. So I'd call someone and they'd ask me for my name, and I'd say 'Emmanuel,' and they'd say, 'Okay Emmanuel, what's your last name?' As soon as I began spelling it out, I was in difficulties. As a non-Danish speaker,

I found it hard to differentiate the letters 'u', 'y', 'o,' and the 'a' with a circle on top [å]. These sounded very much the same to me. So my name is Munyaruguru. 'M', I would say. They would say, 'N?' 'No, M as in Moses, then 'u.' When I say 'u,' they hear 'y,' so I would have to say 'oo,' but this would confuse them more. So, for simplicity, Nanna and I decided that I would use her last name, which is very common. I thought this would avoid any more frustration, but it only made matters more complicated. I should really have persisted in using my own name or just using initials for my own name and calling myself Emmanuel M. M. Olsen. If someone wanted to know what my middle initials stood for, I could write them down. It was even worse when the short version of my name appeared: Emma Olsen. They would be expecting a Danish woman, not an African man! Sometimes they would phone me and ask to speak to Emma Olsen. I would say, 'Yeah, yeah, this is Emma speaking.' 'No, no, we wish to speak to Emma. When she comes back, ask her to call us.' I could stay on the phone, trying to explain the history of why I am Emma Olsen, but it would cost time and money. I think I may have missed one job because of this name business. I went to an interview and there were three people sitting there. They said, 'Uh, I don't think it's your time yet; we have someone else before you.' I said, 'No, they called my name—Emma Olsen.' They said, 'Yeah, we have an Emma Olsen on our list. What has happened to her?' I said, 'No, it's me, it's me.' At that moment I knew that nothing positive could come out of it. So after sitting there for ten or fifteen minutes, I saw how resigned they were. Unfortunately, it was a job I probably would have qualified for if they hadn't had that suspicious feeling in them."

HELP THE HELPLESS

Had Emmanuel *not* finally secured a job, I doubt whether our conversation would have included these risible digressions, in which Emmanuel appeared to take great pleasure in recounting his recent tribulations not as tragedy but as farce.[33] But I was intrigued to discover what Emmanuel's Ugandan names actually were and what they meant.

"Munyaruguru was my father's name. Mulamila was given to me by my father's friends. They were Masai, living in the Arusha area of Tanzania."

"Was this a nickname?"

"No, it became my official name. According to my mother, the Masai elders came up with that name. It means 'Help the helpless.'"

"Was this a reflection on how the Masai saw you?"

"Saw my father, perhaps, or my family. Arusha is on the Kenya-Tanzania border, but the Masai don't recognize the border—they cross and recross it, looking for food for their animals. And my father was in the area, working for the East African Community—"

"Perhaps your father helped the Masai in some way—"

"I think that is right. Even when we went back to Uganda and moved to Mbale, my mother used to welcome strangers to our home and offer them food. 'Come, come, let's eat together,' she'd say. I don't know if she did this for the Masai around the time I was born. But I think this is why they gave me that name."

"It's very appropriate, given what you've been telling me about the way you helped and protected your younger siblings and went out of your way to help other people."

"It was like that in Mbale. But during my high school years, when I was bullied so badly, a boy was actually killed in this way. In Namilyango College, the best boarding school in the country, he was beaten to death with a cricket bat. So when I reached senior two, I began to be what you might call a local protector of the first-year kids because, trust me, you don't want to come to a boarding school and your first day somebody comes and pours shit and piss on your bed. You don't want your blankets and sheets to be put in sewage and put back on your bed. You don't want someone to come and attach an electric wire to your bed. These were the things that were happening, you know. Older kids carrying a younger kid outside while he was asleep, so he wakes up in the grassland or bush—you don't want that happening. I'm sometimes surprised I finished school because of that bullying. At primary school, I knew I was bullied because I was different from the others and didn't speak the same language. At boarding school it should have been different. We were all speaking English, coming from different places—the children of bishops, the children of priests, the children of people who are sensible—but they were all bullying the younger kids. So I started protecting these kids, from when I was in senior two until I was in senior four. To tell you the truth, Michael, most of my friends in Uganda now are the kids I protected during that period, not because I was strong or anything, no, I was just loud, speaking out all the time, giving the older kids reasons why a smaller kid shouldn't be beaten. Most of these kids were thirteen-year-olds, fourteen-year-olds, green, protected, from homes where they hadn't faced a slap, let alone been kicked and boxed and caned at night, so it pained me a lot, and that is what

I insisted on, and even when I left school I continued to have the same feeling. Even now, if we're in a school group, and someone wants to know, 'Who did that?' I want to say 'Me.' I've always felt that I can handle the punishment. I want the others to go free. I can handle things better than anyone else. Even at home, when something is misplaced or broken, and mum comes and says, 'Hey, who broke the glass here?' I would say 'Uh, it was me.' I don't care who did it, I just say it was me.

"So when I left school, I left with that legacy. Protecting the weak is one of the things the strong should do, not the reverse. 'Don't beat the weak,' as my mum used to say. 'If you want to fight, join the army, because that's where you can fight.' So I've grown up with that, no question about it. To swallow a lot of punishment has never been my problem. No, no, no, I can take it for a very long time. I think that's why I stayed so long without having a job, not having a steady source of income, and not being able to help my family in Uganda, not being able to take Nanna for a coffee even. Not being able to afford things that one might want. I'm a keen photographer, for example, and I thought of borrowing money to buy a camera. But I hate debt. From my mother I learned to really hate debt. I could take out a loan for school, and I borrowed money for a driving permit here in Denmark, because I was tired of asking Nanna to take me here, drop me off there, that kind of thing. But I paid those loans back immediately. But not to be able to afford some of the things everyone has in a country like Denmark, that is hard. I've always said it's worse than being called a poor man in my country, because at least, as we say, 'Poverty grows on you,' and you know you're poor and can't afford to buy things."

"If most people are poor, perhaps it is easier to accept your own poverty. You may not even think of it as poverty."

"Yes."

"Something else I find compelling in what you say, Emmanuel—that you can take a lot of physical punishment, but psychological punishment is something else—"

"To tell you the truth, you can only survive so much punishment, so much torture. You reach a point where you say, 'Of what use am I here, on earth, if by this time I have achieved nothing. What am I worth?' When you start thinking that way, it means you are withdrawing. Your war is lost. It means you are now going back—that's my thinking. Not that I could do anything about it, but basically I was withdrawing. I had reached the point where I could not even greet Nanna in the morning. I knew that was it. I think my psychological container was empty. There was nothing left anymore. Luckily,

I've never thought of suicide or ending my life immediately. No, I've always thought of alternatives, like running away. I would rather run away, go and stay in a tree and die of snakebite, than put a rope around my own neck. No, no, no."

"So that is the kind of suicide where you get someone else to put you out of your misery?"

"Precisely, it would be easier for me to go and box a soldier in Uganda so that he shoots me dead than shoot myself. I would prefer it that way. And I was basically reaching that level, the level of giving up and going back, failing my marriage and my family—"

"But to go back to Uganda would have been an admission of failure, would it not?"

"That's the point, that's what I'm telling you. That was giving up. I used to tell Nanna, 'When I leave, I will carry my certificates and go. No trousers, no extra shirt, just my certificates in a folder, airport, home.' I was actually going to tell everybody who cared to see me or listen, 'I'm done, that's it. If I have failed in Denmark, how am I going to succeed in Uganda?' Ironic as it sounds, or illogical as it sounds, it's true. If you fail in Denmark, where you probably would succeed if you were given just a crack or an opening of a door, it would be impossible for you to succeed in Uganda."

"But you said you had many friends there who would be willing to help you."

"Let me explain. To start a business in Uganda could be easy. It could be like you waking up in the morning with your money, your piece of land, then building a hut and putting your shop there, and selling your peanuts or whatever. In Denmark, it's complicated, getting your papers and permissions, all that red tape. In Uganda you don't have that problem. The problem there is that as soon as you open your shop, people will start asking, 'Why is he opening such a small shop and selling bananas?' You see, you're already telling everyone, 'I'm a failure.' You've been to school, you've been to Europe, and all you can do is open a small shop and sell bananas. You're a failure."

"So going back to Uganda was like jumping out of the frying pan into the fire?"

"This time, this period when I was giving up, going back to Uganda, I knew it was going to be tough. Actually, tough could be an understatement, but there was one thing that kept me going—my sister and my brother-in-law. I was going to start from there. Either I was going to accept working for him, even if the pay sucked, or I would accept help from the two or three people

out there who were in positions to offer me a job. That was my hope. I also had colleagues I had known from university who were now running departments and companies and so on. I was also hanging onto that. In fact, the job I did get was from an old university friend. He told me, 'I'm giving you six months. I'll keep the position open for that long, dodging the board of directors until you reach your decision. So in six months' time, please write me.' I will now send him a letter explaining that I have found a job in Denmark."

"Will he be happy for you?"

"Yeah, because strangely enough he would prefer that I'm employed here. He will have the chance to visit us here, and he will also be happy, because we assisted each other so much at university. He will be happy if I succeed. One thing that pained me when I went back to Uganda in January was being constantly reminded that I was in Europe but had nothing to show for myself. In the two months I was there, I was all the time saying, 'I'm not going to drive through here, I'm going to drive through there.' It was very painful."

"When I last visited Sierra Leone, I went with a friend who is living in London. Although he has two jobs in London and took home several boxes of gifts for family and friends, he was constantly harassed by people who expected more, who complained bitterly to his face and behind his back about his failure to share his good fortune. When we finally went back to Sewa's village, we spent only a few hours there. He could not satisfy the demands people were making of him. And not because he was considered a failure! Because he was seen as such a success! I found it ironic and poignant that at the same time Sewa was having a house built in his village, he doubted he would ever be able to return there to live."

"It is the same in Uganda. The measure of success is, first of all, doing well at school, then building a house. It's the first question they ask. 'Hey, Emma, what have you built?' Because I was in Europe, everyone assumed I was working there, so they were asking, 'Hey, Emma, where did you build?'"

"Having a house back home was proof you had made it in Europe?"

"Precisely, or you had at least made it somewhere, that you had at least a two-room house. You tell them, 'No, I haven't.' They ask you, 'Why? Don't you know that it's important to build something while you're still young? You *have* to, man, before something goes wrong. You'd better do it.' I tell them I don't have a good job. They say, 'Why? Aren't you the one in Denmark?' Then you know, nothing good is going to come out of this. All the critical questions: 'What in heaven are you doing there? Why don't you

come back?' Or telling you, 'Perhaps you should have stayed here.' So I was pressed between two places that I didn't really want to be in and unable to find any middle ground."

HEAVENLY INTERVENTIONS

"Hope" is a word we give to the confidence that we have the capacity to move and to act, albeit within limits. Insofar as movement and action carry us into a situation that surpasses the situation we started from, it evokes what Hannah Arendt calls a sense of natality—of something surprisingly and refreshingly new that makes life full of promise rather than static, repetitive, or terminal.[34] It is, moreover, this quest for life as vital potentiality that defines the ethical project. But this quest is always fraught. Our hopes may be dashed, or the price we pay for staking everything on the future may be the loss of our foundation in the past. Even the joyous birth of a child may signal the ultimate demise of those who brought it into the world. And so, considering Emmanuel's comments on being stuck and arrested, I asked him to share with me his thoughts on hope and hopelessness.

"I lost hope. I didn't think anything would happen for me here. I didn't know what tomorrow would bring. It was killing me, this loss of hope."

"I don't know how you managed to keep going for so long."

"My mother taught us one thing: the ability to wait, to be patient, and to do what is right. Not always what is legal, but if you break the law, then do it for the right reasons."

"For example?"

"Like dressing up your CV to get a job. In Uganda, people do this all the time. You fake recommendations in order to get a job. You bribe people. You forge your school records. You use tricks. But you have to have the right reason for doing this."

"And the reason is to stay alive, to have a life, to do something rather than nothing?"

"Yes."

"But you didn't break the law in getting the job with FLSmidth?"

"No. That happened very differently. It was one of the summers I was working for the tourism company. My workstation was at the airport, the departures area, waiting for guests from a cruise ship who were flying home that day. On the arrivals side was this lady, Anna, also a foreigner, from

Romania I think. Anyway, we'd met at CBS [Copenhagen Business School] though she was taking different courses. I had several friends from the former USSR, from Lithuania, Romania, Bulgaria, all those countries. And so, this Saturday after work, we're coming back to town on the same bus when Anna tells me she is working for the FLSmidth Company. She says, 'Emma, I know you haven't got anything to do yet that is related to your education, but are you willing to work without pay? Because there's an opening—we need two assistants to help us with product analysis.' I asked her for details, and she said, 'If you're interested, just send me the application. Go to our website— I'll direct you to the link. Send your application on Monday. On Monday I will check for it, print it out, and send it to my boss.' I said okay. I left her at the Tivoli, where she was meeting her husband, then literally ran back here, straight to the computer, and wrote my application. It was the shortest application I have ever written, because inside me I was still skeptical—I was not sure this was going to go through, because at the end of the day the decision would lie with those people there. So I sent her the application. I did not tell Nanna; I didn't want to disappoint her again. Anna got the application on Monday. She said, 'Okay, we're going to study your application and your CV. Then we'll get back to you.'

"Two days down the road, she sends me an e-mail: 'Emma, are you willing to come for an interview?' I said, 'Just tell me the time and place.' She said, 'It's nine thirty in the morning. Come to this place, this building. We will be waiting for you.' I said, 'Fine, I will be there.' So it was the twenty-sixth of June, if I'm not mistaken. I had told Nanna I had an appointment, and probably the way she saw me dressing up and so on, she had the feeling that maybe this was big. But she never asked for any details, and I didn't want to tell her anything unless I had something positive to say. The interview lasted an hour, I think. The unit manager was there and Anna herself. They asked questions, asked me what I was going to do for them, what I knew, what duties I had done, the whole shebang. Afterwards, of course, I said, 'Oh well, at least I went. We'll see how this goes. If I don't get any positive reply, that's okay.' After the interview, I told Anna, 'Anna, regardless of how this turns out, I owe you big. Trust me when I say I owe you big. Whatever the situation, just call me and I'll be there.' A few hours after the interview, Anna calls me back and says, 'We've just gone through your responses and had a discussion, and everything looks positive. We'll keep you updated.' This was illegal, but she did it anyway. The next day she called me again. 'Emma, I've talked to the unit manager, and it seems like he's very positive. But he's questioning why

you are so qualified and have never been employed, whether you are not over-qualified for this position.' I told her, 'Anna, do I need to say anything?' She said, 'No, no, Emma, I'm just telling you what we discussed, but I know that this is what they are going to ask. So I would suggest that regardless of what they say, just accept the conditions and come in.' I said, 'Anna, I will. I don't care what the conditions are.' So that's the second day. The third day she calls me again and says, 'Emma, the department heads and the unit manager are still discussing you and the other guy, but on Friday we'll give you a response.' That was the end of June.

"That Friday they send me an e-mail: 'Can you start work on the fourth of July?'" Emmanuel laughed. "You know, Michael, even at that moment I gave no thought to what I would be paid. I don't know when I have ever been so excited, not even when I got married." Turning to Nanna, Emmanuel apologized and hurriedly explained. "Inside me it was as if someone had just opened me like this [Emmanuel made a gesture as if pulling open a closed jacket]. I had never felt like that before. Nothing surprises me in life, but when that was said to me, 'Can you start work on the fourth of July?' I listened for a moment, then said, 'Anna, that's a Monday, what time?' She said, 'Come preferably at eight thirty and we'll go from there.' I was holding the phone. She had actually put down the receiver, but I was still holding the phone, and that's when I told Nanna. I think she sensed it, but I hadn't told her because I was not willing to go through the old business of getting our hopes up, then being disappointed. I told Nanna, 'I think on Monday I'm going to start work.' But even then I was not sure of anything. Because of the skepticism that had been growing in me for all those years, I was still not sure. So I called Anna and said, 'Can you send me an e-mail to tell me what you said on the phone just now?' And she said, 'Yeah, I'm sending it now.' On Monday I woke up, I think it was at five thirty. I was supposed to be there at eight thirty and it's a fifteen-minute ride or a twenty-five or thirty-minute walk from here. But at five thirty I was up, thinking, 'Is it true, today, Monday, I'm going to work? In FLSmidth?' I was light, I was very very light, I was on the moon. The problem is, I didn't want to share the excitement."

"Were you nervous about whether or not you would measure up?"

"That didn't occur to me. Not at that moment. I was wondering if I would be allowed to enter the building. That's what I was thinking about. Jump on my bike, I go, I reach there, Anna comes down, because I hadn't got an access card yet, she opens the door for me, we go inside, and to my very big surprise, she shows me a very big desk. Two screens, a laptop, all the things that go

with an office. And I say, 'This is where I'm supposed to sit?' She says, 'Yes, this is yours.' And there is a big poster there, 'Emmanuel, FLSmidth welcomes you.'"

"Wow!"

"I was humbled, I was very quiet. I sat there for three hours, but even if they told me, 'Oh we made a mistake,' I knew I would carry this with me for the rest of my life. And to tell you the truth, I thought they had made a mistake, because who would really employ me at that time? So Anna came and said, 'How are you feeling?' I said, 'Well, Anna, to tell you the truth, I don't believe I'm here, but let's wait until tomorrow.' Anna said, 'Today, don't do anything, just relax, walk around, find where the kitchen is, the toilets, and you know, read the office signs a lot, whose names are on what doors, and so on. Just do that. Then try to access your computer because everyone gets an access code, and try to use your access card for different places.' But I couldn't. I was lame, I was paralyzed, I was just sitting in the swivel chair and I was just quiet. I don't know about others, but for me this was the first time going to work for a big company like that, and my whole life I've been working for shady organizations, shady companies, some jobs I couldn't even describe what I was doing, but this one had a job description, a job title, and a desk, for heaven's sake. I was humbled. I went back to Anna. I told her, 'Anna I owe you big. Big, big, big,' and I don't think my offer to her is going to elapse today."

"What motivated her, what moved her, to go out of her way to help you like that?"

"I think it was her experience of being a foreigner, like me. Having spent probably eleven years here and never getting a break like the one she gave me."

"Was she also married to a Dane?"

"No, the husband is, yes is Danish, but he's also, and this is the most interesting part, he's Danish-Argentinian, so he also looks different, and not being 'a Viking,' as we say, was a serious issue for him too. Anna has been here longer than me, so she knew my situation—"

"You had told her of your difficulties in finding work?"

"Yes, and we had been to the same university, and I was the only one of our class who had not found work. I have not yet asked her why, but I would really bet that that is what moved her to help me."

"I'm sure this has been the same for you. Like helping smaller kids at your boarding school because you had been bullied and knew what it was like."

"I don't think those people in the municipal offices, the training courses that we go to, which are supposed to help us penetrate the job market, know

what our situation is like. They have our profiles, and they are supposed to help us, but they don't. And then I meet a girl with whom I have no relationship apart from the fact that we met once at the university and have been working in the same organization, and everything falls into place."

"Did you see a lot of each other when you were working for the tourist company?"

"Maybe every ten days. When a Princess ship came in. We'd usually talk on the phone because I was at the departures end and she was at arrivals. I'd ask her how her family, how her husband was doing, wish her a good day, that sort of thing. Maybe I sounded kind, concerned for her well-being, I don't know. If we did meet face-to-face it was usually at the end of the season party, when we all got together and swapped stories about how we helped this person or that person. Anyway, it was a miracle. Two months after she gets a job, she helps me. That selflessness is not something you get in everybody; it's something you have to appreciate whenever you wake up.

"So you asked me a question about the pressure of performing. On my second day I started feeling it. I said, 'Now I have to show Anna that I can do something. I have to show the department what I can do.' But first, it's Anna, Anna, Anna, yeah, because she was the one who stuck her neck out to help me. So my drive is to basically do something that she can hear about and appreciate because she is a very diligent employee. On Friday, just this last Friday, she even got a prize for being one of the most hard-working employees and for having helped the department hire two new people."

"But you have these two degrees, so you must feel confident in your ability to—"

"Yes, I have this feeling that if I put myself to doing something I will do it, as long as I have the qualifications for that kind of work. I will not say, 'No, I don't think I can do that.' No, I will try it, even if I have to say, 'I can't go beyond this point.' Computers, for example. My knowledge of computers is from the short period I've been in Denmark. I attended a course at the university called 'Financial Modeling in Excel,' using Excel as the basic program for modeling. I was not very fast on the keyboard because I was still getting used to learning how to do that, but I *had* to. I had to learn this thing—I didn't care whether I was slow, whether I took two minutes looking for the 'B' letter or 'A' was lost and I couldn't find it, no, I had to do it, and so I survived and passed the course with good enough grades to do what I am doing now. When I came to Denmark, I learned that everything is possible. It's you who limit yourself. I said I would do anything that I put my mind to, and

that's what I did until I met a brick wall. Actually it was not a brick wall—it was a concrete wall, and when I hit it I said to myself, 'Why should I even struggle?' Because I had gone as far as I could in qualifying myself to a level where I would be fully employable, and when that didn't happen I said, 'There is nothing else I can do.'

"To start a private business here, you need capital, and to borrow capital you need somebody to stand in for you. I didn't have collateral or anything to begin with. The other disadvantage is that people have had bad experiences with Africans. There are people who have dealt with Africans here and have lost a lot of money. So I was lost. It was then that I began to think about going back to Uganda. I had to do something. After my summer job ended, I would go crazy. One of my last efforts was to get a job driving a bus. I saw an advertisement on the side of one of the yellow city buses for a driving school that trained bus drivers. You got half salary while you were training. So I had an interview and applied, thinking that anything would be better than going back to Uganda. But thank God, I met Anna that same day. Even though she had started working for FLSmidth, she came to the airport that day, helping a colleague, I think. If I were religious, I would say it was . . . I don't know how to put this . . . a godly thing that she appeared. What you might call a heavenly intervention, something like that."

"What would our lives be like if it were not for lucky breaks like this, people appearing at the right time and throwing us a lifeline?"

"If it hadn't been for Anna, we would not be sitting here recording my story. I would have e-mailed you that I was leaving in October to go back to Uganda. I had even marked in my calendar the day I was going to leave."

"In fact, you did tell me this, in an e-mail a couple of months ago."

"Yes, the date was set. I was to leave a couple of days after running a 13.2-kilometer race—a very old Danish sporting event—and I had told my running mate that I would be there for it. The problem was that a lot of consequences would flow from my decision to leave Denmark. I didn't talk it through with Nanna. I just gave up and said, 'If Nanna cannot understand this, I'm not going to sit down and talk it over with her, because there is nothing to talk about anyway.' I was determined to go to Uganda and do something for myself before ever coming back to Denmark. Either personally or through salvaging the remaining network I still had there, I would succeed in doing something in Uganda. And, painful as it was, this was what I was going to do, because I'd reached the point where even facing Nanna's parents was becoming more painful for me. I could no longer face this old lady who

was looking at her daughter who had married a loser. Much as she could say she understood my situation, inside her heart she was probably thinking I could do more, there must be something more I could do. So sympathies were there, but I also thought people might turn around and start blaming me for my situation, and when people reach that point and you don't think you have an alternative, then things only get worse. And I also felt bad telling them that I probably would've got a job if I had been different. It sounds very flimsy. It's a reality, but it sounds flimsy to people when you are explaining it. Not only flimsy, but there are many of my kind who are working here; it doesn't matter where they are working, but they have jobs, so what is so strange about me, why am I not employable?"

"What do you mean 'many of your kind'?"

"People from different countries. Younger people. To get into investment banking, financial analysis, it helps if you're younger. If you are open to be indoctrinated in how to sell your product, sell yourself—"

"And you are too old to—?"

"Precisely, it's like the limit for joining the police or military. Most countries set an age limit for joining certain institutions. So it was a problem. For me it became such a big problem that I started breaking myself down into pieces: my age, my origin, my names, my qualifications, the universities I went to. The Islamic University—that could also be a problem. In fact, one person I consulted on getting a job told me, 'In your CV, avoid using the word 'Islamic.'"

"I don't believe it!"

Emmanuel laughed. "It's true. I did it. I changed my CV."

"It's a wonder they didn't suggest that you change everything else about you. Or cease to exist as you were."

"That was it. That was the problem. Everything I looked at—my age, my appearance, my qualifications—I would ask myself, 'How can I change this?' And the answer always was, 'I can't. I can't change who I am.'"

It was getting late, but there was a question I needed to ask Emmanuel before our conversation came to a close. I wanted to ask him how, given the vicissitudes of his childhood in Uganda and his years of frustration and tribulation in Denmark, he appeared to be so generous and caring, so bereft of bitterness.

"Let me tell you, Michael, how I used to sort out my anger. I would think of things in reverse. If I made myself think of the consequences of losing my temper, I would not lose it. Also, whenever I felt angry, I would look for an

outlet. I would go into the garden and cut a sugarcane, or cut down a banana plant. Or I would break a plate, except this cost money to replace, so I had to look for other outlets. Sweating, tiring myself out, cooling myself down. In Denmark I would go running rather than argue with Nanna. I also fear my anger. I don't know where the limit is, and I don't want to test it. If I got into a fight, I might start remembering the beatings I got from teachers at school or from my mother's relatives, and I might kill someone. In Uganda, men beat their wives. For some people it is entertaining to watch. I swore I would never do it. Why should I go to prison for losing my cool?"

The light was fading in the courtyard, and I told Emmanuel that I had promised my friends Hans and Anne that I would join them for dinner at six.

"I'm sorry our time has been so short," I said, "but we've packed a great deal into a single day."

"I think so. But as you said, we can exchange e-mails and continue working on the story."

"I look forward to it."

I got up from the table, shook Emmanuel's hand, and thanked Nanna for providing us with food and drink and for all she had done to help us accomplish so much in the little time we had. Then I pulled on my jacket, negotiated the tiny entranceway to the apartment, and descended the stairs into the street.

TALKING TO HANS LUCHT

Emmanuel's story had impressed upon me that a person's life unfolds unpredictably within a complex field of forces. First are those oppressive and largely contingent forces that we call natural, historical, or political, such as the Ugandan famine of 1980–81, the ethnic conflict in Rwanda, or the Amin dictatorship. Second are the forces of one's cultural upbringing, to which Emmanuel frequently alluded—the protocols of in-law avoidance and respect, the expectations that children work for their keep and learn to endure hardship without complaint, the stigma of being born out of wedlock or being parentless, the value of placing the care of kin before the care of self. A third set of factors might be called psychological, since they cover character traits that are not wholly determined by culture nor natural nor historical— the school bullies, the malevolent aunt, the loving stepfather, the devoted

mother, the heroic grandmother—the significant others in Emmanuel's life. But one is also struck by Emmanuel's resourcefulness, for though his life was shaped by a concatenation of forces acting upon him, he discovered within himself remarkable ingenuity in getting around obstacles, saving his skin, helping others, and negotiating the limits that had been set upon his freedom.

Viewed from an ethical perspective, Emmanuel's story impressed me for several reasons, not the least of which was his resilience in the face of hardships that would have broken the spirit of many. Although it is undoubtedly difficult to acquire this ability to endure, it may well be, as Spinoza pointed out, that all living things seek to persevere in their own being—increasing their capacity for life, while avoiding whatever diminishes that capacity.[35] However, Spinoza is silent on the question of how much a person can endure without giving in. It was not until the Second World War that psychologists concluded that any soldier, regardless of his training or personal qualities, would be prone to trauma if obliged to remain in combat without respite or relief. For all his forbearance and determination to succeed, there proved to be a limit beyond which Emmanuel could not go: a breaking point when he contemplated suicide, an unbearable ethical impasse over whether he should remain in Denmark, unemployed and demoralized, or return to Uganda and suffer separation from his wife and daughter. To use Emmanuel's own recurring metaphor, both courses of action would have "killed" him. I was also struck by the fact that even though Emmanuel's actions showed fortitude, courage, and generosity, he did not reify these actions as virtues. No moral value is ascribed to anything he did; rather, he gives the impression of simply doing the best he could to survive and, in turn, doing the best he could to help others do so.

Consider Emmanuel's adroitness in avoiding the bullies and tormenters that cast their shadows over his childhood, and how he learned to protect the weak, putting the care of others before the care of self. The Danish ethicist Knud Løgstrup makes an invaluable observation here: that it is in "the sovereign expressions of life," when we spontaneously forgo or forget self-interest and literally "put ourselves out" to help less fortunate others, that we attain true freedom. Though I reject the idea that acting without self-interest is necessarily a free choice, and therefore a genuine virtue, Løgstrup's main point is that "norms and principles are subordinate to moral experience."[36] Spur-of-the-moment acts of kindness, courage, selflessness, or mercy are all expressions, as it were, of an ethics before ethics. Such actions, Løgstrup

argues, are not necessarily informed by moral principles, which is why those who spontaneously show courage or compassion often disavow such moral language on the grounds that they acted without a second thought and did not for a moment calculate the costs or consequences of their acts.[37] "The sovereign expression of life precedes the will," Løgstrup says. "Its realization takes the will by surprise. It is one of those offerings in life which, to our good fortune, preempt us, and in whose absence we should be unable to carry on from one day to the next."[38]

To embrace Løgstrup's view that ethical action is not necessarily an enactment of a moral rule, nor open to post facto conversion into a categorical imperative, is to shed doubt on the possibility of gleaning from any human life moral lessons that might help us alleviate the suffering of others or prevent future tragedy. As I observed in my study of Kuranko storytelling, the fervent discussion of ethical dilemmas that follows the recounting of any story may change a person's experience of her situation in life without, however, changing the social world in which that person is bound to live. Our attempts to wrest moral meanings from a life story may be as misguided as our attempts to identify causes or allocate blame. To exhort us to remember Auschwitz lest it happen again may bolster our hope that we can improve our coexistence on earth, morally and materially, but history offers us no examples of how such gestures alter the future, even though they help us understand how we come to terms with the horrors of our past.

What I find compelling about the sovereign expressions of life is not only that they cannot be reduced to some moral principle or instinctual drive, but that such acts are timeless, as if they lay outside history, outside natural causation or cultural determination, outside any original intention or preexisting design. To act without a second thought in aid of someone whose life is in peril may spring simply from the fact that one is in possession of life and the other is not. Levinas speaks of this as a sense of the precariousness of the other and reminds each of us of the shocking experience that an-other, in whose presence *I am,* could, in suddenly becoming absent, render *me* incomplete, wanting, impoverished.[39] If, for a moment at least, one feels that both oneself and the other are in life together, then the other's peril is experienced as one's own. It is as if one acts, not in terms of one's own life or the life of the other that is at risk, but for life itself.

It may be impossible to predict or explain moments when the gap between self and other closes and one becomes aware only of a shared space in the here and now, encompassing self and other equally. It would be comforting to

believe that this kind of suspension of historical, cultural, and moral determinations might provide a cleared space for addressing some of most vexed ethical impasses of our time. As the descendant of settlers in a land that was not, properly speaking, theirs to settle, I have sometimes thought that there must be some point at which the sins of my forebears cease to be my sins, or even my responsibility, if only because the past was another time, another place, inhabited by others to whom I am not beholden. I like to think that responsiveness or responsibility to the present situation in which I live can best be achieved by bracketing out considerations of how that present was historically determined or culturally shaped. And I imagine an ethics based wholly on what is present to me, what is at hand, as if history and causation were irrelevant. But as Løgstrup observes, it is rarely possible to convert the sovereign expressions of life—which often imply ahistorical, acultural, and amoral forms of consciousness—into actions that change the world at large, even though they offer us glimpses into what we mean when we invoke the human, or the divine, or simply the human condition.

As I walked through the familiar streets of Frederiksberg in the falling night, two trains of thought preoccupied me. First was the pivotal role of human kindness in Emmanuel's life. It is hard to imagine how he could have survived his many trials and tribulations, both as a child in Uganda and as an adult in Denmark, had it not been for what Emmanuel called the "heavenly interventions" of decent, caring people like his stepfather, Nanna, Anna, and his grandmother, who fed her grandchildren at a time of chronic food shortage despite pressure from within her household to deny them food. It would be gratifying to see these redeeming moments as Emmanuel's moral reward for his own devotion to the needs of his younger siblings and his junior schoolmates. But this is the preserve of folktales, in which good is ultimately repaid in kind and supernatural saviors are always waiting in the wings, prepared to thwart evil schemes. Nevertheless, variations on the closely connected themes of reciprocity and exchange appeared in every episode of Emmanuel's story. As I trudged through the deserted streets toward the Tycho Brahe Planetarium and then along Sankt Jørgens Lake toward Norsvej, the theme of natural justice dominated my thoughts—the reasoning that leads us to conclude that when the wherewithal of life has been taken or withheld from us, we are entitled to retrieve it, even though we may infringe custom or break the law in doing so. And so we conjure images of some

daemon who will redistribute what has been unfairly and unequally allocated. Or we fantasize a person or place that will offer us the life we feel we are owed, much as a deprived child steals objects in the hope of reclaiming the parental love that was withheld. What is the spirit of utopia if not this universal search for what is missing from our lives and the hope that we finally may get our due? And what is migration, imaginary or transnational, but the expression of this impulse to be recompensed for what fate, circumstances, or the malevolence of others has denied us?

When I arrived at Hans and Anne's apartment, Anne was placing bowls of vegetarian food on the table, while Hans made fruit smoothies for their two children. This picture of warmth and homeliness was in such stark contrast with the images of the Bagisu village where Emmanuel languished as a child that I had a sudden and shocking realization of how tenuous our happiness is, and how the bounty and well-being we take for granted is, despite its illusion of permanence, utterly dependent on a regular income, social services, and the manifold tokens of belonging that guarantee us a secure place in the country we call our own—fluency in the language, deep knowledge of local lore, familial connections, long-standing friendships, and a physical appearance that ensures we will be seen to belong there. I found it difficult to imagine what it would be like to be born into an environment so bereft of the basics of life that one had no option but to travel far afield, to places where one was anomalous and unwanted, in search of food, shelter, and safety. Yet there is, in the global South, a growing disenchantment with the West as a land of plenty. For many, Europe and North America are no longer mythologized paradises, but rather places "where one's life is filled with poverty and problems concerning money, jobs, papers and housing, where one feels unwanted and undesired, where one is often confronted with racism and with the huge human cost of broken marriages, families and friendships, in short, with all the collateral damage of migration."[40] As a Congolese pop song from the 1990s put it, "They go to Europe but land in the desert instead."[41]

Hans had recently published his compelling study of African migrants living on the margins in southern Italy. *Darkness before Daybreak* documents the plight of Ghanaian fishermen who lost their livelihoods as a result of European Union boats overfishing West Africa's coastal waters. Faced with dwindling fish stocks and an uncertain future, many of these young dispossessed fishermen undertook the grueling journey across the Sahara to Libya, and thence on unseaworthy boats to Italy, sustained by the hope that the

future denied them at home might be found in Europe. When Hans asked one of his Ghanaian friends how he justified leaving his family and village, risking his life by crossing the Sahara and the Mediterranean, and exchanging a familiar world for a bleak Neapolitan suburb where buses did not stop for you, where you were preyed on by local criminals and subject to racist assaults and slurs, and where day labor was underpaid, intermittent, and dangerous, his friend replied that while his life in Italy was full of bitterness and disappointment, it was "always better than to rot away in the village in Ghana."[42] In the village there was no hope. To return there would be to face ignominy, unpaid debts, and social death. In Europe there was always the chance of a breakthrough. Another informant couched his answer in religious terms: "I keep hoping that one day the Lord will smile down on us and we'll get our documents, so that we'll be allowed to find regular work, and change this life-style and the life-style of my family, as I have promised to do. That keeps me going. I have been tempted on so many occasions to say that God has forgotten the Africans. . . . I don't know whether God is still having his eye on us, because things are tough, really tough."[43]

Given this persistent and often anguished search for how promises might be kept, debts paid, suffering redeemed, and faith justified, it is not surprising that these erstwhile fishermen should draw an analogy between their present situation and their traditional relationship with the sea. Fishermen will sit in silence, watching the sea, the seabirds, and other crews, waiting for the telltale signs of fish before leaping into action and casting their net. "It's like that [here]," one informant told Hans. "You have to pay attention to whatever is around you and grab it. . . . You have to be very careful [at the roundabout]; maybe someone will be calling you or inviting you, but because you're not paying attention or looking at the cars, you'll not notice the person calling you, and somebody standing afar will rush to your place. This also happens on the sea. You'll be at a place and there's fish right there—only you wouldn't know it. But somebody will see it, and before you know it, they'll come from afar and drop their net."[44]

The connection between looking for fish and looking for the wherewithal for life itself reflects a deeper reasoning, which Hans calls "existential reciprocity."[45] Just as the sea will only yield its bounty if given respect in the form of periodic sacrifices and conformity to the protocols of fishing, so the world at large will only open its doors to those who are prepared to yield a portion of their agency to the powers-that-be, submitting themselves to the hardship of prolonged waiting. This existential yielding is compared to the dutiful

sabr.
pause.

relationship of a child with its parents. "The sea is our source of everything; we depend on it, like a parent. That's the sea; it's our father and mother, everything, the parent of the fishermen. So, when things are not going the right way, we get very disturbed; we get disappointed that the sea is not favoring us."[46] Not only does this reasoning explain why one can only hope to gain life by giving something of one's life away, in the form of risk, sacrifice, or deprivation; it explains why a reversal in one's fortunes requires greater sacrifice and yielding, not less. In the case of the Ghanaian fishermen, this logic is complicated by the fact that their situation has deteriorated not because of any failure on their part but because external events have disturbed the equilibrium they so painstakingly established with the natural environment. Illegal overfishing by foreign boats has degraded the marine habitat, and an ethic of reciprocity now finds expression in syllogistic form:

The sea gives us a livelihood
Europe took that livelihood from us
Europe owes us a livelihood

The syllogism may be elaborated:

The sea gives us a livelihood
(on condition we pay it respect)
Europe took fish from the sea
(but gave the sea nothing in return)
Europe now owes a debt to the sea
(that gave us a livelihood)

Hans and I talked at length about the affinity between his notion of "existential reciprocity" and the principle Michel Serres calls "natural justice"—which adds "to the exclusively social contract a natural contract of symbiosis and reciprocity."[47] Individuals like Emmanuel and the Ghanaian fishermen with whom Hans had lived and worked on the outskirts of Naples found themselves in the position of giving or giving up everything they possessed, only to receive nothing in return. Persecuted or exploited by parasites who take all and give nothing, they had in effect been naturalized, like the sea—transformed into undifferentiated members of an anonymous host, bare lives,[48] an invasive plague, a teeming mass, an elemental horde—and like the

sea, which those in power treated as a possession, they were denied any presence as subjects or any legal status.

I asked Hans what writers like ourselves had to give that might justify our relationship with the individuals we sought out on the margins of Europe. What kind of existential reciprocity governed our relationships with them? When Hans threw the question back at me, I said that for Michel Serres, it is necessary to "set aside mastery and possession in favor of admiring attention, reciprocity, contemplation, and respect."[49] We thus mimic, in some ways, the Ghanaian fishermen's relationship with the sea. But Hans insisted that the critical question was not the attitude we might adopt but the repertoire of practical skills we needed to acquire. For it was not enough to inspect the sea for evidence of fish; you had to know exactly what to look for and where, not to mention all the ritualized rules that governed what you could and could not do when out at sea. All this could only be learned through a long apprenticeship and arduous and repeated endeavor.

Where Hans and I found much contemporary anthropology wanting was in its paucity of descriptive detail, closely observed events, complete life stories, and records of sustained conversations in which the give and take of ethnographic fieldwork was fully disclosed. We also shared an astonishment at how much can be communicated between two people in a relatively short space of time. Hans had recently been in northern Niger, where migrants gathered before embarking on their hazardous journeys across the Sahara. After a group of rebels (affiliated to al-Qaeda in the Islamic Maghreb) kidnapped seven French nuclear reactor builders, Hans was obliged to abandon his fieldwork and return to Denmark. Despite his short sojourn, however, Hans had collected some rich and remarkable material.

Reflecting on the day I had just spent with Emmanuel, I agreed. "Whenever I embark for the field I feel that I leave myself behind. And for as long as I am in the field I possess an almost hallucinatory hyperalertness.[50] Successful fieldwork isn't a matter merely of being open to others, but of receiving what is given, seeing what is simply *there*, being responsive to what is in front of you. For this, one needs to put from one's mind much of what one has read." Undoubtedly this cavalier attitude to my profession had undermined my chances of getting research grants. But I had the satisfaction of knowing that in ignoring current paradigms and conventional methodology I gained more than I could reasonably have expected to get, especially after a few days or weeks in the field.

"Perhaps this is because we are writers first and anthropologists second," Hans said, adding that our inclination to work narratively, allowing small details to illuminate or encapsulate larger patterns, was more typical of creative writing than social science.

THE ETHICAL DEMAND

My Icelandair flight from Copenhagen to Boston involved a two-hour layover in Reykjavik, where I found a table overlooking a rain-swept tarmac and resumed writing in my journal, recalling as best I could snatches of my conversations with Emmanuel and Hans that had either slipped my mind or previously seemed insignificant. When I had asked Emmanuel to tell me more about his mother, he mentioned that she had joined a Pentecostal church, which prompted me to ask if she found in her religious community the kind of social bonds she had failed to find in her village. Emmanuel's response was an unequivocal no. "My mother joined the church only after the last of her six children had graduated and left home," he said, explaining that the money she had once used to put her children through school and university was now wholly dedicated to her church. "Enough money, in fact," Emmanuel added, "to build a new church." But she sought neither friendship nor community, Emmanuel said. He explained how the church segregated boys and girls and sought to cleanse itself of the evils of modernity—drugs, corruption, licentiousness, slovenliness, and selfishness. "She did not seek pleasure in the company of others or material rewards," he said. "She wanted to find inward fulfillment."

Emmanuel's comments set me to thinking about my late friend, Noah Marah, without whom my first fieldwork in Sierra Leone might never have succeeded. Indeed, when Emmanuel spoke of his friend Anna's intervention in his life as a "godly" or "heavenly" thing, and how he had incurred a debt to her he could never repay, I thought immediately of my relationship with Noah. Just as Emmanuel described himself as "lost" at the time Anna offered to help him find work, I too felt lost when I arrived with my wife, Pauline, in the dusty northern Sierra Leone town of Kabala in November 1969. But unlike Emmanuel—or the Sierra Leoneans in London whose experiences I have recounted elsewhere, who encounter racist insults, social rebuffs, closed doors, and bureaucratic indifference—I met with nothing but friendliness in Sierra Leone. Indeed, within twelve hours of arriving in Kabala, disoriented,

exhausted, and not knowing where to find food or shelter, I was introduced to Noah, who unhesitatingly found my wife and me a house to rent with tables and chairs to furnish it, and offered to teach me the rudiments of the Kuranko language. What had I done to deserve such generosity of spirit? How could I hope to repay such goodness? And how could I reconcile such hospitality, generous despite its guardedness, with the debates raging in Europe over pedantic distinctions between morally legitimate and morally impermissible criteria for selecting migrants for admission to the EU, and the questions over whether migrants who had passed the "first gate of entry" could aspire to "the rights and duties of permanent residents (denizenship, the second gate of entry)" or be assigned some compromised form of citizenship?[51]

As Noah helped ease my way into a wary community, acting as a go-between, translating my obtuse questions, and trying to satisfy my childlike curiosity, I became aware of the subtle workings of reciprocity in everyday Kuranko life. For example, when I first went to Noah's village of Firawa, I was lodged in the sergeant's house because, as Noah explained later, I had done the sergeant a favor by trucking his cement from Kabala two weeks before. Chief Sewa Marah welcomed me in the same vein. If I had come to live among Kuranko people, then I must be positively disposed toward Kuranko, and therefore Kuranko were positively disposed toward me. Commenting on the favor I had done Sergeant Marah, the chief went on to say that to do a favor for one is to do a favor to all; similarly, to offend one is to offend all. It was not surprising, therefore, that my fieldwork would lead me to explore the ramifications of the Kuranko image of paths—paths along which people, goods, and services move in the give and take of everyday life, paths that connect people, which become blocked or darkened by ill will or selfishness, yet cleared by sacrifice and opened by ritual appeals to the ancestors.

There was another connection between Emmanuel's and Noah's stories that also came to mind as I sat in Reykjavik airport, watching mist envelop the rock-strewn landscape that extended toward the sea. It was the theme of separation and loss, of dispossession and eviction, and how events occurring long before one's birth presage one's future. I remembered Noah's nostalgia for the Kuranko past and his eagerness to create a record of traditional life for posterity. I used to wonder whether his attachment to the past was a projection of his attachment to his childhood, and whether a primordial sense of loss permeates every human life. For the old, the world was a happier

place when they were young. For many Palestinian refugees, the lost homeland was a place where the well water was sweet, the sky always blue, and the streets filled with laughter.[52] Ironically, such thoughts echo the longings of the Jews in Europe dreaming of next year in Jerusalem, and the poignant theology of Christians mourning paradise lost. Before is always preferable to after. *Elsewhere* is always better than *here*.

These reflections on loss had a direct bearing on the question of whether there exists anything that we call our common humanity. Knud Løgstrup writes that there is "a characteristic of human life that we naturally trust one another" and that "human life could hardly exist if it were otherwise." Although this "ethical demand" may well constitute a *minima moralia* to which most human beings *aspire or pay lip service,* we must address the indifference or distrust with which many in Europe and America regard migrants from the global South and the sense of violated trust that often informs the migrant's attitude toward the affluent North. For me, the ethical demand[53] is not that we should trust one another but that we should never lose sight of the humanity we share with others, so that rather than seeing them and acting toward them solely in terms of their ethnicity, age, gender, or status, we see and act toward them as if they were ourselves under other circumstances. To speak of a shared humanity is not to invoke a transcendent category or universal essence but to recognize the extent to which human beings are able to work out ways of communicating and coexisting with one another in the face of seemingly insurmountable differences. That these forms of mutuality are only randomly or rarely attained is no more a proof of ineradicable difference than their occasional attainment proves a common humanity. To invoke the human is simply a way of acknowledging one's potential or capacity for seeing oneself in the other and finding the other in oneself. Such moments are, as Judith Butler observes, often associated with the loss of someone dear to us and the sudden sense of vulnerability that follows. Such grievous loss, she writes, makes "a tenuous 'we' of us all." And "this is how the human comes into being, again and again, as that which we have yet to know."[54]

Roberto

A COUPLE OF MONTHS AFTER my conversations in Copenhagen with Emmanuel, I was sitting in an espresso bar in Boston's North End, killing time before attending a ceremony at Faneuil Hall, where I would take an oath of allegiance, receive my certificate of naturalization, and "enjoy my new life as a United States citizen." My mind, however, was not on the day ahead, but on Emmanuel's story and the opening lines of Woody Guthrie's "Talking Columbia," where he describes watching the boats entering and leaving Bonneville lock and

> thought 'bout the river goin' to waste,
> thought 'bout the dust, thought 'bout the sand,
> thought 'bout the people, thought 'bout the land.
> *Ever'body runnin' round all over creation,*
> *Just lookin' for some kind of a little place.*

It was raining by the time I made my way to Faneuil Hall and joined the other candidates for citizenship, forming lines outside and sheltering as best we could under umbrellas, briefcases, or sheets of newsprint. When we were finally ushered into the historic hall, I was surprised to see how many we were—and how many family members, dressed to the nines, filled the upstairs gallery. As I waited for the ceremony to begin, I chatted with the Haitian guy to my left and, later, to a Colombian woman to my right. I was humbled by their stories—the arduous and often soul-destroying roads they had traveled to reach this point, where they were reunited with families, given a chance at a new life. Their experiences bore so little comparison to my own untroubled passage to citizenship that I felt fraudulent and somewhat guilty that I had treated the naturalization process skeptically or taken it with a grain of salt.

Usually, I begin work around seven o'clock. But this particular morning in the early fall, only a few days after my citizenship ceremony in Boston, I arrived an hour earlier at the Center for the Study of World Religions, where I have my office. It was barely light, and when a figure hailed me from across the street I did not at first recognize who it was. Roberto Franco had taken a course with me the previous year called "The Politics of Storytelling," a course in which I encouraged students to integrate their personal experiences with the critical analysis of texts.

I had not forgotten the day Roberto told his story to our class. He did not look up once during the fifteen minutes it took for him to describe, in minimal yet compelling detail, his childhood in Mexico, his harrowing journeys across the U.S.-Mexico border, his life working in the fields of Central California, and his efforts to gain an education. It was clear to us all that it had taken a lot of courage for Roberto to share these experiences, and when our tutorial ended we were all moved to thank him individually for his moving testimony. To my own remarks, I added the hope that he would one day commit his story to paper and share it with a wider audience. I had read nothing that brought home so sharply and poignantly the ethical dilemmas faced by every migrant. Roberto confessed that this was one of his long-term aims, and several months later he agreed to share his story as part of this book.

Here is how Roberto later described our predawn encounter: "When Michael shared the story about his citizenship process, I told him that, for a long time, I had avoided becoming a citizen and that I had an ambivalent relationship with the U.S. because of the discrimination and violence against nonwhite immigrants that I had heard about and directly experienced. Yet it was inevitable that I would take this step. I had already adopted the language and completed most of my education in the U.S. According to Frantz Fanon, speaking a certain language is an act that carries deep political implications: 'To speak means to be in a position to use a certain syntax, to grasp the morphology of this or that language, but it means above all to assume a culture, to support the weight of civilization.' It was this supporting element that I was wary about. After much deliberation and considering of the privileges and responsibilities of citizenship, I overcame my initial reluctance. I then began the arduous process of filling in applications, sending money orders, and waiting for a response from the U.S. Citizenship and Immigration Services (USCIS).

"A few months later, I was approved for citizenship and had to appear at Faneuil Hall for the official ceremony. It was a rainy day, and the judge was twenty-five minutes late. I remember telling myself, half jokingly, that he probably assumed that Latinos are never on time, so why should he bother? On the other hand, I was critical of him for setting a bad example. Although I thought I had overcome my reservations about becoming a U.S. citizen, my anxieties returned during the pledge of allegiance. I found myself crossing my fingers during the first part, 'I pledge allegiance to the flag of the United States of America.' Looking around, I could not help but notice the ethnic diversity of the multitude of people gathered there: Asians, Africans, Eastern Europeans, and Latinos. 'Have we no shame?' I thought. I crossed the fingers of my left hand tighter while hiding my hand behind me. 'One nation under God,' the crowd repeated. Suddenly, I remembered that it was in the U.S. that I learned that effort could potentially pay dividends, regardless of one's class, gender, or status. In my case, at least, this was no myth, for, after all, hadn't I, a Mexican immigrant from impecunious and obscure beginnings, ended up studying at Harvard? My great-grandmother had taught me to be grateful for small mercies, or, as they put it here, to never bite the hand that feeds you. 'With liberty and justice for all,' the judge pronounced. My fingers were no longer crossed, and the crowd started clapping. After the ceremony I went back to the day when I stood in line with my family on a cold morning waiting for the green card interview. More than ten years had passed since that day and now at last the fears of deportation, of the 'three strikes and you're out' law, dissipated. In the end I came to terms with my citizenship through 'naturalization.' This is the country where my family is, the country where my sons and daughters will be born. This is now, for all intents and purposes, *my* country."

BEING OF TWO MINDS

This curious metamorphosis, which entails distancing oneself from one life and becoming ineluctably absorbed into another, is, as Roberto suggests in his remarks about citizenship, never entirely natural nor completely consummated. One remains susceptible to the sharpest memories of the past, though for days or weeks on end one may be oblivious to one's former existence or it may seem like a previous incarnation that happened to an avatar of oneself, or that one simply imagined. Nor can one ever explain the suddenness with

which the past can overwhelm the present, blotting it out in a squall of disturbing emotions, only to pass as quickly as it came, returning you to the reality of here and now. This oscillation between a sense of being relatively sure of oneself and being profoundly destabilized, as if the solidity of the ground beneath one's feet and the motives of other people could no longer be trusted, found expression in Roberto's mixed emotions about sharing his story with me and, as I would discover, pervaded his narrative.

"The feeling emerges," Roberto said, "when deep-seated, anti-immigrant prejudices make the news headlines, or I hear slanderous comments from conservative news hosts like Lou Dobbs, or when I'm verbally attacked by a racist individual in Allston, Dedham, or Malden. Then I can't sleep. My mind becomes a vagabond in long vigils of the night; it runs desperately, always looking back to establish distance from its perceived threats, but also looking up for answers, anticipating multiple scenarios, and finally, praying and asking God for peace."

PARENTAGE

On Martin Luther King Jr. Day, 2012, with Roberto just back from visiting his family in California, we met in my office and spent almost two hours discussing how we might proceed. Initially, Roberto felt more comfortable writing installments of his story than tape-recording an oral narrative, but we finally settled on an ad hoc method that mixed freewheeling conversation with e-mailed exchanges.

One of my first questions concerned Roberto's parents—where they hailed from and how they met.

"My mother came from Cortazar, Guanajuato, and my father from Victoria, Guanajuato, both small towns close to the mountains, where water is scarce (though that is no longer the case) and people depend on *el temporal*. They were both migrant workers who moved to Mexico City in the 1960s looking for work, pressed by the idea of making money and fleeing family problems. Though they came from the same state, they didn't know each other, but the city's lure of progress snatched them both. She was fifteen and he was thirty when they met. He was a construction worker and she was a housemaid. Since she didn't know anybody in the great capital, she stayed with another housemaid and her family over the weekends. It was at this maid's home that she met my father.

"After they married, they chose to settle in la colonia Higuera, near Atizapán de Zaragoza, on the outskirts of the historic capital. There, my three older sisters, Hortencia, Guadalupe, and Cecilia, were born, and so was I."

"Did you spend your childhood in la colonia Higuera?" I asked.

"No. Ours is a story of migration. From the very beginning we were on the move. You might say that in the long registry of our migrations, we were born along the way, born during our several attempts to leave Mexico City and our failed ventures at settling elsewhere."

"So you moved—"

"Yes, not long after I was born—to San Francisco Soyaniquilpan, about fifty miles north of Mexico City. In contrast to Atizapán de Zaragoza, San Francisco was much like the rural towns from which my parents had come. It was primarily an agricultural town, surrounded by *milpas de maíz y frijol* (fields of maize and beans), and like most towns in the area, it had a rich colonial past. Through his 'connections,' my father secured a job as a farmer, and since this offer included housing, my parents determined to carve out a new beginning. There, my younger brother, Jesús Nicolás, or 'Chuy' as we called him, was born. I still remember playing with him in the front yard and reprimanding him for chasing the chickens away while they were eating. My sisters also adjusted well to the local school system. In one of their class pictures, they are all smiles, and my mom says Hortencia and Lupe (Guadalupe) were highly regarded by their teachers. But despite their initial enthusiasm, my parents developed a love-hate relationship with the town. On the one hand, it was the ideal place to raise a family, and to this day my mom says she regrets moving away. 'I had dozens of chickens, which translated into a generous supply of eggs, and pigs, and we also had fresh milk from our cow,' she once told me. But it was hard to make ends meet. The lady who owned the farm would often delay payment or not pay at all, so my parents faced real financial hardship. My mother recalls a day when my brother fell gravely ill with a high fever. She went to the landowner's house but was again refused the money due to my father. 'Had it not been for *la Santa Virgen María*,' my mother says, who miraculously provided her with five hundred pesos, she would not have been able to pay the doctor, and my brother would not be alive today. She also purchased another piglet!"

"How about you and your siblings? Did you like San Francisco?"

"Generally speaking, we didn't like San Francisco, because it had snakes in abundance. One could find *coralillos, cascabeles,* and *alicantes (Pituophies*

deppei deppei), which tend to live in the cornfields. The latter were the most feared because, according to the locals, they would climb trees or door lintels and drop down, coiling around peoples' necks and pressing to the point of asphyxiation. However, they were more notorious for inviting themselves for lunch at one's house. They would creep into your house, or so say the locals, and whisper some sort of soothing sound that would cause nursing mothers to fall asleep while breastfeeding their babies. Once this hypnotic effect was achieved, the snake would stealthily climb up to the woman's breasts, push the baby's mouth out of the way, and help itself to the mother's milk. As if this wasn't enough, the snake would place its tail on the baby's mouth to keep the baby from crying. But the snake's acumen transcended the banquets it set up for itself. The locals also noted that *alicantes* would spy on the man of the house from a distance and wait for him to go to work. Not only that—they would also follow the workers for a large part of the way to ensure that they were actually going to work and would not interrupt their feast."

Intrigued by these stories of a dark and dangerous snake that preyed on the poor, stealing their nourishment, sapping their strength, and endangering their lives, I asked Roberto if this imagery reflected the kind of situation in which he grew up—anxious struggling to sustain self and family under conditions of chronic scarcity.

"It's possible," Roberto said. "But for my family, the stories were not simply apocryphal, because one day my father noticed a snake was following him to work, and when he came home at noon he found an *alicante* coiled around one of the roof beams while my mother was sleeping. In the blink of an eye, my father pulled out his machete and in one move deprived the *alicante* of its head. After that event we all wondered, rather jokingly, if the *alicante* had been suckling at Mama's breast. We all argued that since my little brother looked pathetically skinny, he must have been sucking the snake's tail, but then again, most of the kids in town, including myself, looked rather bony. Looking back, I realize that we all had to account in some way for the rough reality of malnutrition in those rural areas of Mexico. There weren't enough *frijoles* or milk or *maíz,* and snakes ended up picking up the tab for all of us. Besides, they fed primarily on rodents. Since the crop owner continued to refuse to pay my father, we increasingly had to rely on the *milpa,* farm animals, and, above all, the Virgin of Guadalupe. Unable to make ends meet, we reluctantly returned to Mexico City."

"Why return to Mexico City? Why not go elsewhere, perhaps to one of your parents' hometowns?"

"Even to this day, there is a huge stigma against those who return to their hometown empty-handed or without achieving any success. In those days, Mexico City, or *La Capital,* was seen as a place of opportunity, so to return home with nothing to show for oneself would have been a social disgrace. People don't like to see the faces of failure. Thus the fear of shame and the city's centripetal forces once again drew us back to it, laying claim to our lives even as it now offered a space for us to live.

"One of my father's connections had told him that the government was giving land grants in a recently created barrio on a hill called Las Águilas, named because it was where eagles supposedly nested. The place was just ten minutes north from la colonia Higuera, where my older siblings and I had been born. My dad's nephews, who were married and in their midtwenties, were already there and had laid claim to an entire block, a quarter of which my father secured for our family. I still remember the morning we moved in, because we had to spend the night at one of my cousin's houses and share a bed, which meant that my siblings and I had to sleep on the floor while my parents and my little brother had the bed. The next day was filled with excitement. The morning was fresh, and the noise of trucks, cars, and voices created an atmosphere of excitement as we joined hundreds of people who had come to settle their own Tenochtitlán.[1] Men and women, both young and old, hurried back and forth carrying construction materials to the plots of land given by the government. From that location we could look down into the vast expanse of concrete pyramids that dominated the view of the city. Majestic but impenetrable, there was no place for us there. Our hopes were now in this place. For me, the best news was that I could now play with my cousins, who had a twelve-volt Ride-On plastic car. I remember jumping on it and being pushed toward the left side of the hill and suddenly seeing how the landscape and the smells changed as smoke clouds rose from the valley below. The noise of people talking, dogs barking, and trucks reversing filled that horizon. As my playmates and I reached its edge, we beheld a raw and apocalyptic vision of the Abyss. There, before our eyes, was a dump covering several miles, where the trash of Mexico found its resting place and mountains of trash burned day and night. If there was a hell, this was surely it. We saw people whose appearance was zombie-like, rushing after the trash as it was dumped by the trucks, fighting one other for the spoils. Once the load was delivered, they'd screen it carefully for valuables, food, and furniture. This was a place populated by strange creatures and demons, a terrible frontier. As we beheld this vision, my older sister explained that the site was

called La Viña (The Vine). 'It is also a shantytown of *pepenadores* (garbage pickers),' she said, 'who feed on the waste dumped by the trucks.' Suddenly, she pointed to the right side of the Abyss and, as if by magical power, the curtain of smoke that had hidden it from our eyes now dissipated. There was a shantytown below, extending for many miles. La Viña had taken hold of my imagination."

I was immediately put in mind of Zygmunt Bauman's vivid account of the vast numbers of human beings who are cast out from the dominion of modernity, written off as wastrels, outsiders, *sans papiers,* and disposed of in ghettoes, prisons, and dumping grounds as so much human waste.[2] And so I asked Roberto to say more about how La Viña affected him.

"Stories circulated that a lot of the people below were rich, though they pretended to be poor. They had found wallets filled with money but lived as poor people so that no one would deprive them of their wealth. But would anyone in his or her right mind choose to remain there? La Viña was also a place where toys and spare parts could be found, and occasionally people from the barrio descended to search for metal scraps and objects they could use to adorn their houses. Most importantly, La Viña was a place where candy was abundant! 'Oh boy, *los veñeritos* (little kids from La Viña) must have a good time there,' we'd say to ourselves. 'They get all the candy they want and it's free!' This was partly true, for it was also here that the candy factories dumped their trash, and this included tons of candy. Trimpies, for example, those marzipan-like candies made from goat's milk, were a real prize for us. I remember venturing down there with my friends, our own descent into hell. We would come down a hidden path to avoid being spotted by those below. As we approached La Viña, the terrain changed and the dirt was pitch black, composed primarily of burnt dust, with pieces of metal and broken glass embedded in it. And a foul smell permeated the scene, as did the smoke. We would encounter *viñeros* here and there, some too old to do us any harm. As the Book of Revelation points out, the abyss indeed burns day and night, and this scene before us lent credibility to the catechist's warnings that bad kids will burn in hell.

"Yet, as terrifying as the scene and the admonition were, we did not hesitate to venture into the abyss in search of candy. Making our way through an unstable terrain that was composed primarily of partly burned plastic bags and mountain after mountain of trash, we spotted the candy truck and carefully crafted our plan. 'Let's color our faces with the burned dust and pretend we're *viñeros,* so we can get the candy first,' a friend said. 'No,' another said,

'they'll recognize us. Let's wait until they're all over the place, and then sneak up from behind and grab what we can.' 'I have a better idea,' said another. 'Why don't we trade with them?' We all concluded that was a great idea, except we had nothing to trade, so in the end we had no plan and would have to watch from a safe distance as a circle of people formed behind the truck and waited for it to dump its load. At the very moment this happened, we rushed in and filled our bags with all sorts of candy. But in a matter of seconds we rushed away, because the *viñeros* didn't suffer others stealing their food. We were chased away by children and women and could not always avoid being hit by a stone or a shoe or whatever was thrown at us as we struggled to find our way up the cliff. Once we reached one of the houses bordering the barrio, we were safe, for people there defended us and threw stones at our persecutors. What we could not escape, however, were the visits to the dentist and the constant reprimands from our parents, who imposed various seasons of candy prohibition on us!"

"So you gained insight at a very early age into a world divided into haves and have-nots, a world in which even the most desperately poor often fought one another for things that the rich discarded or trashed."

"Yes, even at that time it was clear to me that we lived in some sort of liminal geographical space. To the right of Las Águilas were the apartment complexes of the so-called middle class, or *los profesionales*—teachers, doctors, engineers, and so on. We hardly went there except on our way to school. Beyond that neighborhood was a beautiful forest reserve that I now wish we had visited more often. It was unusual to find such green places filled with trees and animals, and we went there only once a year, if that. To the left, of course, lay the Abyss, threatening to swallow us up. And I was aware that we were much closer to falling into the abyss than to ever moving up the social ladder. Anyway, these social boundaries were fiercely enforced. We were not welcome in either the wealthy neighborhoods or La Viña because in both places we would be suspected of being thieves. We didn't get along with the people in these places, either. In our view, these people had no codes, no moral laws, or no law at all. They existed in some sort of prelegal status, living in complete anarchy. The police didn't dare to go in there and only did so when *los viñeros* killed somebody, and even then it was only to save face, because the cases were seldom solved. 'You should never play, eat, or have any sort of interaction with them'—that was the rule laid down at my house, and in the entire barrio for that matter. Whenever somebody broke this rule, disaster ensued. At the age of seven, I saw this vividly.

"One of my dad's cousins had gone to a tavern where some of the *viñeros* often drank and played cards, and he decided to play cards with them. Somehow, at noon, while my friends and I were playing soccer in a field that bordered the Abyss, we saw him emerge screaming and bleeding profusely. We rushed to him but then saw a mob of *viñeros* coming after him, so we rushed back and told his relatives, who lived near the Catholic church facing the football field. By this time, he had reached midfield, but the mob had caught up with him. They kicked him, punched him, and threw him back and forth while he cried for help. Incensed, the people from the barrio came out and lined up in front of the church. Some women cried at this barbarism, and the men said they would not let the mob cross the line. We and *los viñeros* had come face-to-face on this fateful day. They were angry and said they'd kill the man because he had cheated them playing poker. As they yelled all sorts of blasphemies, the police arrived and stopped right in between the two crowds, us and them, weapons in hand. To my amazement, they didn't intervene and allowed the violence against my dad's cousin to continue. When the mob began to stone him, he turned his face to us and pleaded for help, yet no one moved, no one dared to defy the angry *viñeros*.

"Suddenly, my relative's mother appeared from behind our line and rushed to him despite attempts to stop her, despite warnings that she'd die. '*Mi hijo, mi hijo,*' she screamed, '*mi hijo . . .* what have they done to you?' Her face, her countenance, cannot be described, but it is forever engraved in my memory. She threw herself over him, taking the blows and the stones, and was almost knocked unconscious. 'They are going to die! Please do something,' people urged the police, but they did nothing. Others started pleading with the *viñeros* that they were acting sacrilegiously by stoning a man in front of the church, but they didn't listen. It was only when the mother threw herself over her son that the women in the mob backed down and urged their men to do the same. While these people obeyed no law and adhered to no religious codes, they saw the love of a mother for her son. They dropped the stones at the site, and others rushed away from the scene with embarrassment. There lay a mother, still crying out, 'My son, my son,' her face disfigured and bleeding from the stones and the blows she had received. He was in shock, shaking and mumbling, right in front of the church quadrangle where he had managed to drag himself and where we thought he was going to die. When the mob left, all the barrio people rushed to help. An ambulance arrived and took both of them to the hospital, while an old man uttered the warning we had heard so many times: 'You must never play, eat, or interact with *those* people.'

On the following Sunday, the priest sermonized on the stoning of Saint Stephen and on the woman Jesus saved from stoning. During the last sermon, a heavy silence reigned in the church, and I'm sure it was because, unlike Jesus, no one had intervened to save this man except his mother. To my surprise, I encountered this man again in California decades later. He lives in Pasadena with his wife and children."

I made a mental note to return to this theme, for it echoed moments in Emmanuel's story when sheer luck had made the difference between life and death or a fortuitous intervention proved critical to a person's survival. I was fascinated by this presence of an ethical sensibility, in this case expressed as maternal love, which, as Roberto put it, "obeyed no law and adhered to no religious code." I mentioned to him that I had recently read Tracy Kidder's book, *Strength in What Remains*,[3] in which Kidder recounts the story of Deogratias, a young medical student from Burundi who escapes the 1993 genocide in his homeland and, after a succession of traumatic ordeals and fortunate encounters, makes his way to America. On October 22, 1993, Deogratias was working as an intern in a rural hospital in northern Burundi. Despite signs of an impending disaster, Deo was so focused on his work that on the day Hutu militias arrived at the hospital bent on hunting down and murdering Tutsis, Deo cheated death only because, in his panic, he had hidden under his bed but left the door to his room wide open. Because it was assumed that the "cockroach" had fled, Deo survived the massacre.

For days and nights on end, he stumbled across an unknown countryside, witness to further killings, hoping to cross the border into Rwanda and safety. Hungry, exhausted, and terrified, he found himself one gray, rainy morning in a banana grove. When a bedraggled group of thirty woman and children approached, he was afraid for his life but lacked the energy to flee. "Are you alive?" one woman asked him. "Yes," he said. "But please don't kill me." The woman, aged about forty-five or fifty, assured him that she wanted to help. She was a Hutu but declared, "But I'm a woman and I'm a mother." That, she said, was her *ubwoko,* her ethnicity. The woman led Deo to the nearby Rwanda border. She told him that she knew what he was going through; many of her friends had been murdered, Tutsis for being the enemy within, Hutus—including her own son—for refusing the join the killing or because the militias wanted their land. She had once been married to a Tutsi, who had been accused of being a traitor and killed. As they came close to the militias guarding the border, the woman told Deo to pretend to be her son.

She protected him, protesting when the militias suspected him of being a cockroach and threatened to take him away.

Roberto reminded me that my notion of an ethics beyond the pale of any specific legal or moral code was reminiscent of the Cynic's emphasis on living according to nature *(kata phusis)* rather than social law and custom *(nomos)*. Conformity to the polis is supplanted by a cosmopolitan sense of self that transcends particular geopolitical allegiances. The figure of the migrant could be genealogically linked, therefore, to the Cynic's view that one's home was the world.

"I suppose we all imagine somewhere we can escape the social distinctions and discriminations that determine our destinies," I said.

In response, Roberto began to describe the affluent neighborhood that adjoined Las Águilas. "On the other side of Las Águilas was Las Lomas Lindas, or the beautiful hills, and this was an upper middle class residential area, where lawyers, teachers, and architects lived. The condos there always had a nice front yard, covered with lovely green grass where people washed their cars or left for work, smartly dressed in suits and ties. I remember these scenes vividly. This was the model of success for us, and our parents invoked this place as a point of reference when they wanted to encourage us to study and work hard at our schoolwork. 'You can be like one of them, making money, living comfortably, and eating good food, but you have to study.' In fact, I could hear their voices even on my way to school, as our bus, *el pitufo* (the Smurf, as it was called, due to its blue color), passed through Las Lomas Lindas on its way to Las Arboledas, where the truly wealthy people lived and where we went to school. I've always wondered why *this* place was not our model of success, since people here were so rich, and I wondered if it was because, for my parents, it was so far beyond our reach or because these people were ignorant of that hell on earth that we lived so close to."

"Did you ever come into contact with the people from Las Lomas Lindas and Las Arboledas?"

"Yes, my older sister worked as a housemaid for one of her teachers on the weekends. She would bring me along, and I'd get to play with the teacher's kids. They lived in a two-story condo, well furnished and decorated. The house had carpet, and there were toys, new toys, all over the place. Best of all was their food. They ate cereal every morning with pancakes and all kinds of fruit. Every Saturday before we arrived, my sister would lecture me on proper manners and warn me not to eat too much so as to not give the impression that we were *muertos de hambre* (starving to death) or dirt poor. Sometimes

I listened to her, sometimes I did not and risked disappointing my sister and her teacher/boss. My father also worked in the area on various construction projects. These people were always doing home renovations or building new houses. They had the money, and we had the need. However, if the interactions between the have-nots (us) and have-nothings (*viñeros*) were often violent, our interactions with the haves were far from amicable. One would assume that by virtue of their education and higher socioeconomic status, these people were 'civilized' or occupied a higher moral ground than the anarchists from La Viña. Such was not the case."

SCHOOLING

Although exhorted by his parents to work hard at school, it was clear that Roberto had, from a very early age, more than an aptitude for study. It came naturally to him, the expression of an inchoate curiosity to understand the world into which he had been born *and* to move beyond its limited horizons. It seemed to me that, unlike his parents, education was for Roberto not merely a means of social mobility but an end in itself. And so I asked if he would tell me more about his schooldays.

"The school we attended in this wealthy suburb was built in honor of José Clemente Orozoco, a great Mexican muralist who painted the *Man on Fire,* and whose other magnificent murals are on display at Dartmouth College, where I had a chance to see them during a speaking appointment there. Since our family was poor, we sometimes convinced my sister Hortencia to leave home early and walk to or from school so that the bus money could be used to buy candy or food. It was a two-and-a-half-hour walk, involving several bridges, roads, and alleys, but we managed to get to school on time, and walking with a full tummy was never a nuisance. The school was a lovely place for me. There, children of the wealthy and the poor experienced conviviality, though our realities kept us in check. It was there that I learned how to read by trying to decipher some graffiti the class bully had written on an outside wall. On my way to the restroom, I saw the letters and started putting the syllables together, one by one, until they started to form a coherent whole, and I spoke the word. This exercise continued silently in class, where I drifted from listening to the teacher's lecture to reading the textbook. At dismissal, we had to walk home, and I read the business advertisements, the bus timetables, the road signs, and suddenly understood.

"Apart from this, I remember this school for a nearly fatal accident I had one morning. Dreading the long walk, we had taken the bus to school, but it was more crowded than usual, and I was all the way in the back, while my siblings were in the front, closer to the door. When the bus stopped, they were able to get off easily, but I had to fight my way past fat ladies, pregnant women, and grumpy old men who resented me pushing through, as well as people who were trying to get on the bus. By the time I reached the front door, the bus had started to move away from the stop. My sisters ran back, shouting at the driver to stop, but he would not. Not wanting to be left on the bus and carried to some place I did not know, I jumped onto the sidewalk, but the momentum made me fall over and suffer some serious bruising. By the time my sisters reached me, my nose was bleeding and they feared I had broken a leg. As they picked me up, the bus stopped and the people who were nearby started cursing the driver, whose response was to drive away. That afternoon I arrived late to class for the first time. When the teacher saw me, she immediately pulled out the first aid kit and put antibiotics on my bruises and took care of the bleeding. That day, I was the center of attention and, for the first time ever, commanded the respect of the bullies, who bragged they would have done the same had they been in my position and had to decide between jumping off and getting lost. This was good news to me, for it meant they'd leave me alone for as long as I had those bruises."

MOVING AND BEING MOVED

Stories of great hardship and sorrow often suggest that experiences which take us to the edge of what we can endure—and almost destroy us—are sometimes preludes to extraordinary transformations. That a near-death experience should have had a positive outcome for Roberto seemed to echo a paradox that ran through his story like a red thread: that in losing one's humanity, in being robbed of one's dignity, and in moral degradation, a person sometimes comes into possession of the very humanity his persecutors lack. As we saw with Emmanuel, the moral qualities of humility and care for the well-being of others are born more often of suffering than security. Perhaps this explained Roberto's sense that his suffering might be a down payment on a better life, as if his season in hell logically and ethically entailed some kind of paradise, much as the path from the smoldering dump at Las Águilas led to the verdure and affluence of Las Lomas Lindas. I wanted

Roberto to talk more about this passage from being a bewildered witness to violence and injustice, unable to comprehend or control the forces that impinged upon his family's life, to being someone capable of playing some small role in deciding his own fate.

I mentioned to Roberto that I had been impressed by Paul Ricoeur's emphasis on ethics as action *(praxis/pragma)*, where action is predicated on a sense of what is possible and the feeling that one is capable of realizing that possibility.[4] I was interested in how Ricoeur's "phenomenology of being able"[5] entailed a phenomenology of movement, since the realization of one's power to act or speak demands bodily and emotional movements of the larynx and tongue or the hands and limbs. If, as Ricoeur suggests, we emphasize the self not as "interiority in relation to itself" but as "an opening onto the world,"[6] then being fully alive means moving out into the world and making that world, in a sense, one's own. Robert agreed that Ricoeur's comments captured something crucial about his childhood experience, and he spoke of his "own perceived powerlessness" as his family suffered the slings and arrows of outrageous fortune, by turns helped, criticized, and ostracized by "people who didn't know what we were going through."

"The final epiphany came when I was eight. We were living in Apaxco, Estado de México. As you know, we had already moved to San Francisco Soyaniquilpan, then to Las Águilas in Atizapán de Zaragoza; Apaxco was my father's latest attempt at a simple life. Although he argued that he moved the family to Apaxco to protect us from the city's violence, poverty, and danger, my mother believed he moved us there so that we would not know about his escapades. In any case, the place seemed promising at first. The name Apaxco comes from Nahuatl and means 'the place where water flows.' It was here that the Aztecs held their second fire ceremony while on their way to the valley of México, where they would eventually settle. Surrounded by a small mountain range, Apaxco is home to a major cement-producing company called Holcim-Apasco. Most people in this small city and its surrounding barrios, such as Pérez de Galaena, work for the company or for the small family-owned companies that grind materials like quartz, dolomite, limestone, calcite, and marble. However, wages are often low and the labor backbreaking. In view of these conditions, my father opted to pursue construction jobs in Mexico City, even though this involved staying in the city all week and coming home only on the weekends, which further increased my mother's suspicions that he had another woman in the city. As newcomers, we were actually welcomed by the locals—many of whom were descendants of those who worked at the

Spanish colonial haciendas of Las Águilas and Guadalupe—and we were often invited to celebrate baptisms, weddings, first communions, and *quinceañeras*.

"In the early 1980s, however, my mother became critically ill with continuous hemorrhages, and this event would eventually uproot us all from Mexico and drive us to the United States. Initially, my mom's bleeding was not as pronounced as it later became. She could still attend her doctor's appointments, and I'd often go with her. As hospital visits and medical expenses increased, so did the bills. My father started selling his construction tools— hammers, pliers, wheelbarrows—and other valuable items, such as the sewing machine he had purchased for my mother some years before. Despite these sacrifices, her health continued to deteriorate, and the doctors gave us no hope. The Gospel of Mark 5:27–29 narrates a similar story of a woman who suffered hemorrhages and spent all she possessed on medicine, but no doctor could cure her.

"To this day I still remember the time when my mother started bleeding while on the bus, and we had to get off before our stop so she could clean herself. We went from house to house, but people shut their doors in our faces, despite the fact that she pleaded with them to the point of tears. I'd often wonder how people could be so indifferent to another person's pain. It was a premonition of things to come. As her hemorrhages increased and she was either unable or afraid to walk, the responsibility to seek help fell on me, the oldest male, even though I was only eight years old. Sometimes late at night or early in the morning, I'd venture out into the dark, knocking on people's doors to ask for help. The fear of evil spirits and creatures—such as La Llorona (the woman who had drowned her children in the river and afterward appeared at night with a shrieking cry of '*ay mis hijos*'), El Naual (a man that turned into various animals), Las Parturientas (the spirits of women who died in childbirth and rode the wind)—which had long haunted my imagination, was set aside. I was facing a greater foe: death herself. It was always the local Pentecostal who would open the door and heed the call for help. A man named Meliton would often drive us to the hospital, but when my mother's situation worsened, we had to rely on the ambulance. My mom grew increasingly weak and was unable to take care of my two-year-old sister, María Magdalena. She would lie gravely ill in bed at home or spend several days at a time in hospital. One day, returning from school, I saw an ambulance in the distance, parked at the back of my house, but seeing the ambulance at home was not unusual. What shocked me was that the ambulance

was of greenish color. As a child I had heard that a green ambulance is sent when a person has no hope or is already dead. With these thoughts in mind, I ran as fast as I could to my house, wanting to see and hear my mother, wanting to feel the touch of her hand on my face for one last time. When I got there, the crowd was so huge that it blocked the entrance.

"When they saw me, people moved aside until I suddenly found myself standing in the center of our living room surrounded by a circle of women and men praying. For a moment, time seemed to have frozen, and I could not believe my eyes. Half the circle was composed of nuns and Catholic devotees who were arduously praying the rosary: '*Santa María, Madre de Dios, ruega por nosotros, pecadores, ahora y en la hora de nuestra muerte. Amén.*' The other half consisted entirely of Pentecostals, Bibles in hand, reciting parts of Psalm 23: 'The Lord is my shepherd, I shall not want.... Even though I walk through the valley of the shadow of death, I fear no evil.' One could say that the scene reflected the powerful ecumenical spirit in the area, but the truth is that both Pentecostals and Catholics had been trying to recruit my mother for quite some time. Despite their doctrinal differences, they had all come to bid my mother farewell. I still could not believe the scene but had no time to account for it, or for the gracious but pitiful looks they all cast upon me. I made my way to the bedroom, where all my siblings and close friends had gathered. My father and siblings were in tears. When my mom saw me, she asked me to come closer, caressed my hair, and murmured certain words that for the life of me I cannot remember, but I know she was saying goodbye. Then she asked to hold my little sister, María Magdalena, but the child started crying because, since my mom had spent so much time in hospitals and away from home, my sister no longer recognized her. Suddenly, the priest appeared and began to administer the last rites. The room was soon filled with incense and the application of *la extremaunción* (last rites): '*Per istam sanctam unctionem et suam piissimam misericordiam adiuvet te Dominus gratia spiritus sancti ut a peccatis liberatum te salvet atque propitius allevet.*' My mom, however, became uneasy and interrupted the priest so much that at the end of his prayer he leaned forward and told her, '*Mujer, muere ya y descansa en paz*' (Woman, die now and rest in peace). Unable to cope with the situation, I went outside and sat under the shade of our jacaranda tree in resignation and waited for the end. According to the Gospel of Mark, 'When she [the woman with hemorrhages] heard about Jesus, she came up behind him in the crowd and touched his cloak, because she thought, "If I just touch his clothes, I will be healed." Immediately, her bleeding stopped and she felt in

her body that she was freed from her suffering' (NIV, Mark 5:27–29). After the Pentecostals and the Catholics had left, I went back inside to be with my mother, fearing she had already passed away. To my surprise, she was still breathing, and the next day she even had chicken soup for lunch. Somehow, she had found the strength within to touch Jesus's cloak, not with her hands but with her faith, and she was healed! As the weeks and months passed, she recuperated and soon returned to her regular housewife duties.

"Whenever I read the gospel narrative of 'The Woman with Hemorrhages,' I value it in a very special way, for it vividly resembles my mom's story. But such similitude makes me raise questions that the author chose not to comment upon. Since the woman had spent all her money on doctors, how did she recover financially? Did she borrow money, or was she perhaps taken in by a relative? Or did she have to migrate elsewhere looking for work? In our case, my mom's illness and the expenses we had incurred with hospitals, medicines, and ambulance rides made it impossible for us to recuperate financially. It was this event that would uproot us all from Mexico and drive us to the United States in search of a new start.

"Having heard about our situation, Honorio, one of my father's nephews living in California, encouraged my father to migrate to the U.S. and offered him a loan to pay for travel expenses, the coyote, and housing in California. When he came back to Apaxco for the weekend, my father told my mom he was leaving 'pal Norte' (El Norte means 'the north' but is also used as a metonym for the U.S.—the place where he could make lots of money and get us back on track).

"A few days later, after lunch, he and my sister set out on their journey. We walked outside with them to the gate. Then my little brother and I followed them to the bus stop, and even ran for a few seconds after the bus. Only my sister stuck her head out the window to say goodbye. I would not see them again for several years. Had I known the hardships that awaited us, I would have jumped on that bus too or asked my father to take us all with him. Surely we could start again elsewhere, but I figured my dad knew better.

"A month after my father and sister left, we received news from them. Their circumstances were difficult, but they remained hopeful. Every first of the month, my mom went to the post office to collect the mail and see if my dad had sent money. The first months my father and sister did their best to send money and letters, but eventually we received neither.

"Without a source of income, our situation in Apaxco became unsustainable. People started to turn against us, and our security was also at risk.

Knowing that my father was away, men from the town would attempt to break in. Many nights I had to sneak out through a window and run to plead with the neighbors for help. Being only eight or nine years old, I feared the darkness, but these situations forced me to overcome my fears. My family's safety was at stake, and it fell on me to ensure they'd be fine. One day I came home late from a friend's house and found a man in the backyard searching for ways to break into my house. He looked at me and even had the audacity to ask me what I was doing there. I didn't answer but ran to get help instead. The neighbors, however, had grown tired of my calls for help and doors were shut, and others were never opened. As a last resort, I turned to a forty-year-old woman who was known for her feistiness, and after I explained the situation, she was more than willing to help. She called a few of her daughters and escorted me back to my house. When we arrived, the man had been joined by at least four other men. The woman, however, began to slap the men and, calling each and every one of them by name, forced them to disband. Although I was relieved to have obtained help from this group, it was clear to us that we could no longer live safely in that town.

"Though extreme, our situation was not the exception but the rule. When the breadwinner of the family migrates to the U.S., his family often becomes susceptible to unspeakable abuses and deprivations, but this is a part of the story that most people never hear. Under such circumstances, the familial roles and hierarchies are also altered. The wife becomes the head of the household and strives to find ways to put food on the table. The task of rearing of children and household chores are then transferred to the oldest daughter, whereas the oldest males assume the protection of the family, as in my case. But even despite such concerted efforts to keep the family afloat, difficult choices must be made. Without money and news from my father and sister, my mom decided to move the family to her hometown, El Huizache, in the state of Guanajuato."

EL HUIZACHE

"The name Huizache means 'thorny bush.' It is a primarily agricultural town, and my mom had an extensive family network there. When we arrived, everybody turned out to be an aunt, an extended cousin, or an uncle. And yet I had no roots there. Everybody in the town, young and old, knew each other, and most of them worked for local agricultural companies that harvested

barley, wheat, tomatoes, corn, and chili peppers. A few of them had their own *milpas* to tend and worked on these 24/7. During our first month there, people were polite, and we were amazed at the beauty of this town. My father also started sending money again, and with it my mom built a small house on a plot of land she had purchased from her brother. However, a few months later my father disappeared from the picture again, and this time we didn't hear from him for at least a year. Due to our dire circumstances, my mom and my third oldest sister, Cecilia, started working in the fields, but the low wages made it impossible to support a family of six. Realizing that my father would not be returning, my mother decided to leave and start a new life on her own. After all, she was much younger than my father, though she realized she could not make this fresh start with all of us. One afternoon she suddenly came home and said she was taking my two youngest siblings, María and Alejandra, to Baja California, close to the U.S. border, where a man had offered her work. The very thought of what was unfolding before us prevented us from uttering a word. So we cried, and so did she, which simply confirmed that this was not a see-you-later but a farewell. She asked her relatives to keep an eye on us, but our situation had made us more vulnerable, and they tried to take advantage of us in every possible way. Hunger and need tend to make people forget family ties and turn against each other in quite dark and unspeakable ways. Water sources were denied, doors were shut, and we began to deal again with people trying to break into our home. One night we had nothing to eat and had to steal corn from our relatives, whose cornfield was a few minutes away. Under cover of darkness, we entered the field and collected as much corn as possible in order to turn it into *masa* (corn dough) and make tortillas. As we made our way home, a man appeared from nowhere and asked us to stop. He turned out to be Chente, my mom's uncle who was working for another uncle guarding the field. At first, he scolded us, saying that he had come close to shooting us. After we explained our circumstances, he was so touched or embarrassed that he offered protection and food but said we should stay away from the field. Under these conditions, and with both our parents gone, the task of making difficult choices befell us. We decided to split up in order to survive. My brother was 'adopted,' so to speak, by his best friend's mother, who was a bit wealthy and liked my brother (who was eight years at the time) because he looked so much like her son, to the point that people thought they were twins. My sister, who was thirteen, went to live with another aunt, and I, then eleven, had to stick around with Candelaria, my ninety-five-year-old great-grandmother."

I was hesitant to ask Roberto to speak more about his mother's disappearance from his life, and how he endured not knowing where she was, whether she was alive or dead, or if she would ever return. I was well aware that these recollections were emotionally harrowing for him, for he had already mentioned to me that several episodes in his childhood had been blocked out but would suddenly return with overwhelming and often devastating effects hours or days after he had completed writing an installment of his story. I therefore suggested that he take his time, writing only as much as he could manage and waiting until he felt ready to revisit the more painful events of his past. "Even I am finding it tough, at times," I confessed, "reading about your separation from your parents and the dispersal of your siblings."

I was also fascinated by the question of how a human being rationalizes the gross inequalities in the distribution of wealth *and* well-being in this world—how we individually live with the fact that fortune smiles on some but deserts others, irrespective of their personal qualities or needs. But again, I was determined to exercise patience and allow Roberto to share his sociological and theological views on these matters in his own words, and in his own good time.

A week passed before I saw Roberto again, and when he resumed his story it was as if he had read my mind and knew what I hoped he would expand upon.

"When my mom left, she promised to return within a month to take us with her. Although we knew she had left forever, we had to believe she'd return, perhaps because to accept the truth would have amounted to accepting that our family as such had failed. After the month passed, my siblings and I would go to the bus station every Saturday to wait for her. We imagined she would bring all kinds of goods we lacked at the time, such as clothes, shoes, food, and lots of candy. It's difficult to recall this memory because we waited for hours until the last bus came and went at sunset. We searched for our mother among the many people coming to town, only to encounter mockery and pity. We must have been distressing to behold. When the wait was over, my little brother would look at me for answers. I had none, and we'd walk home in silence. In time, my brother got used to his new family, so I would make the journey to the bus stop alone. I always came back home disheartened. Sometimes I thought that my mother had forgotten the way back, or that the bus had mistakenly dropped her elsewhere, or that the

driver had refused to open the door for her and she had to get off at the next town. Hence, even as the bus departed, I would look intently at the windows. Finally one day, I got so upset at the situation and at my mother lying to us, that I decided to go and play soccer instead of waiting for her. I don't recall the day I stopped hoping she'd return; perhaps I never did. But rather than wait at the bus stop, my siblings and I started to gather at Candelaria's house every Sunday night to spend time together and tell stories of previous times when we were all together and had it good. We'd laugh, remembering the time my older sister Hortencia, my father's favorite, broke her arm and blamed us all. Fearing a beating, some ran to the neighbors' houses, while others climbed a tree and were quickly found and took a beating. When the candle was spent, my sister and brother would go back to their new homes, and I'd stay with Candelaria, whose long prayers and continuous cursing of witches and demons provided a sense of safety, allowing me to fall asleep."

"How old were you at this time?"

"Thirteen."

"What sustained you through those hard times?"

"In those tumultuous years, school was not only a safe haven but also my only joy. I represented my school in two academic contests where students were tested on math, history, and cultural literacy. I came in third and fifth respectively. Furthermore, my instructors, such as *el maestro* Hector, were always there to cheer me up. I completed all my homework in class and turned it in before class ended. My peers despised me as the teachers' pet and often threatened me with after-school beatings, which were nothing unusual for me. During that time I even joined an adult literacy campaign and was teaching three adults how to read. Despite my achievements, it was still difficult to learn on an empty stomach, to stand alone at award ceremonies, and to graduate from middle school without my parents cheering me on. While most students in my grade graduated from middle school, the majority went off to work at their family's *milpa,* waiting to become old enough to pursue the American dream. As an outsider, I also had hopes of making my journey out of El Huizache, for there I had no land, no roots, and no future."

"I get the impression," I said to Roberto, "that you were desperate to escape the stressful situation at home more than you entertained dreams of a better life across the border. Or did these considerations merge in your mind?"

"The myth of the American dream constantly haunts the imagination of young Mexican men living in rural areas, and it is fueled by all the success stories of those who return with trucks, cars, and money. Some even bring

several boxes of beer and liquor that they drink in the town's plaza to assert their newly acquired status. Daring ones, like Jaime, a thirty-year-old guy from El Huizache, even brought a white girl back—a tall, blue-eyed platinum blonde who embodied the success of a guy that people had previously regarded as a failure. What is more, he now had his green card, so we knew he was not going to stick around. In any case, the bar was set high for single would-be migrants. From then on, it was not enough to simply return with a car and money. You must also marry a white girl, and as if this wasn't enough, you had to convince her to come to Mexico! However, not everyone who ventured out to the U.S. made it alive. There is no need to create high-voltage fences at the border, as some bright U.S. politicians suggest; the journey is filled with perils, and many people die along the way. Thus, when someone does not write back after a few months, it's clear they are not well; when you don't hear from them for a year, you can assume they died on the journey at the hands of cartels, in the deserts of Arizona, or crossing the treacherous Rio Grande, as was the case with one of our cousins. He had gone north but got carried away by the currents while crossing the river, and those who accompanied him were unable to find him. However, he remains alive in the memory of loved ones, his mother in particular, who prefers to think he opted to forget entirely about Mexico and his family and is living the good life in the U.S."

MARÍA INÉS RETURNS

"One Saturday night, as I was sitting in the plaza of El Huizache to rest, I saw a taxi going in the direction of my house, which was located in the east side of town. For a moment, I imagined it was my mother, but the pain of hoping made me dismiss the thought right away. Besides, it had been at least two years since she had left. When I finally reached Candelaria's house, I heard the voices of my grandmother, aunts, and cousins inside. This was shocking to me, because they all disliked Candelaria's continual reprimands about what she regarded as their wasteful lifestyle. When I opened the door, I saw my mother sitting on the floor with her suitcases open, giving presents and clothes to everybody. I could not believe my eyes. As soon as she saw me, she tried to hug me, but I didn't hug back. Here was the woman I had waited for at the bus stop, and she had all the goods she had promised she would bring, but she had taken too long. Sensing my resentment, she apologized to all of

us. With tears in her eyes, she explained how she had crossed into the U.S., made amends with my father, and become a Pentecostal Christian. Now she had returned to take us back with her so that we could be a family again.

"Within a week, we had geared up for the trip, and we departed on a Saturday morning. The same bus that had disappointed me so many times was now taking us to reunite with the rest of our family—my father, my sister Hortencia, and my little sisters Alejandra and Magdalena waited for us in Bakersfield.

"We reached Celaya, Guanajuato, late in the afternoon and boarded a train to Guadalajara around eight that evening. Next morning, we arrived at Guadalajara, where we took a break to eat and wait for 'El Burro' (The Donkey), as they call the slow and beat-up passenger train that goes all the way to the border town of Mexicali. When the train finally arrived, we boarded and prepared for a three-day journey.

"Most of those in the train were migrant hopefuls, bound for the border, with the same dreams and expectations as mine—"

"Were you consciously in search of the American dream, or in search of your family, or both?" I asked.

"You are right," Roberto said. "What filled my mind at this time was not so much the American dream, but the possibility of being reunited with my family. The journey in 'El Burro' was complicated in many ways. In an effort to save as much money as possible on our trip, my mother purchased snacks for lunch and ramen noodle soups for dinner. Moreover, at almost every stop, the army conducted searches for drug dealers and contraband. Yet the journey was also exciting in that I got to see how beautiful Mexico is. In Apaxco I only saw bare, dry mountains, but passing through Sinaloa the landscape was green, filled with all types of fruit trees. The sight of women knitting on their front porches, men rushing home on their horses before sunset, and little kids playing soccer made me realize the vitality of the country I was leaving. But regardless of how green and fertile the soil appeared, my family had been unable to take root there.

"The nights on the train were long and cold, but at least now we had our mother to care for us. On the third day, the train arrived at Mexicali in Baja California. We then took a bus to Tijuana, where we were to wait for a coyote who would help us cross the border. As the bus descended into Tijuana, we caught sight of a huge American flag in San Ysidro.[7] A high steel fence extended for miles on end. It seemed as though America was at war with the third world. Even the hills on the American side appeared to serve as some

sort of second line of defense, with border patrol cars positioned strategically along them. The noise of a helicopter, or 'El Mosco' as migrants call it, flying back and forth still haunts me to this day. Indeed, the American fortress seemed impregnable, though it allowed 'legal' Mexicans and American 'spring breakers' to travel back and forth."

THE BORDERLANDS

Tijuana is the largest city on the Baja California peninsula and a flourishing industrial and financial center. For the migrant, however, Tijuana is the gateway to the U.S., a place to rest before the crossing is undertaken, and a point of no return. "The mere sight of the mighty steel fence drills a hole in one's hopes and sobers up even the most enthusiastic migrant." Roberto said. "A heavy silence reigned as we came in sight of the border. '*No será nada fácil*' (It will not be easy at all), one migrant said, rather prophetically, while a Pentecostal shouted, 'God didn't bring us all the way here to go back.' When our bus finally reached the station, we caught our breath and proceeded to a plaza where our coyote was supposed to meet us.

"Once at the plaza, we sat on a bench waiting for our coyote. But unbeknownst to us, we had become targets of a scam that now began to unfold before our eyes. In her book, *Borderlands/La Frontera,* Gloria Anzaldúa describes the border as '*herida abierta*' (an open wound), a place where the first world grinds against the third.[8] On the Mexican side, however, the border is a jungle with its own rules and expectations, where one is either the prey or the predator, the hunted or the hunter. Needless to say, migrants are often associated with prey, as the term *pollo* (chicken), which is ascribed to them, clearly illustrates. Ironically, one of the first moves in surviving is to identify oneself as a *pollo* but as one who has already been claimed or taken by a *coyote*. Learn this rule and you will live; miss it and you'll probably become a statistic.

"While waiting on the plaza, I noticed different groups of *pollos* talking to a coyote. You can identify a coyote because he or she is usually better dressed and well fed and has a certain air of assurance. Furthermore, he or she is often doing the talking while others listen attentively.

"My observations were interrupted by my mother, who had just spoken to my father over a public telephone and announced that our coyote should arrive soon. After waiting for at least an hour, which seemed like an eternity,

we were interrupted by a kid my age riding a bike around us. 'Señora, I can cross you guys over to California,' he said. But how could such a ragged, tiny, and skeletal character make this claim? We all laughed, but he continued talking. 'I have relatives in San Diego, Los Angeles, and San Francisco.' His insistence drew an answer from my mother: 'No thanks, we are going to Bakersfield.' 'Bakersfield?' the kid replied with apparent perplexity, as he continued to encircle us. 'I've never heard of that city.' My mother explained that it was just two hours north of L.A. This indirect Q & A continued for about fifteen minutes until finally he left. Ten minutes later a coyote arrived. He approached us and asked for María. He said he'd been sent by my father, Bartolomé, to take us to Bakersfield. My mother answered politely but asked why he had been delayed. Meanwhile, I screened the guy from head to toe and concluded he was not to be trusted. He mumbled when he talked and did not look my mom in the eye. My mom asked us to pick up our things. The guy smiled, offering food, but still I did not trust him. Finally, as if she had been having an internal monologue, my mom began to interrogate the guy, and I noticed a certain exasperation in her tone. 'When did you last talk to my husband?' she asked. 'Last night,' the coyote replied. He was wrong! My dad had sent the coyote our way only three hours ago, but we said nothing. My mom pressed on. 'Where did you make arrangements with my husband?' she asked. 'Oh, downtown,' the coyote replied, very self-assured, since everybody knows that all deals are made and closed downtown. However, my dad had met our coyote while working in the fields and sealed the deal there, and this my mom knew very well. 'You are not our coyote,' my mom asserted, while looking him in the eye. He smiled like an impostor who has been caught out, but quickly offered us a better rate to cross us over. As he departed, our actual coyote arrived and my mom gave him the update. We were all quite anxious at this point. We looked around and saw the kid on the bike and the impostor talking to each other. They were soon joined by other people, but our coyote instructed us not to look at them and led us to a taco truck nearby. Although we were still being watched by the impostor and his decoy, our coyote said we were safe. We had been claimed, and other coyotes had to respect this fact. But leaving in a rush would be a sign of fear, and it would only attract these predators to us. We were left alone."

When Roberto went on to describe Tijuana as "an entirely new space, governed by its own rules and expectations," I was immediately reminded of my

weeks in southeast London with Sierra Leonean migrants, and their persistent, sometimes paranoid, sense of being in breach of unspoken rules and regulations, their experience of being socially inept or ignorant, constantly afraid of taking a wrong step, arousing the suspicion of the police, attracting the minatory stares of locals—struggling not for visibility but invisibility. You crave a guide, someone who knows the ropes, who possesses the practical and social know-how without which you cannot hope to navigate this bewildering and alien environment.

"To survive," Roberto said, "you must remember that you are at the border and your entire journey is contingent on that immediate reality. The border towns have their own rules, and you must quickly learn them, adapt to them, or negotiate them. You see, the border crossings at Tijuana, Juárez, or Reynosa attract a lot of lowlifes and predators—wretches who are afraid to dream or to hope for themselves, and who opt to live off the dreams of their *paisanos*. They gather in groups like cunning lions, observing, taking notes, and identifying their prey. Usually, they zero in on the weakest link of group or a disoriented migrant—one who has just arrived and does not know the rules, one who can't get help from relatives in the U.S., or one who has been deported several times and is utterly demoralized. Then the decoy moves to collect information, goes back to the group, and the impostor coyote is deployed. No one will ever know what happened to that migrant. Two or three years later, one might read that a mass grave has been uncovered, or read that El Pozolero (someone who makes pozole—a traditional Mexican pork and vegetable stew), the guy who worked for the cartels dissolving enemies in acid barrels, has confessed to unspeakable deeds, or learn, as we have recently, that members of Los Zetas, Mexico's bloodiest drug cartel, kidnapped seventy migrants from Central America, took them to a secluded location, and shot all of them. We know of the event only because two migrants survived and notified the army. The police could not be trusted."

THE CROSSING

"That evening we checked into a motel around seven thirty, and I fell into a deep sleep. We were all woken up at midnight and instructed to get ready for the crossing. We were to take only what we needed for that night's journey. The coyote drove us to the border point, dropped us there, and then crossed the border with our luggage, parked the car, and returned about

thirty minutes later. We then made our way to the actual border fence, which was just beyond the railroad tracks. The night was cold, but at least we had clear skies with the moon lighting our path. As we reached the border fence, a Mexican undercover officer pulled us aside and demanded identification, which we provided. He wanted to know where we were going. 'Are you crossing?' he asked. 'Yes,' the coyote said, perplexed that we had to explain ourselves at all. We were in Mexico, our own country. When the officer realized that we were not about to give him any money, he let us go, and we finally reached the border fence. It now seemed more intimidating than when we had seen it from the bus earlier that day, but there was no time to lament. Someone from the houses near the fence came quickly to our aid with a ladder, but even then we had difficulties, because the ladder did not reach the top of the fence. When the four of us—my mom, my sister Cecilia, my brother Jesús, and I—had finished going over the fence, the coyote asked us to quickly take cover, so we ran up into the hills and hid behind the bushes. Three minutes later, El Mosco flew by several times, which led the coyote to think we had been spotted by someone on the hill. We moved deeper into a nearby canyon and found what we thought was a good hiding spot in a small cave surrounded by bushes and overlooking the canyon. From a distance, we saw how El Mosco located pocket after pocket of migrants. It flew over them, giving warnings, until the border agents arrived in SUVs or on motorcycles. Some tried to run in desperation, but they were rounded up like cattle. My heart was beating so intensely I felt it would explode. I was sweating. Fortunately, our hiding place was not close to any road or trail, but we still could be spotted from above. The coyote told us not to look at the spotlight; our eyes would reflect it and we'd be caught.

"An hour passed. The roaring of engines and the sound of El Mosco were truly a torture. The climax came when we heard the sound of footsteps cracking the dry bushes and approaching our hiding place. We held our breath and ducked closer together. Then, suddenly someone tapped the coyote's shoulder and whispered, 'Hey señor, would you like to buy some hot chocolate, *empanadas,* or *tortas de carne asada?*' We could not believe our eyes. There before us was a Mexican man carrying a huge pot of hot chocolate and bags of bread—a border entrepreneur!

"To make the most of the situation, or normalize it, the coyote bought hot chocolate and bread for all of us. The border entrepreneur told us he had his own business near the plaza on the Mexican side, but this was a way he supplemented his income. When we asked how he had been able to find us, he

said he knew the best hiding spots on the hill, as did the border patrol. After giving us some information about the peak and the hours of relaxed vigilance by the border patrol, he encouraged us to change hiding places or descend into San Ysidro. At three o'clock, following his advice, we moved closer to the city. But we could not enter the town because there were at least three border patrol vehicles parked on the roadside between the hills and the city proper. We waited for at least another hour, but the SUVs didn't move. The border merchant had told us that such vehicles were usually unoccupied. Should we believe him? What if he was wrong? What if we got deported? At four o'clock, we decided to pass right in front of these vehicles. As we approached them, we heard the sound of El Mosco and ran faster, but when I passed by one of the vehicles I didn't see anyone inside. As I entered the city, I was struck by its tranquil atmosphere, its wide and well-lit streets, and the number of fast food restaurants that flanked each corner. McDonalds, Burger King, and Jack in the Box ruled the intersections. I had never had a burger before nor, given my circumstances, did I crave one. The coyote asked us to walk normally now, to smile and pretend we were a family that had just left one of the restaurants. This was a tough act when police cars were driving slowly past us. At four thirty, we reached the parking lot from where we would make our way to San Clemente, our last checkpoint within the U.S. Though the morning was cold, we were excited and felt we had made it. We were also reassured by the coyote, who spoke as if the worst had passed.

"As we reached San Clemente, however, we saw a huge traffic line. The coyote's demeanor changed radically, for it was clear that a random check was under way and all traffic had to stop. Immigration officers would go from car to car for a certain period of time, interrogating people, opening trunks, and ensuring that no migrants were being smuggled in. If caught, a coyote could face years in jail for human trafficking, and our coyote was obviously well aware of his possible fate. He started to sweat and mumble and said we needed to get out of the car and hide in the mountains to our right, since we could not hide in the beaches or the ocean on the left. My mom demanded more specific information, because we didn't have much food or money with us. The coyote said he would go through the checkpoint and then return for us. In a matter of seconds, we were literally kicked out of the car. With no time to process the situation, we ran toward the hills, only to realize that they were farther away than they appeared. So we hid under a tree. Besides, we needed to stay close to the road to make sure we were able to board when the coyote returned for us. At quarter of seven, we realized that the coyote was

not returning for us. It was a windy and cold morning. As dawn broke, we saw border patrol cars combing the hills. We knew it would be only a matter of time before we were caught. As we huddled together, we saw that our hiding place was close to a nest of scorpions, so we could not stay there too long. We heard the roar of an engine approaching and actually felt a sense of relief. It was indeed a border patrol car, though they were not coming for us."

THE FACE OF THE OTHER

"The agents parked their SUV about twenty feet away from us and walked toward an area of long grass near the road. Out of nothing, the two agents grabbed a migrant by his hair, hauled him to his feet, and hurled all the insults at him that they could muster. 'Get up, you son of a bitch!' they yelled. The terror in this old migrant's face haunts me to this day. Disoriented, starving, and surely unwanted, he was powerless in such a situation. I will not forget this man as long as I live. He must have been in his late sixties, of wiry build, with gray hair. There was something dark and magical in the labels and terminology used by border patrol agents—such as 'wetback,' 'piece of shit,' 'motherfucker'—terms that turn human beings into animals.[9] This old man was actually just one of five migrants pulled from that hiding place. They were thrown into the back of the border patrol vehicle. My brother Chuy, who witnessed the entire scene from our hiding place and was only ten at the time, broke down in tears and started shaking. Upset, I reprimanded him and asked him to keep his cool, but looking back I wish I had cried with him. Of my childhood and teenage years, what I hated the most was being 'the oldest male,' because I could not cry, I could not laugh, I could not be afraid, and I could not break down. At around eight thirty, we were debating whether to turn ourselves in voluntarily, not only because our coyote had left us stranded but because of the scorpions."

There were times when Roberto confessed that his story might seem unbelievable and that many people would not take it seriously. I saw this in part as an expression of the incredible distance that lay between his present and past circumstances. Indeed, Roberto was sometimes troubled by the gap between his life in the U.S. and the lives of those who had stayed at home and made the best of their circumstances there. Not only did the latter imagine

the migrant to be wealthier and more powerful than he really was, but the migrant's experiences were often dismissed as unbelievable. In writing about a recurring nightmare among Holocaust survivors, Primo Levi touches on one of the deepest sources of loss among migrants: "Strangely enough, this same thought ("even if we were to tell it, we would not be believed") arose in the form of nocturnal dreams produced by the prisoners' despair. Almost all the survivors, orally or in their written memoirs, remember a dream which frequently recurred during the nights of imprisonment, varied in its detail but uniform in its substance: they had returned home and with passion and relief were describing their past sufferings, addressing themselves to a loved one, and were not believed, indeed were not even listened to."[10]

I told Roberto that the issue might not be credibility per se; it was, perhaps, the gap between the reader's world and the world he described. As such, it was a question of not knowing how one could respond, what one could possibly say or do in response to the journeys that migrants undertake, staking everything on a new lease on life. For several days, the face that haunted Roberto had also haunted me, reminding me of the points Emmanuel Levinas makes about the face "as the most basic mode of responsibility.... The face is not in front of me (en face de moi) but above me; it is the other before death, looking through and exposing death.... [T]he face is the other who asks me not to let him die alone, as if to do so were to become an accomplice in his death."[11] Levinas's challenging remarks make one acutely aware that in doing ethnography one does far more than gain self-knowledge through one's encounters with the other; one is taken beyond oneself, undergoing an eclipse of one's familiar identity, effectively becoming an-other. Sometimes, this finds expression in the uncanny sensation that the other's story is one's own story from another lifetime or previous incarnation. At other times, one imagines that the other is affording a glimpse of what life would have been like had one been born into that other world rather than one's own. There is, accordingly, a compelling analogy to be drawn between the psychology of narcissism and the politics of global capitalism. The narcissist assumes that "I am everything to myself and must be everything to others, but others are nothing in themselves and become something only as a means for me."[12] For the privileged, those on the global margins seldom exist for them *emotionally;* they do not exist as human beings whose raisons d'être can be placed on a par with their own.

We touch here on the transformative implications of entering deeply into the lifeworld of an-other, and of the open-ended, aporetic character of

conversation as ethnographic method.[13] In my view, the justification for ethnography is not epistemological but existential. It cannot presume to *know* the other, for this would be to claim the last word, to bring dialogue to an end by declaring that something is now settled and grasped. Rather, the ethnographer seeks to provide an ethical justification for engagement with the other—answering the ethical summons to enter into that other lifeworld, not to achieve perfect comprehension of it but to call into question, and place in brackets, all that he or she customarily privileges as natural, moral, legal, or human. As Neville Symington puts it, "We shall make no progress in the transformation of the human condition until we understand that its root lies in the emotional state where the other does not exist; where reality is cancelled out; where a pseudo-self dominates the scenario."[14] Reading the next installment of Roberto's narrative, this existential imperative of being recognized in one's humanity—and not simply reduced to some categorical term or vernacular tag—seemed to define the borderland experience itself.

DEPORTATION CENTER

"Although one expects to be caught and deported at any time, one is never entirely prepared for it. After the border patrol caught the group of migrants near us, we stood up and became visible from all points. It was around nine o'clock. I put my hands over my brother's eyes and ears so he would not see or hear the insults and instructions that were yelled at us by the border agents as we were led to their van. As we were driven to the deportation center, which is close to the San Clemente checkpoint, we became aware of how impregnable the border really was. We had jumped the steel fence and survived the mountains, yet were caught only a few miles from our objective.

"When we arrived at the deportation center, we were 'processed,' then asked to sign a form in which we consented to voluntary deportation. Then we joined a long line of about fifteen people and were led into a cell. At the entrance of the cell stood a short immigration officer who looked like the wrestler Hulk Hogan (bandana and mustache included). I will always remember his smile, though, to my surprise, he was not there to mock us but to cheer us up. 'Next time, amigos, don't give up. I'll see you mañana!' At that moment, however, his words felt quite insulting, for none of us could see how we could possibly make it back.

"Inside the deportation center, migrants don't speak much to each other, nor do we look each other in the eye. The reality of our failure weighed heavily on us. We had traveled hundreds of miles, spent money on coyotes, and endured unspeakable humiliations. We were deportees. For some, this was their last chance, and they were probably already considering the prospect of returning to their hometowns. In short, we were licking our wounds and mourning quietly as we waited for the final hour. Finally, we boarded a bus and were driven to the Tijuana border. Once there, we were expelled and had to cross a bridge back into Mexico, where a group of human rights activists wanted to inquire how we had been treated in the U.S. I was annoyed because regardless of what we'd say, we all knew little would get done. Even to this day, Mexico simply reacts to U.S. immigration policies. Most of us chose to remain silent and keep our heads down."

Many months later, after several more unsuccessful attempts to cross the border, Roberto and his family made it to a safe house in San Ysidro.

"The atmosphere was tense, as more migrants, including a pregnant woman, were brought in by coyotes throughout the night. We were instructed not to open the door to anyone to avoid being deported yet again. At around midnight we were nearly asleep. The coyotes had completed their rounds and were beginning to draft plans for getting us all to our respective destinations. While they were discussing, however, someone knocked violently at the door. Immediately the lights were turned off and silence reigned, with the exception of the coyotes whispering to each other, 'La migra, la migra' (border patrol). After a few minutes, the knocking stopped and we heard the footsteps of someone going away. We all sighed with relief, for we were all tired and feared that another deportation would make us vulnerable to the coyotes looking for game in Mexico. As the lights were turned on and we began to relax, my mom pulled a package of cookies from her sweater and fed us. We all cuddled close to her and were beginning to fall asleep when the knocking resumed, this time more violently. We heard the coyotes whispering and debating among themselves. 'Let's give up,' one said. 'It's too much money, we can't let them in,' the others responded. Finally, they asked us to throw ourselves on the floor or hide behind the furniture. Then, five coyotes pulled their guns and took aim at the door and the window while one of them asked: 'Quien es?' 'It's me, the husband of Ana María, the pregnant woman,' a voice replied. The coyotes opened the door and pulled the guy inside. They

were incensed and so was the husband. 'We told you not to come here. We agreed to deliver your wife at L.A.,' said one of the coyotes. 'I just wanted to make sure she was OK,' said the husband. At last, the coyotes decided to turn the wife over to her husband, though without the deposit he demanded back, arguing that he had broken the deal and put everyone else at risk. The coyotes now went back to their planning and decided that the San Francisco group should go first, then the San Jose group, and then the L.A. group, of which we were a part.

"When our turn came, the coyotes gathered us around a table and explained the plan. We were supposed to travel in a Jeep Cherokee that accommodated five people; we would pretend to be a family. I could tell these guys were professional and had all their bases covered. My mother interrupted, asking where I figured in the plans. The coyotes responded that I was supposed to travel in the back of the car, head down and covered with a blanket. We boarded the white Jeep Cherokee and made our way to San Clemente. However, they had sent another coyote ahead whose job was to drive to and from the San Clemente checkpoint so we would know whether the checkpoint lights were red or green. (Red meant all cars must stop to be inspected, and green meant a free pass.) After he radioed us with instructions to move forward, our coyote accelerated. We were ecstatic and thought we were finally on our way. Unfortunately, just a mile or so before reaching the checkpoint, the light went red and the immigration agents began to inspect all the vehicles—asking people for their documentation and searching the trunks of their cars. Our coyote panicked and begged us not to turn him in. We should say he had picked us up along the road and given us a ride. He kept on repeating, 'Is over, is over, please don't turn me in.' Hearing his distress, I peeked and saw that the immigration officer was just about five cars away from us and quickly approaching. Finally, my mom interrupted the coyote, saying that God had everything under his control and that if it was his will, we would cross without difficulty. The coyote asked my mom to pray for us all, and we all prayed. Still a Catholic, I prayed to my mom's God, the Pentecostal God, saying, 'If you allow us to reunite with the rest of our family, I will serve you for as long as I live.' No sooner had our prayers ended than the light turned green, and I watched the immigration officer return to his post and signal with his hand that all cars should now move forward.

"After we were past the checkpoint, we thanked God for such a miraculous intervention. We arrived at L.A. around three in the afternoon and waited for my father until six. Apparently, he hadn't expected us that early

and had gone to work. After he got the message from the coyote, he phoned my sister, and they drove two hours south from Bakersfield to L.A. to pick us up. The final transaction was made at a grocery store parking lot, where my father paid the coyote and we boarded a 1974 Oldsmobile Cutlass. We then searched desperately for Interstate 5, or El Cinco, as it is often called by Mexicans. Once on the road, my father and mother started to catch up while my sister spoke with us. We descended rapidly into San Fernando Valley, then passed Gorman, and finally reached the Grapevine area, from which we obtained our first glimpse of Bakersfield and the San Joaquin Valley, where we were to settle for good."

THE COST OF REVISITING THE PAST

It was early summer. Classes had ended. Heavy rain had sluiced away the yellow pollen from the sidewalks, replacing it with rusty drifts of pine flowers. Although Roberto was engrossed in his dissertation research, he found time to write further installments of his narrative and occasionally visit me in my office for a long conversation that ranged from the work we had done thus far to our common preoccupation with questions of belonging.

On May 29, at one in the morning, Roberto had completed his account of arriving with his family in the San Joaquin Valley and e-mailed me his installment with a note: "I've finally made it across the border." When I saw Roberto the following day, he explained, "The past days have been draining emotionally, and I'm just glad I'm no longer writing about my childhood in Mexico." I urged Roberto to take a break and shared with him a line I remembered from Ruth Behar's *Translated Woman*: "We cross borders, but we don't erase them; we take our borders with us."[15] I told him that I understood how difficult it was for him to retrace his steps, revisiting these heartbreaking scenes from his childhood. I also confessed that his story had seeped into my unconscious. Certain episodes kept me awake at night, as if I had been drawn along as a shadowy companion on the dolorous road he had traveled, plunged into a world in which I had lost my bearings, yet guided toward a new understanding of what it means to lose one's life and find it again, over and over.

During this last week of May, I had also been reading Claude Lanzmann's memoir, *The Patagonia Hare*. At one point, Lanzmann says that he could never have devoted twelve years of his life to making *Shoah* if he had been sent to camps. "These things are mysterious," he writes, "or perhaps they are

not. There can be no true creation without opacity, the creator does not have to be transparent to himself."[16] The conclusion, it seemed, was that a writer is most open to another when he or she has no *direct* experience of the other's life. And yet, there must be oblique connections; otherwise there would be no possibility of grasping another person's experience or being moved by it. When Roberto describes his younger brother Chuy's distress as the old man is dragged by his hair from his hiding place and the look of terror on his face as the border agents vilify him, I am there. I am a witness. I am with Roberto's family. And these images of vulnerability and despair blur with images from my own past, though the places and circumstances are not the same. Haven't we all found our way barred by a red light, at the mercy of happenstance? All our resources unavailing, all our efforts come to nothing, we sit and wait for the axe to fall, the end to come. But even then, there is one last hope. We can will or wish the light to change, the barrier to be lifted, the way forward to be cleared. And so we call upon powers that lie beyond the powers of border guards, helicopter spotlights, steel fences, and the state. We summon distant and mythical figures that may until that moment have played no active role in our lives but who personify omnipotence.

"In Bakersfield, my family was at last reunited after nearly six years. But learning to live again as a family would not be easy. Since my oldest sister Hortencia's marriage, my dad had lived on his own in a single-bedroom house that looked more like a shack. My siblings and I slept on couches in the living room, which was also the kitchen! Although we were happy to be together again, tensions with my father quickly erupted. Fearing we would become lowlifes or *cholos* (gangsters), he became overly strict and imposed a curfew on us. Because we were used to doing things in our own time, my brother and I often got into trouble. One day, our father became irritated by the street lingo I used and asked me to shut up. I resented this and told him his chance to mold us had passed; he punched me in the face, and I began to bleed as he left the house. Days later he apologized, and we had peace again at home. I still remember our first meals together. We didn't have much, but we were very happy. Had someone told me that I would get to enjoy such moments, I would not have believed it.

"Despite our happiness, winter arrived and work became scarce. So did the food. Although my father had a steady job at Grimmway Farms, a local and now worldwide carrot producer, it was not enough to pay the rent and feed

us all, not even when my mother worked. My father and mother had to go to the local food bank and wait in line for several hours. At other times, the pastor of their church would bring us clothes and food.

"On Christmas Eve, my mother was not planning any special dinner, nor did we have a tree or expect to exchange gifts. What had happened to our American dream? Grateful to be united again but unable to share in the Christmas spirit with the friends we'd made, my brother and I sat on the front porch watching families arrive at neighboring houses with bags that were surely filled with gifts. One could also hear Christmas carols in these houses, while our home was silent. Around seven in the evening, however, we saw a woman walking in our direction with grocery bags and lots of gifts. We assumed she was going to our neighbor's house, but instead she entered our house, hugged my mom, and said, 'Merry Christmas!' La hermana Carmen (sister Carmen) said she felt guided by God to buy us gifts and food. She was a wealthy member of my mom's church and was determined to help our family! And yes, among the pile of gifts, my brother found the train he had always wanted."

BORDER SITUATIONS

In September 2006, Davíd Carrasco gave the convocation address at Harvard Divinity School. Invoking the borderlands between Mexico and the United States, Davíd described a vexed and ambiguous zone that was not merely geographic or political; it defined an existential situation of being betwixt and between, of struggle and suffering, which Karl Jaspers sums up with the term *grenzsituationen* (border/limit situation).[17] The frontier evokes images of borderline experiences, of a destabilized and transgressive consciousness in which "dreams, repressed memories, psychological transferences and associations" possess greater presence than they do in ordinary waking life, and religious experiences emerge from the unconscious like apparitions.[18] This interplay between borderlands and borderline phenomena—between "the differences we have with others and the conflicts within ourselves"[19] also finds expression in the work of Gloria Anzaldúa. "*Mestiza* consciousness," she observes, may be identified with a "juncture . . . where phenomena collide."[20] This implies "a shock culture, a border culture, a third country" where migrants find themselves at the limits of what they can endure, border patrol agents are stretched beyond the limits of what they can control, and

intellectuals find that orthodox ways of describing and analyzing the world do not do justice to the experiences involved. These images of the borderlands reinforce, for me, a conviction that *all* lives and lifeworlds are more complex and variable than is suggested by the paradigmatic discourses of both the academy and the popular media. The borderlands suggest sites of intransitive, unstable, and intersubjective meanings that call into question the kind of reductive and essentializing language that makes human *experience* appear to be coterminous with the conventional categories of religious, cultural, or social *identity* that people use in *representing* their experience to themselves and others. As Nicholas De Genova notes with a nod to Paulo Freire, this "culturalist" assumption, which underpins so much social theory, policy-making, and popular discourse, detaches living human beings "from their own *historicity*," domesticating and fixing them "in an artificial, mythified reality outside time" and reducing them "to objects—effectively inert, inorganic, dead."[21]

These observations were strikingly relevant as Roberto described his life in Bakersfield. "Not long after our arrival," Roberto began, "I had nightmares about our border crossing experience. I often woke up crying or short of breath after dreaming that I had died locked in a trunk, or that I was being continuously chased through the mountains. The sound of the police helicopter that patrolled our neighborhood only intensified my fears. Whenever it appeared in the sky, I'd drop whatever I was doing and run into the house. My friends started to believe I was afraid of helicopters in general and began to make fun of me. Saturday nights were the worst, for then the sheriff's *mosco* arrived early in the afternoon. I dreaded its sound and its searchlight passing over our house. The experience did not get any easier. Just as the border had its own rules, so did this new place, and I needed to adapt quickly, just as I had adapted to the various places to which we moved in Mexico. Little did I know how much harder this new adjustment would be.

"Although it should be obvious, you must always keep in mind that migrants, primarily those of Indian extraction, are unwanted in the U.S. Some say, as Samuel Huntington did, that this is a clash of civilizations and values. But there is a racial dimension to anti-immigrant sentiments, and it pervades both the media and the political rhetoric of America. At the age of fourteen, I encountered a group of white supremacists as I and two friends walked to a local store. 'Get out of my street and my town, you fuckin' Mexican, fuckin' wetback! If we see you here again, you are dead!' While we understood the insults, which were familiar to any migrant, we didn't

understand the warning, or rather we took it too seriously. So we returned to my friend's house, which was at the opposite end of the street from where the white supremacists were. On the way, we bought snacks and drinks at the local store, which was owned by Saudi immigrants. Halfway up the street, we were stopped in our tracks by the skinheads. It was a sunny afternoon, around five, with the sun just beginning its descent on the western horizon. Migrant families were in their front yards washing their cars, and other kids were playing on the street. In this primarily Hispanic town, the white supremacists were also migrants, though they didn't realize it. They came directly at us and began to insult us yet again.

"Reading the situation quite well, my friend Cheyo, who was in his early twenties, urged us to leave, but before we could move the attack began. Everything happened rapidly. An older man, probably in his late twenties, weighing about 250 pounds and six feet three inches tall, attempted to punch Cheyo. Cheyo leaned back so that the blow missed his face but knocked off his hat. Unfortunately, Cheyo was dressed as a cowboy that day, and his long-sleeved gray silk shirt and leather boots were not suited for the occasion. He slipped and fell on his knees, taking blows left and right but still holding on to his attacker. Before I could blink, another man, probably in his midthirties, winded me with his left hand and knocked me down with his right. My face landed flat on the concrete, where I lay curled up like an earthworm, gasping for air and bleeding profusely. I could not cry, I could not speak, I could not believe this was happening to me. What evil had I done to these men whom I didn't even know or hate? While on the ground, I heard a woman crying from a distance, 'He is gonna kill him, he is gonna kill him, call the police!' Having dispatched us, two of the attackers stepped aside, but the more violent of them continued to engage Cheyo in hand-to-hand combat. To my surprise and that of the white supremacists, Cheyo had gotten up and was exchanging blows with the tall, fat guy. Suddenly, Cheyo knocked him unconscious, and he collapsed like a tower collapsing on its foundations. Then, like a mad beast, tears in his eyes and a bloody nose, Cheyo moved to finish off our aggressor, kicking him in the head and the stomach several times. At this point the other two intervened and dragged their friend into the house. Right after this, the police arrived and arrested the skinheads while we licked our wounds.

"I wish I could say that I put up a strong fight, that I punched the white supremacist in the face and then kicked his balls, that I stood up valiantly until the end. But at fourteen I was a malnourished and feeble teenager. In

Moments of Reprieve, Primo Levi suggests that 'transforming a living person into a character ties the hand' of a writer, because even though he undertakes his task with good intentions, the task 'verges on the violation of privacy and is never painless for the subject.'[22] I would argue that this pain is even more intense when the subject is the writer himself. This task also involves another dimension of difficulty. As Levi puts it, 'Finding oneself portrayed in a book with features that are not those we attribute to ourselves is traumatic, as if the mirror of a sudden returned to us the image of somebody else: an image possibly nobler than ours, but not ours.'[23] This is why I choose to remember my weakness, fragility, and unfitness for protecting my family, fighting older men, or crossing the border. Although I may appear less heroic and less noble than the reader might expect, the portrait is still true of me. It is also true that regardless of how I tell my story, it will always be traumatic for me. It haunts me to this day. I am still uneasy around tall white males with tattoos on their arms and shaved heads. My muscles tense, and my mind automatically begins to devise a fight-or-flight plan. In any case, my enthusiasm for the American dream vanished after that bloody encounter."

The passages Roberto cited from Primo Levi preface the Italian writer's account of 'Lorenzo,' a morose and taciturn man from Fossano who risked his life smuggling soup and bread to his starving compatriot in Auschwitz. After the camp was liberated, Lorenzo made his way back to Italy, where he told Levi's mother that before being evacuated he had learned that Primo was ill and that she should therefore resign herself to the worst. Five months later, Levi returned to Italy and went to Fossano to visit the man who had saved his life. But Lorenzo did not appear to want to live. He fell ill and was hospitalized, but ran away. Brought back to the hospital, he died a few days later, alone. "He, who was not a survivor, had died of the survivors' disease."[24]

I told Roberto that I did not want to risk mischaracterizing him, but his comments on 'Lorenzo's Return' suggested an oblique connection between his own situation and the situation of those who survived the camps. "Like being stuck in the nest of scorpions or waiting for the cops to discover you in the car at the San Clemente crossing, the most terrible moments for you were those in which you were immobilized, unable to do anything or say anything that would save you from deportation or worse. You couldn't even protect your vulnerable brother or shut out the derisive and degrading language that was being hurled at you. It seems that this is the trauma of being a migrant— being utterly bereft of any right to be who you are, where you are, having your right to exist as a human being constantly called into question, undermined,

stripped from you. And it seems to me that these humiliating experiences in America repeated the powerlessness you felt as a child, when your father's cousin, who had done nothing wrong, was beaten within an inch of his life by a gang who regarded him as a nonperson; when your mother was struck down by a life-threatening illness and later, after she recovered, left you with your grandmother and did not contact you for several years, not to mention your constant struggle to keep body and soul together as you were moved from pillar to post, without any choice in the matter, without knowing the whys and wherefores . . ."

"Perhaps," Roberto said, "the time has come to tell you about my conversion, when I stopped fighting, when I stopped struggling, when I surrendered to God.

"Because of my fears, and because of the promise I had made to God at the San Clemente inspection point, I finally agreed to go to Templo Sinai de la Assambleas de Dios, the local Pentecostal church in Lamont, California. The congregation was composed primarily of first- and second-generation Mexican Americans, and I had a hard time relating to teenagers who refused to speak Spanish or who, like the white supremacists, hurled racist insults at my brother and me. As a result, my brother and I refused to go back, though months later we did. Why? It was *Tiempo de Avivamiento* (revival time) or *Campaña* (campaign—presumably spiritual warfare against the devil)! At this time, the church fasts, prays, and worships in expectation of a powerful manifestation of the divine, usually in the form of healings, exorcisms, and above all, conversions. Much to my dismay, the revival lasted three days. Church members were encouraged to invite friends and relatives, particularly those who were not Christian and were afflicted by any type of sickness. A special evangelist had been invited to lead the revival. Since it was election time, the preacher adopted the theme 'Vote for Jesus.' The first night, the preaching was reminiscent of the acrimonious bickering that takes place between liberals and conservatives in America. The devil was an impostor, a liar, who had only come to kill and destroy. In all, the preacher said, the devil was a bad candidate, so we should not let him rule over our lives. By contrast, Jesus had come to give us all eternal life and break the bonds of sin and death over us. On the second night, the preacher continued discrediting the devil, exorcizing a few individuals and leading several people to Christ. While all this was not new to me, it was a wild night and I decided to keep a low profile. On the third night, the preacher stopped lambasting the devil and focused on exalting Jesus. 'The Lord came to set the captives free—free from all fears

and terror—and to give eternal life, but you must choose today where you will spend eternity.' Admittedly, this was a fire and brimstone sermon. That said, if Jesus *was* in the business of setting captives free from fear and terror, I'd vote for him. So when the preacher asked those who wanted to accept Christ into their lives or receive healing to raise their right hand, I raised mine.

"Subsequently, he asked those who had raised their hands to come to the altar. At this moment I became self-conscious, aware of the people around me, particularly girls my age, so I sat down. However, an old lady, Sister Castillo, who was sitting behind me, poked my back and said, 'You raised your hand, so now go.' Unable to hide, I got up and started making my way down the aisle as the worship team sang the hymn, 'I surrender all, I surrender all, all to thee my blessed savior, I surrender all.' As I walked down the aisle and opened up my being to the divine, I began to feel the chains of resentment, hate, and fear break down within me. I felt as if I were clay being reshaped by the potter's hands. In a matter of seconds, the nightmare that my life had been up to that point unfolded before me, and I saw my need for healing. Then I lost all sense of place, time, and self. When I finally regained my composure, I was uttering a prayer in which I surrendered my life to Jesus, just as I had promised at the border. Without exaggeration, I felt like a new human being; everything changed after that moment. It was as if a great burden had been lifted from my shoulders."

I had my answer to the question I had put to Roberto about how we cope with the impasses in life. When we cannot act, when all our efforts come to naught, rather than going on struggling against the blind forces that oppress us from without or within, we may decide to let go. In ceasing to struggle and surrendering our will, the burden lifts, the anger dies, the light turns green. But there is a world of difference between Lorenzo's surrender, which was a giving up of life, and 'engaged surrender,' in which one gains a new lease of life because one surrenders not to the void but to a greater being, a transcendent ideal, a community of kindred spirits, an adoptive family *in which one's suffering is recognized and shared, and in which one has an active, self-determining role to play.*[25]

In *Border of Death, Valley of Life,* Daniel G. Groody describes religious conversion among Mexican migrants as "an awakening to a friendship with God, whom they call *Jesus Amigo.*"[26] So I asked Roberto if this resonated

with his own experience, if he came to see Christ as a friend and *compañero* and God as a provident rather than punitive father, someone who is always there for him, close to him? Had the American dream metamorphosed into another utopian vision?

Roberto said that Groody's analysis of the conversion of Mexican migrants was largely accurate. "The Pentecostal convert does learn to see Christ as a *compañero* and God as a benevolent rather than a punitive father. However, I would not call conversion an awakening or 'the reorientation of the soul of an individual' or the realization that 'the old was wrong and the new is right,' as Arthur D. Nock has suggested.[27] The Pentecostal conversion experience is more than simply changing religious allegiances, awakenings, or going to a different church. It is a rebirth from head to toe that is contingent upon the revelation that Jesus Christ is Lord and Savior. Thus Pentecostals believe, with Saint Paul, that 'if anyone is in Christ, *he* [or she] *is* a new creation; the old things passed away; behold, new things have come' (1 Corinthians 5:17). What does it mean to be a new creation ($\kappa\alpha\iota\nu\grave{\eta}\ \kappa\tau\acute{\iota}\sigma\iota\varsigma$)? It means to be born again. The old regrets, grudges, and failed dreams are not only simply ripped from the pages of your life's journal, but you are given a new journal altogether; it is a new beginning! Without exaggeration, the conversion experience becomes a spiritual GPS of sorts, through which you are able to locate yourself in relation to God, history, and others. One's entire story—the past, the present, and the future—is rewritten. Your otherwise mundane and insignificant existence has meaning—you are no longer alone on the road to Emmaus or Bakersfield, and we sing it: 'Divino compañero del camino, tu presencia siento yo al caminar. Él disipado toda sombra, ya tengo luz, la luz bendita de su amor' (Divine companion of the way, your presence I sense as I walk. He has dissipated every shadow, now I have light, the blessed light of his love). In this manner, the conversion experience transforms our migration journey into a pilgrimage from Egypt (Mexico)—the place of suffering and poverty—to the promised land, the place that overflows with 'milk and honey,' the U.S. In a very literal way, God leads us miraculously through the desert into the promised land, though even here we continue to fight the giants of racism, exploitation, and marginalization. Despite the challenges, we don't give up because, as Latino Pentecostals sing, 'Dios no nos trajo hasta aquí para volver atrás, nos trajo aquí a poseer la tierra que él nos dio. Y aunque gigantes allá, yo nunca temeré. Nos trajo aquí a poseer la tierra que él nos dio' (God did not bring us here simply to go back; he brought us here to take possession of the land he gave us. And even if we

were to encounter giants there, we will never fear. He brought us here to possess the land he gave us!)."

Given Roberto's tribulations in Mexico, I could readily understand why his new life in America might be likened to a rebirth—or might require supernatural assistance if he was to survive the gigantic obstacles that now lay in his path—but I was perplexed by his allusions to taking possession of the land. Did he intend this imagery to echo the Spanish conquest of the Aztec Empire that began in 1519, bringing centuries of misery in its wake and traumas yet to be healed? And did this have any bearing on his occasional references to Aztec cosmology ("Huitzilopochtli's promise," "Moctezuma's city"), or to violence and injustice as "faces of human sacrifice," as if his life journey might be interpreted as readily in pre-Christian as in Christian terms?

"After some time," Roberto said, "we realize that the 'promised land' refers not to an earthly place per se but to the New Jerusalem described in the Apocalypse of John or the Book of Revelation, chapter 21. How can this place filled with so much hatred, injustice, and deprivation be our final destination? Therefore, as the book of Hebrews also notes, people of faith from time immemorial have confessed that 'they were strangers and foreigners on the earth, for people who speak in this way make it clear that they are seeking a homeland. If they had been thinking of the land they left behind, they would have had an opportunity to return. But as it is, they desire a better country, that is, a heavenly one. Therefore God is not ashamed to be called their God; indeed, he has prepared a city for them' (Hebrews 11:13–16)."

"So we are pilgrims," I said to Roberto, "because we are looking and waiting for the City of God?"

Later, as I mulled over this installment of Roberto's story, I was struck by the way his theological reflections condense two quite different conceptions of movement. While the first denotes geographical or mythical locations, the second connotes emotional changes in one's mind or heart, as when we speak of being moved by someone's suffering, carried away by an ecstatic encounter, or transported by an aesthetic experience. Though the migrant is sometimes wholly fixated on a *place* that lies beyond the horizon of where he is born, this place may turn out to be very different from the place he dreamed of. As the word "utopia" *(ou-topos)* suggests, such magical elsewheres exist only in the imagination. And yet, in journeying toward these places, which initially lie at the periphery of our field of vision,[28] we may undergo the kind of inward change of which Roberto speaks. And it is then, and only then, that the place

we finally come to can become a place we can call our own, a place where our new life may begin.

In his fieldwork among Ghanaian migrants in Italy, Hans Lucht was given to understand that suffering was a necessary precondition for a just reward. His Ghanaian interlocutors did not conceive of this "return" on one's suffering in theological terms; rather, it reflected the logic and ethics of reciprocity. In giving up so much, sacrificing and suffering so much, and waiting so long, the expectation grows that you are earning the right to a new life in a new land. Thus, Lucht notes, "enduring the hardships of Naples is an accumulation of good things waiting to happen."[29] As one illegal migrant put it, discussing his experiences in Naples, "There is always darkness before daybreak." This promise of a new day is like the interest that accumulates on an investment—an investment of one's very life in the unpredictable bank of life itself. But more significant perhaps is the implied existential payoff. Years of patience and passivity will lead to a life in which one possesses the right to act as an autonomous subject. "Suffering viewed in this way, rather than being a passive state of affairs, is transformed into active engagement," in which an unresponsive world becomes subject to one's own determinations.[30]

Crucial to this transformation is a changed perspective on time. Rather than standing still (waiting) or going around in circles (getting nowhere), one can see the way ahead, one is getting somewhere. Hence the phrases that Marianne Søndergaard Winther repeatedly heard when working with undocumented Latina migrants in the Mission District of San Francisco— salir adelante and seguir adelante—where "adelante implies a movement forward in time and space, and in combination with salir and seguir . . . means, respectively, 'to prosper' and 'to carry on/to go ahead.'"[31] Lacking the symbolic capital needed to become fully mobile and "free" in American society, the migrant experiences himself or herself as imprisoned in a gilded cage (jaula de oro).[32]

When I shared my reflections with Roberto, he compared the migrant's journey to an obstacle course in which one is striving to overcome both personal limitations—a lack of education, of local knowledge, and of linguistic skills—and barriers or pitfalls in the social environment. "As I mentioned earlier," Roberto said, "the promised land had its giants, and I had to conquer them one by one to get ahead. The education process was the toughest of all. A few months after our arrival, my parents decided that we had to continue our education. So I had to attend high school while my brother went to middle school. The day I registered was emblematic of what awaited

me. My older sister Hortencia took me to Arvin High School, a few miles away from where we lived, and dropped me in front of the school. 'A bus will bring you home,' she yelled from the car as I made my way to the registration office. I was exceedingly intimidated by the place and utterly conscious of my inability to understand the language. Once at the office, I got in line to register, but as soon as my turn came I would sit down and pretend to be waiting for somebody; then I'd go to the end of the line, showing respect, for I had lost my place. I kept on doing this for an hour or so, until there was no line and I had to remain seated, sweating every minute of it. Finally, a woman saw me and asked, 'Can I help you?' Aware of my inability to respond, she asked in Spanish, 'Le puedo ayudar?' When I said I was there to register, she scolded me for not being proactive and requesting help in Spanish. After registration, which took only a few minutes, I was sent to my ESL class. When I opened the door, I tried to introduce myself in English, 'May nahme is Roberto,' but before I could finish, the professor answered in Spanish, 'Pasale [Come in], Roberto, have a seat.' The whole class exploded in laughter. They were all *mojados* (wetbacks), as white people call us derisively. They came from all parts of Mexico and were here to try their luck at the American dream.

"American high schools are their own animal, as people say, and you had to adapt quickly and learn the ropes. With many journeys and adaptations behind him, the migrant is determined to conquer this challenge, but shame and temptations prove stronger than any will. You could let the fear of speaking English overwhelm you, and thereby set yourself up to fail in most classes or proficiency exams. Admittedly, things are stacked against us from the start. I recall that some of our classrooms were located near the football fields, away from the main campus. Our teachers were committed, however, and I remember Mrs. Morse, Mr. Quiñonez, Mr. Arvizu, and my history teacher with gratitude. They worked with what they had and tried to make learning an enjoyable adventure. Their efforts reminded me of how much I loved school, and I determined to do my best. After my first year, I started to get good grades, accompanied by awards and certificates of improvement. My disagreements with my instructors, Mr. Quiñonez in particular, were not over absences or failures to submit work, but over why I had gotten a B when I deserved an A. I remember asking my guidance counselor, Mr. García, to ask Mr. Quiñonez about the matter. I cared deeply about education. The class I loved most was history, and my instructor knew it. From the Civil War to the Great Depression, I answered all the questions.

"Sometimes I completed my homework in class, as I used to do when I was a child in Mexico, and school again began to be a safe haven where I dreamed of one day becoming a history professor. Not all my migrant peers shared my enthusiasm. Some of them, like Alejandro, didn't know how to read or write in Spanish, and this made their learning process exceedingly difficult. Alejandro's family sent him to school only because he was of age. My ESL instructor would often assign me to work with Alejandro and teach him how to read and write. I had attempted to teach adults to read and write before, but this guy threatened me when he got frustrated. A bad lesson in the class could mean trouble in the quad during recess, so I resented helping him.

"It may have been because I was tired of getting picked on by bullies that I joined El Flaco and his gang during my junior year. Unlike most local gangs, which defend a particular territory, El Flaco's gang stood for itself and for respect. Like most gangs, El Flaco's gang provided a sense of community and belonging we could not obtain anywhere else. A few years younger than me, El Flaco was a migrant who had come to the U.S. as a child, mastered English, and now spoke without an accent, unlike the rest of us. My brother met El Flaco in middle school, when the latter stood up for him during an after-school fight. After that, my brother joined El Flaco, but I delayed joining the group, because they were in middle school and I was in high school. However, when they caught up with me, they were hard to avoid, for I didn't have many friends and they assumed some sort of protective role, presumably based on their commitment to my brother.

"During my junior year, a girl from the basketball team who was in my Spanish class became interested in me. Lisa walked with me from the cafeteria to class and pretty much everywhere else. She sat across from me in class, and her continuous staring made me uncomfortable. She started riding the bus with me and would miss her stop intentionally to keep talking to me. The signs of her interest were there, but because I had never before had a girlfriend I could only blush. Disappointed by my unresponsiveness, she started flirting with another guy, whom we called El Gallo (the Rooster), and he would walk her to class to make me jealous. However, when El Flaco saw El Gallo trying to make a move, he and his gang proceeded to make him 'an offer he could not refuse.' A day later, during lunch, El Flaco approached me and told me not to worry, that everything was being taken care off. Baffled by his words, I asked for clarification. He told me they'd seen a guy trying to make a move on my girlfriend, and they had threatened him with an after-school beating. I explained that she was not my girlfriend but that I was thankful anyway.

After that day, I started to hang out with El Flaco, and since he lived on the same block as we did, my induction into the gang quickly followed.

"El Flaco taught us the ropes of gangster life—from proper clothing to selling dope. I had to buy a pair of Dickies and wear a white shirt with Chicano images on the back, usually an Aztec eagle or a calendar, or an Aztec warrior. We'd all eat together and hang out together during recess. If anybody wanted trouble, they'd find it, and El Flaco was not all bluff. I saw him pick fights with whites and Mexicans alike. Apparently he grew up without a father and never knew who he was, so he adored his mother. Anybody who joked about his momma was set to lose a tooth. He was a sober, angry, egotistical young man, a natural leader. At sixteen he was already screwing dissatisfied married and single women. During lunch break in school, El Flaco would point out to us the women who had joined his sex Hall of Fame. Whereas in most gangs initiation is done through a mass beating in which members ruthlessly beat the postulant, El Flaco had his own way of proving how tough we were. In my case, he had determined we would go and steal a car stereo on the south side of town. We stayed at his house until eleven thirty at night, then made our way through town. When other gangs saw us passing by, they rushed to pick a fight, but on recognizing El Flaco they left us alone. He'd known them all from middle school, and they all understood that he made no territorial claims as other gangsters did. Besides, he had beaten up most of them at some time or another.

"Once we reached the house, El Flaco asked the others to wait for us, hidden in a nearby grape field, while he and I took care of business. Under cover of night, we stealthily approached the truck. To my surprise, it was a police car, but it was too late to back down. The front doors were unlocked, and El Flaco handed me a flat screwdriver with which I began to detach the stereo. After five minutes of failed attempts, something, perhaps a cat, triggered the automatic lights in the front yard, and as they came on, the dogs started barking. In the blink of an eye, El Flaco and I were running toward the fields. By the time we reached the others, the police were already at the cop's house, and we were still on the move. Fortunately, El Flaco knew all the town's shortcuts and alleys, and this allowed us to move with speed. Just the same, El Mosco was already in the sky, so we decided to disband, because a large group is easily detected. El Flaco and I made it to his house, from where I walked slowly home. Next day in school, El Flaco recounted our feat to the group. He then equipped me with all types of drugs to sell.

"At the same time I saw my fortunes rising with El Flaco's gang, I saw my academic life beginning to deteriorate. I started missing classes, particularly math, and got into a few fights. Finally, I was caught skipping class and hanging out with friends in the football field. I was taken to the principal's office, where I happened to encounter Mr. Quiñonez, the instructor with whom I had argued over grades. He was the one who called my parents to inform them of my dire situation. He gave me a lecture I would never forget. 'Roberto, you think you are tough because you are hanging out with these losers? You used to be a lion, but now you are just a lamb, another loser.'

"I was assigned to do Saturday work, though this didn't stop my adventures with El Flaco. Finally, one Saturday night while walking to my house after a *quinceañera*,[33] I was stopped by the sheriff and taken to jail on charges of possessing marijuana. While it was true that I had sold marijuana, I had none with me that day and refused to accept the charge. I was thrown into a cell, where I joined drunkards rolling about in their own vomit. At around two in the morning, an officer brought me a blanket and said, "You are too young to end up like them.' His words made me reflect on the choices before me. The fact was that El Flaco and the others would likely end up like these men, if they were lucky. The respect I got from other students at school or in the community was useless if I failed to graduate or got shot. Besides, by that point I already knew that despite his self-confidence, El Flaco didn't know where he was going. He was a blind man leading other blind men, and we were all bound to fall, sooner or later. He wanted to be famous and respected, but such respect was costing him more and more with every new venture. Determined to prove himself, he had driven a car with its trunk full of dope from California to Oregon. With the money he was paid, he bought himself a 1984 turbo-charged Buick Regal with T-tops, painted the car cherry red, and added low-rider golden wire wheels. To further impress, El Flaco installed an expensive Kenwood sound system in the car, with at least two amplifiers. The sound system was so powerful that every time El Flaco rode by in his car, the windows of local houses would shake to the melody of Kid Frost's 'Ain't no Sunshine.' He was taking the gang to an entirely new level, but I had my doubts. Was this the measure of success? Was this the American dream?

"I'd have cars, money, women, and 'friends,' but I knew it was all a mirage. It was money we had not worked for. The women were usually somebody else's, and the friends were not really friends. It was a mirage, and it went against all that Candelaria had taught me. That night in the jail cell, at three

in the morning, during my darkest and lowest hour in the U.S., I saw the light. There, surrounded by drunkards and the stench of their vomit, with tears in my eyes, I made peace with God and asked forgiveness for forgetting my pledge to serve him for as long as I lived, for not going to church in the last three years, and for messing up my high school studies. Then I fell asleep. The next day the officers woke me at seven to inform me they had made a mistake and that I would not be charged for possession of marijuana. Released on the spot, I walked fourteen miles back to my town on a Sunday morning, and that same day I went back to church with my parents."

GOD IS LIFE

Roberto's narrative constituted a test of all that I had written (after my conversations with Emmanuel in Copenhagen) on the proto-ethical. Faced with Roberto's commitment to God, could I sustain my argument that God was but a condensation symbol, a powerful metaphor, for life itself? It was significant to me that Roberto should refer his epiphany back to his grandmother, Candelaria, before referring it to God. It was as if his sense of what lay in store for him, what was possible for him, had been formed long ago, glimpsed in a myriad of moments and held, despite the crushing weight of evidence against his aspirations, as a dream is sometimes held well into the day. In Paul Ricoeur's dense yet memorable account of Spinoza's *Ethics,* I found insights that I now wanted to share with Roberto.

Ricoeur avows that he is not concerned with Spinoza's "theology." Spinoza's alleged pantheism or atheism is irrelevant; only the notion of *conatus* matters. In this sense, "God is Life."[34] But life is more than the impulse to passively "persevere in being"; it consists in the search for "adequate ideas" that enable us to *actively* sustain our sense of presence and purpose.[35] God, for Roberto, proved to be such an idea, for the adequacy of any idea, Ricoeur insists, consists in its ability to help us realize our capacity for speaking, acting, praying, and even narrating our story.[36] To submit to a higher power is not, therefore, to forfeit one's own agency *but to recover it through a relationship with something beyond oneself,* be this a supportive friend, a divinity, a diviner, or a material object. Here the divine and the utopian coalesce as alternative symbols of what William James calls "the more." For we are all susceptible to the uneasy sense "that there is *something wrong about us* as we naturally stand," and what we call religion is a set of ideas and practices for

getting in touch with an "elsewhere," an "otherness," or a "wider self" that lies beyond the horizons of one's immediate lifeworld, especially at times when our "lower being has gone to pieces in the wreck."[37] This process of othering, which places one's own agency in abeyance, is a precondition for clearing one's head of confusing subjective preoccupations and returning to oneself as someone capable of taking a hand in determining one's own fate.

Roberto appreciated my remarks, noting that some possibilities open to us for achieving that sense of a "wider self" are not so much illusory as disastrous—as El Flaco's gang proved to be for him. But the church was different. "My return to church inspired me to become a responsible individual and reinforced all that Candelaria had taught me—hard work, determination, commitment, and discipline. However, picking up the pieces of my life and my academic studies was not easy. When El Flaco learned that I had returned to church, he ordered that I be isolated from the gang. They were not to talk to me, and some made fun of me when they saw me walking by with my Bible: 'Hermano (brother), come preach to us and have a beer to spice things up!' One time El Flaco showed up at my house to make peace and invite me back. He said he was throwing a party and led me to the trunk of his 1984 T-type Buick Regal. The cargo was impressive: Jose Cuervo tequila bottles, cases of beer and liquor. I thanked him for the invitation but said I didn't drink anymore. He couldn't really understand but said he respected my choice and left disappointed. I lost my so-called friends for good that day, but I was not sad.

"In church, I focused on developing my friendship with Christ and attending every church revival. But this didn't completely determine the course of my life from one day to the next. In school, I was on track to join the ranks of those who fail to graduate. I was missing units and still had not passed the writing proficiency exam. Most unfortunate of all, I was failing history and could not remember the last day I had been to class. Armed with the grace of God, I took the bus to school rather than riding with El Flaco, and went to talk to my guidance counselor. He agreed that only a miracle could help me graduate. He arranged with the migrant education office for me to do extra work and pick up some units. Then I had to face my instructors. Because it was near the end of the quarter, they were reluctant to help me. Knowing how much I had liked his class, the history teacher made me a deal. He'd allow me to take the final exam and let that be my final grade. With only a few weeks to go, it was a gamble and an opportunity. I accepted the challenge, applied myself, and passed the exam with a solid A.

"My work through the migrant office also paid off, and all I needed now was to pass all my classes, including the writing proficiency exam, which was a nightmare for most ESL students. By this time, however, my faith in Christ assured me that all things were possible. I prepared for the test as diligently as I could. The prompt I chose asked the student to describe a major life difficulty and how he or she had faced it. Going against advice, I chose to write about the exam itself and the challenges and terrors it signified for the ESL student, since if you do not pass this exam you cannot graduate. A few weeks later, I was waiting for the results in my writing class, when the instructor informed us that our respective guidance counselors would be calling us individually to give us our scores. I was discouraged when student after student returned to the class with defeat written on their faces. Some were in tears, while others tried to pretend the test was insignificant, that nothing was at stake. However, we all knew, for instance, that John Gonzales wanted to be a professional writer, that he wrote poetry in both English and Spanish, and though it was both bad English and bad poetry, we knew how much he cared about his dream. What had gone wrong? I'm not entirely sure. He was not a gangster, but he liked to party. Who knows?

"At last, Mr. García sent a note requesting to see me. I took a deep breath and made my way to his office. Once there, Mr. García, in his usual way, gave me an update on the situation. 'The test was difficult for most ESL students,' he said. I thought he was trying to comfort me or make the impending news less painful. 'But,' he added, 'you passed with the minimum score. Congratulations.' I was ecstatic at the news and could not hide my joy. Here again, I thought, God had opened a way where there was really no way. I would be the first in my family to graduate from high school, though only if I obtained decent grades for that last quarter. I made my way back to the classroom and debated whether to share the news or not. How could you say you passed when most of your peers had failed? But I could not hide my smile, and before I said anything they all congratulated me.

"Now only that quarter's courses stood in the way of my graduation. I had to meet individually with each professor and inquire how I was doing before even thinking about buying a cap and gown. When I shared my quandary with the Pentecostals in a Wednesday service, they all encouraged me to buy the graduation gown on faith, which I did. I'm not sure if they were taking revenge on me or not, but most teachers waited until the last week of that term to inform me about my grades. All was contingent on passing my economics class, and Mr. Pritchard gave me a hard time to the very end. During

graduation week, I had to ask him directly, 'So, I'm graduating or not?' He smiled, pretending to be surprised. 'You should know that,' he said. I replied, 'It all depends on this class.' A bit annoyed by now, he said, 'Look, if you want to be really sure, why don't you go to the football field where they've already arranged seating for graduating seniors. Go through each list, and if you find your name, then you will be graduating.' I didn't wait for the class to end or the bell to ring but made my way to the football field as fast as possible. He was right—each row had attached to it a list with the names of each graduating senior. I rushed to find the F section, and when I found it, I started to look desperately for my name. Farias, Fernandez, Flynn, Fogglesong...I was getting nervous but finally located my name.

"Graduation was one of the happiest moments of my life. I thanked God because, without His help, I would have ended up elsewhere. I thanked my parents for their support and the brothers and sisters from Temple Sinai, Juan Palomino in particular, for cheering me along the way. While I was not the commencement speaker or an honors student, I determined that I would do better next time. However, that next time seemed far away. Because of my legal status, I didn't qualify for financial aid, and I had to return to working in the fields. My dream of becoming a history professor would have to be deferred."

"It must have been terribly demoralizing," I said, "to have struggled so hard to graduate, only to find yourself again at an impasse."

"I cannot tell you how awful it was. That feeling of emptiness and despair in the pit of your stomach, that sense of having been worn away to nothing. What was the benefit of passing that writing exam or graduating? Some of my friends, who had failed at both and were now working alongside me in the fields, said, 'We always knew we'd come to this.' I was silent.

"I was eighteen and had to work hard, just as Candelaria had taught me, but I had a hard time adjusting to the fields. We'd get up at five o'clock, be ready at five thirty, then drive to the ranch, where we would harvest grapes, oranges, watermelons, whatever. Picking grapes was the hardest work for me because I'm tall, and I had to kneel down to get under the vine and cut the bunches. Sometimes my head got stuck in the branches, and it sometimes seemed like I was fighting the vine rather than harvesting grapes. It was on these days that memories of my dream became exceedingly painful. 'What happens to a dream deferred?' Langston Hughes asks in his famous poem. 'Does it dry up like a raisin in the sun? Or fester like a sore—And then run?' But I was convinced that though the dream may fade, it never dies. We carry

it along with the long list of what might have been. It becomes like a butterfly fossilized in amber. Every time we look at it, we recognize its shape, its features, and can say that it existed, that it was real, though this cannot mask the reality that it is long dead. This is perhaps the most painful and frustrating part of it all. Perhaps that is why some people don't even dare to dream. Perhaps this is why my high school peers turned cynical when, unable to go to college because of their financial, academic, and legal status, they had to go back to grape picking. Why did I cling to it even though my dream was dead? I believed that Christ could open a new door of opportunity for me. I had no reason not to believe. He had brought me from Mexico, he had put my life back on track, and he had allowed me to graduate. There was a door and I needed to find it.

"Convinced of this, one spring morning, before dawn, alone in a vineyard, pulling excess leaves from a vine, I prayed to God, asking that I be given an opportunity to go college. 'If you help me, I will do my best not to waste the opportunity and to honor you.' I confessed how much I disliked the fields and how it was killing me within. I had not come so far to end up like this. After this prayer, I was not visited by angels. Nor did Jesus appear in a cloud to give me comfort. But my anxiety went away. From that day on, I began preparing academically, so that when the door of opportunity opened, I'd be ready to enter it. I took my books with me to the fields and read them during my lunch breaks. My peers would laugh at me and call me a fool, and on their good days they asked me to give it all up. 'You don't need history in the fields.' I applied myself regardless. On my free afternoons or the days there were no church services, I'd spend my time reading in my room. My determination was such that my mother thought I was going insane and expressed concern. 'Son, why don't you go with all the guys your age and play soccer in the park? I'm worried that you spend too much time locked in your room. You shouldn't read so much.' But I was already too immersed reading about Josephus's adventures during the Roman invasion of Palestine in the first century C.E. How could I restrain my imagination from picturing his dexterity in preparing the defense of the Galilean cities? Or not marvel at how he survived the Zealots' determination to commit suicide when the Romans were approaching? My friends in the fields were right—I was no longer going to school. Nevertheless, school was now coming to me every day in these books I had purchased, as I sought to satisfy my growing fascination with the historical and social world of early Christianity and Second Temple Judaism."

I reminded Roberto about a short essay by Primo Levi describing the power of amber—which in Greek is called *électron,* from which we get our word "electricity." If you rub amber with a cloth, "small, curious phenomena are produced: one hears a crackling, in the dark one sees sparks, small bits of straw and specks of paper brought close dance about madly." Apparently, it wasn't until well into the nineteenth century that someone interpreted this trick with amber as a sign to decipher and suspected that this "was the annunciation by enigma of a force that would change the face of the world, and that the graceful sparks shared the nature of the lightning bolt."[38] I told Roberto that I was intrigued, not only by this image of dormant potentiality—of life about to be awakened, or "galvanized into action"—but by the analogy between rubbing a piece of amber with a soft cloth and praying to God. When Roberto had remarked that no angels appeared and no sparks flew when he appealed to God for guidance, was this because some kind of acquiescence attends every action? To illustrate my point, I mentioned my experience with Kuranko diviners. A client passively assents to the diviner's advice, just as the diviner passively channels the inspiration he receives from his spirit guides. But as soon as you have received this guidance, *you* must assume responsibility for making the sacrifices required to avert misfortune or realize a positive prognosis. There is thus a delicate balance between submission to the spirits and assuming an active role in determining your own fate. If you fail to make the sacrifices directed, then you have only yourself to blame if things don't work out the way you want them to. Roberto agreed. Without a leap of faith, you would venture nothing. Nothing would be possible. "And you are right—it sometimes takes us a long time to realize that we cannot leave everything to God. But four years went by, and I saw no hope of my fossilized dream being resurrected or moving at all. My faith was dwindling, my dream slipping from my grasp."

RESIDENT ALIEN

"A crucible in and of itself, obtaining a green card can take up to ten years, and not everybody qualifies to apply for it. My father obtained the privilege during an amnesty granted by the Reagan administration in the 1980s, and soon after submitted an application for all of us. After we arrived at the U.S. in 1991, we had to wait nine years for approval of the application. During this time, we all had to work illegally, drive without a license, and be subject to

deportation. When the letter approving our application finally arrived in 1999, my parents began to prepare for the final stage of this process. We all had to get physical examinations, be fingerprinted, and ironically, obtain Mexican passports, for which we had to present proof that we were Mexican citizens. Since my parents only had copies of our birth certificates, my father had to go to Mexico City, where we were born, and request official copies. Once we secured the official copies of our birth certificates, we set out to complete the rest of the process for the green card. The two-hour trips from Bakersfield to the headquarters of the United States Citizenship and Immigration Services (USCIS) in Fresno were constant and draining. Furthermore, my parents had to borrow money not just to pay for the paperwork, but also to pay a fine imposed on all eight of us for coming to the U.S. uninvited.

"When the day of the final interview arrived, we left Bakersfield around three in the morning and arrived in Fresno two hours later. We were shocked to find a long line of people; others had even camped there the whole night to secure the first places. Since we still needed to obtain the passports, my mother took me off the line and dragged me with her to the Mexican embassy, where we had to join another line. This was just as long and packed with people waiting to certify that they in fact were Mexican citizens. The Mexican officials looked at us with disdain, as if we had betrayed our country. It is not unusual, in fact, to encounter Mexican officials, whether at the embassy or special events, who still claim that migrants leave Mexico on a whim. One in particular, here in Boston actually, argued that Mexican migrants don't actually have to come here, because Mexico has plenty of jobs available. 'How do you actually define jobs?' I asked her, incensed. 'One could wash cars, or gather aluminum cans, or do heavy labor, but I would hardly call that a job. Migrants come not just in search of work and opportunity, but to find a place where they can be fully human.' She then challenged me, saying that we only come here to be mistreated, and this forces the government to intervene on our behalf. 'It is not easy to be a Mexican immigrant in the U.S., and it never has been,' I replied, 'but I and thousands of others would rather risk our lives and everything we own to carve a future here.' She proceeded to inform me that she had worked with Mexican immigrants in meat-packing plants in the Midwest, advocating on their behalf. In her view, they all regretted coming here. I then told her that I was an immigrant myself, and she listened in disbelief since I was now a doctoral student at Harvard. Looking back, the only regret I have about this conversation is that it didn't take place sooner,

perhaps even that day while I waited in line with my mom at the Mexican embassy. However, these Mexicans didn't even look at us in the eye, as if we were unworthy of acknowledgment, yet in my heart I knew they were not any better than I was. How did they land these positions? They hardly spoke English, and their camaraderie seemed superficial. Surely, I thought to myself, they got their jobs through 'connections'—a friend of a friend or the relative of a relative in high places procured the position for them.

"But there was no time to waste. We returned to the American consulate to join the rest of the family in the line. To our surprise, the line had moved inside, and we waited our turn anxiously. When our number was about to be called, my parents gathered us for a final briefing in preparation for the interview, since we had heard that American officials could be quite unpredictable. 'Always tell the truth but don't say more than you are asked,' my mother said. So we were called in groups of two and asked random questions about when, how, and why we had come to the U.S. Nervously, we answered as best as we could, and after some cross-examining our case was approved. We could now get real social security numbers, tax refunds, and a driver's license. Above all, the threat of deportation was gone. Unfortunately, my sister Ceci, who is two years older than me, was not qualified since she had turned eighteen before she applied, and so didn't fall within the grace period granted by the government. Despite our sadness, the family's lot did improve significantly. I started working for Grimmway Farms, in their packing line, with the opportunity to drive a forklift. 'You can make it big here,' my supervisor said.

"One day I arrived earlier than my coworkers and started to prepare for the day. The mist in the cold storage reduced visibility in my workstation, and I was alone. So once more, I began to pray and question God. Had he not heard my prayer, or was I not reading the signs properly? 'If this is all you have for me, I'll take it, but I had expected more,' I said. While I was not making huge amounts of money, it was a decent job and I had finally legalized my status. What, then, was missing?

"That same day, during lunch, I realized that God would not come down from heaven to fill out my college application. So I picked up the phone and called a college I had heard about during a Pentecostal retreat to request an application. A few weeks later, I was anxiously waiting for my letter of admission or rejection. I say anxiously, because when I graduated my GPA was a meager 1.9. But I kept faith, 'because without faith it is impossible to please God' (Hebrews 11:6). To walk in faith means to trust in God even when all the pieces of the puzzle are not in place or available. 'Abraham, when called

to go to a place he would later receive as his inheritance, obeyed and went, even though he did not know where he was going' (Hebrews 11:8). I could not do otherwise.

"Finally, on 7 August 1999, I received a letter from the admissions office informing me of my acceptance to Bethany College that fall. Because of my low GPA, I was admitted under academic probation and was required to attend the learning center, take a study skills class, and attain a GPA of 2.0 or higher. Even though I didn't qualify for any institutional financial aid, my family was jubilant. My mother immediately shared the news with her friends, which put pressure on me. Though I was excited, I didn't know how I was going to pay $12,000 a year. But walking by faith demands that you take such challenges head on. That same month I communicated the news to my pastor, but he was not at all excited. He needed me by his side to serve in the congregation, even though I had already given it all I had as a youth leader, Sunday school teacher, and leader of cell groups and evangelism.

"The day before my departure to Bethany College in Santa Cruz, the brothers from the church raised a $200 offering. Combined with my paycheck, I had a total of $350. That night I began to doubt the whole enterprise. Was this really God's will or my obsession with college? Sensing my doubt, my mom came to talk with me at midnight and told me not to surrender before the fight had even begun. Besides, she had already told all her friends, and I could not let her down. She had prepared lunch and made transportation arrangements for the journey. 'Your brother will drive us tomorrow to Santa Cruz,' she said. This was another moment of truth, and I commended my life to God.

"The next day, my brother showed up at five in the morning, and we loaded my luggage into the car and made our way to connect with El Cinco, Interstate 5, the same road along which I had traveled from Tijuana to Bakersfield. As we left town, tears came to my eyes. I recalled my hardships in the fields, my adventures with El Flaco, and my days at the Pentecostal congregation. I was also leaving family and friends behind to answer God's call, without really knowing how a few hundred dollars in my pocket would pay for my tuition. But had not Jesus also multiplied the fish?"

COLLEGE

Bethany College was a private Christian institution founded in 1919. Formerly called Glad Tidings Bible Institute and located in San Francisco,

Bethany's mission was to train pastors and missionaries of the Assemblies of God, one of the largest Pentecostal denominations in the U.S. Sequestered among the redwoods of Scotts Valley, the college was only a ten-minute drive from the beaches of Santa Cruz, where surfers, poets, and dreamers congregated in the late afternoon to admire the sunset and the sea. Roberto's cohort comprised students from all over the world seeking an education and hoping to discover their true vocation. Daunted by the uncertainty of what lay ahead, Roberto felt as if he were entering a wilderness. "This was a place where I would have to learn to trust God completely and believe that he can make a way where there is no way. It was all a matter of faith, of keeping going when all the odds were stacked against you."

"What were you afraid of?" I asked.

"I was afraid of fear. Fear can paralyze you mentally and lead you to accept defeat before the battle has even begun. In my first weeks at Bethany, my fear of failure was so overwhelming that I could hardly concentrate on the task before me. Academically, it was an uphill battle, because I was on academic probation and had several requirements to fulfill, which included taking courses I had failed before, such as Algebra and English Composition. The very thought of getting through this process so paralyzed me that I began to have second thoughts about my venture. However, as with most obstacles, I turned to God in prayer. The last day of orientation I went to a small prayer room that adjoined the chapel and surrendered my fears to God. 'You know I have failed all these courses and related subjects in high school, but I also know that you are the fountain of wisdom and knowledge. Grant me that I may be a wise and knowledgeable student, and I will do my part.' I slept well that day, but the fear of financial collapse threatened the entire enterprise. With only a few hundred dollars in my pocket, I had to take a loan and have my oldest sister, Hortencia, as cosignatory, because, as the financial aid officer was quick to highlight, I was not 'creditworthy.' Although God didn't show up with a $12,000 check to pay my tuition, I had no doubt he could do it, and I saw the loan as a test of faith. Taking stock of my situation and covenant with God, I decided to attend classes every day, complete every assignment, and take time to study. Furthermore, I had to secure a source of income and be frugal in my expenses. I applied and was hired for a part-time job at Wendy's. Although it was tedious, it was not even close to the heavy labor jobs I had in the fields or when growing up in Mexico. The owner of the restaurant was so impressed with my work ethic that she raised my salary. For me, this was not only providential but also an assurance that God was with

me. During the summers, when the college served as retreat center for various youth groups, I worked as a janitor and security officer, and I also did small construction jobs for some of my professors. Making about $250 per month and working about fifteen to seventeen hours a week during the academic year, I earned enough to make small tuition payments not covered by the loan, buy clothes, and pay gas for my 1984 Pontiac Trans Am with T-tops. Even after all these expenses I still had enough to open a small savings account with Bank of America."

"And you were living at Bethany?"

"Yes. And that meant another set of challenges, though these were social rather than financial or academic. My first days in the dorm involved setting boundaries and priorities as well as identifying potential friends and foes. I received phone calls from the student life director inquiring about my well-being, but she would not say why. Later that month I learned that my two roommates were men of ill repute, one a drug addict and the other a sex icon. Since I didn't talk much and didn't pry into their business—a sound principle I learned in the barrio—they left me alone. But I was bothered by the stench of weed and all the eager freshmen girls knocking on the door, wanting to meet 'hot stuff.' I needed a quiet place to study, complete my assignments, and rest after flipping burgers at Wendy's, so I was transferred to another unit. But the issue was not solved. My new roommate, Matt, was a prankster who lived in a constant state of paranoia about potential 'avengers.' One night he suggested that I avoid answering the phone because he was getting nasty phone calls from girls he had aggravated. Since I talked to my mother at around ten o'clock before going to bed, I could not agree to this request. Used to getting his way and assuming that my quietness implied an even temper, he waited to see if I would answer the phone. At ten sharp, the phone rang. I picked it up, talked to my mother, and updated her on my situation. I had a job, was working hard, and was now dealing with roommate issues. She asked me to pray for them, but before I could do anything, Matt, who weighed about two hundred pounds and was about five feet nine, exploded in anger: 'I told you not to answer the fuckin' phone. Are you deaf?' He then proceeded to take the phone from my hands and place it under his pillow, hurling all sorts of insults at me as he did so. Incensed, I jumped on him, grabbed him by the neck, and broke things down for him. I raised my right hand to punch him, just as the resident assistants, who had heard all the commotion, entered the room and dragged me off him. Since they knew about Matt's reputation and had been victims of his pranks at

some point or another, they were more concerned about me, but I refused to move again."

"Did you meet other students that you felt positive toward? Who became friends?"

"Yes, soon after my arrival I met a guy called Jerry who later became my best friend, and the members of a group called the Council, whose goal was to grow spiritually, academically, and professionally. These individuals not only taught me how to be a competent student, but they spent long night hours teaching me how write and speak proper English, and also helped me enjoy learning and life. Leaving college was hard because it also meant the dissolution of that community, but we have found new ways to keep in touch."

FINANCIAL BORDERS

"At the end of my first year at Bethany, I ran out of money and received constant calls from the financial aid office. The message was clear and difficult to digest: I needed to pay all my debt to be able to register for the following academic year. Although I worked and took classes the entire summer, I still didn't have enough to pay my remaining debt or make any installments for next year. Defeated and with a sense of uncertainty, I returned to college that fall knowing that I had reached the end of my rope. I turned to God in prayer again and hoped for a miracle. After discussing the issue with my study skills instructor and mentor, a psychology professor to whom I'm heavily indebted, we decided to take my case before the president of the college. My mentor said he had sponsored students before and perhaps he'd be willing to help me. It was a difficult time, and several of my classmates were dropping out due to financial difficulty. A promise was unfulfilled or a huge sum of money was never delivered, so they had to leave. The prospects of returning to my hometown empty-handed were high, but I resolved not to return because, as I mentioned before, there is a strong stigma attached to failure in the Latino community. I had come by faith, so I decided to trust and hope until the very end.

"The day of my interview arrived, and my mentor came with me to talk to President Wilson. A Latin Americanist who had completed his PhD at Stanford and served as a missionary in El Salvador, Dr. Wilson knew the culture pretty well. When he heard my case, he stated that I was not the only

one in need and that he only supported people he knew. For all intents and purposes, I was a *desconocido,* and his words fell on me like a bucket of cold water, so to speak. 'This is over,' I said to myself. Suddenly, his semblance changed. He approached me and placed his right hand on my shoulder and said, 'But I will invest in you. From now on, do not worry about your tuition. Whenever you receive calls from the financial aid office, tell them to talk to me about it. My only condition is that you excel academically and remain focused on your studies.' I thanked him and my mentor and walked out of that office renewed. That day I knew for sure that God had heard my prayer that cold morning in the vineyards below Bear Mountain. I was in God's hands, and my financial worries ended that day. Although I continued to make monthly installments on my remaining debt, the president paid for my tuition that entire year. Because by that time my GPA had climbed from a 1.9 to a 3.8, I was now eligible for academic scholarships. I was getting straight *A*s, and I know the president was proud, and so were my professors. One of them encouraged me to apply to grad school and suggested Harvard and Princeton Theological Seminary as two options. 'Harvard?' I replied in disbelief.

"Getting into any of the ivy league schools is surely complicated, and despite my academic achievements, at least one professor refused to write a letter of recommendation on the grounds that my potential rejection could ruin our friendship. I applied to Harvard and Princeton Theological Seminary and was admitted to both with a full scholarship. The day I received Harvard's letter of admission was one of the happiest days in my life. I started jumping, dancing, and thanking God in the hall of my dormitory. One by one, all my friends came to congratulate me and rejoice with me. (I still keep that letter framed side by side with my admission letter to Bethany, which stresses in bold that I had been admitted under academic probation.) Once again, for me this was entirely a faith journey. Following a professor's advice and considering the historical educational challenges that Latinos face in this country, I opted for Harvard and do not regret making that decision.

"A few months before graduation, I received a call from the president's office regarding selection of commencement speakers. Accompanied by three close friends of mine, Arsene, Justys, and Nathaniel (Jerry had graduated the previous year), I made my way to the fourth floor of the administration building, where I was joined by two other students. With his usual serene semblance, the president said, "After long deliberation, the faculty has decided that Roberto will be our commencement speaker, and both of you will speak

at the baccalaureate service.' 'You have been awarded a great privilege,' he said to me, 'so prepare accordingly and do your best to represent your peers and the best of your school.' While my competitors digested the news, I asked the president to thank the faculty on my behalf for conferring such privilege upon me, then I shook his hand and had a brief conversation without speaking any words. The last time I had been to his office was to ask for an opportunity to stay in college, and I had obtained his support. We exchanged looks. He smiled, and I knew he was proud. He had invested both time and money in me, and I had honored his trust the best way I knew how, with a high GPA, a full ride to Harvard University, and now this speaking appointment. Thereafter I made my way down the stairs to the lobby, where my friends awaited the news. Since I was all smiles, they read the good news in my face and took me to my favorite Mexican restaurant to celebrate. At commencement, I related my hardships in the fields, my efforts to go to college, and the intense nights of study at the tutoring center. After thanking the president, my family, friends, fellow students, and professors for their continued support, I also thanked God for his faithfulness.

"After graduation, I went back home to Bakersfield and spent the entire summer with my family. Since I refused to stay at home, I joined my father and brother in their construction work, and the company's owner was surprised that despite my admission to Harvard I still wanted to do that heavy labor. 'It's about family,' I said to him. However, he did not understand, nor did the other construction company owners who gathered around us during lunch to criticize my move and suggest I needed to find a job worthy of a Harvard student. Yet for me, it was really all about family, for I well knew this would be one of the last times I'd work side by side with my brother and father. Finally, the night before my departure, all my siblings, along with my nephews and nieces, came to bid me farewell. They brought small monetary offerings and food, and spent time talking with me and taking pictures until late at night. Then they all gathered around me, and my mother prayed for me, reciting a well-known benediction: 'The Lord bless you, and keep you; may the Lord make his face shine on you; the Lord turn his face toward you and give you peace.' The next day, I woke up at five o'clock, and my mother and sister Alejandra drove me to Los Angeles airport, and I boarded a plane to Massachusetts, where Harvard awaited me. I completed the master's program in 2006, took a two-year break and got married, then returned to Harvard in 2008 to pursue a doctoral degree. I'm now in the fifth and last year of my doctoral studies and hope to return to California soon, though

I may have to go where I can find work. Although my journey from an unknown town in Mexico to Harvard has been long, perilous, and painful (though at many moments joyful), I know there are more borders to cross, more fears to overcome, and new limit situations to transcend. Yet I already know that 'though I walk through the valley of the shadow of death, I will fear no evil,' for the Divino Compañero del Camino walks with me and my family."

Ibrahim

IN 2007 MY COUSIN LOUISA JACKSON and her friend Evelien Kuipers were working as volunteers for an NGO in Ghana. Louisa was helping out in an orphanage; Evelien was teaching English in an elementary school five hundred miles away. When they first met, Evelien responded instantly to Louisa's unconventional personality, and both quickly discovered a shared commitment to protecting the environment and helping the poor. The two young women (Evelien was thirty, Louisa twenty-three) kept in touch by telephone and began planning a seven-week tour of Togo, Benin, and Burkina Faso when their contracts in Ghana ended. Evelien had dreamed of visiting Burkina Faso for many years. Raised in a Dutch Reformed Church family with strict Calvinist rules against working or enjoying pleasurable pastimes on the Sabbath, she would pore over her family's atlas and fantasize about one day going to Mali and Burkina Faso. Her father was an avid traveler, despite being a farmer. He thought nothing of finishing the milking in the morning, then driving his family to Rotterdam or The Hague for the day. Evelien's mother was, by contrast, a homebody, reserved and reticent. Her focus was her four children and the deeply conservative region of Overijssel in which she had been raised.

When Evelien was four, her father was killed in an accident on the farm. She was given no details and was not permitted to attend the funeral. Years later, when she asked her mother why such a conspiracy of silence surrounded the death of her father, she was told, "You were only a child," as if Evelien's innocence might protect her from such a tragedy or would have been lost had she known exactly what had happened. Evelien's mother never really came to terms with her husband's death. "My father had always wanted to see Russia," Evelien told me. "When he died, my mother sometimes dreamed that he had

gone to Russia. She felt abandoned and angry and has never really worked through the trauma of her loss. When I broach the subject of my own loss, she tells me I was only a child, or that she wanted to protect me 'from all that,' or she turns to how her loss was as great or greater than mine." It wasn't until Evelien returned from Africa that she asked neighbors and relatives to share reminiscences with her and help her flesh out a picture of her father as more than a shadowy figure at the edge of the landscape of her early life.

When Louisa and Evelien arrived in Ouagadougou, they checked into a budget hotel called the Hotel Yennenga, next to the Grand Mosque. The hotel manager, Ibrahim Ouédraogo, was a direct descendant of Princess Yennenga Naaba Ouédraogo, whose son founded the third great Mossi kingdom in the mid-fifteenth century.

Louisa was suffering from a bacterial infection, and a couple of weeks passed before she was well enough to venture out. Louisa remembered Ibrahim vividly. "I first met him when I was sitting on the balcony looking out at the mosque. He was a very composed man and very concerned about Evelien and me." When Louisa was well enough to travel, she and Evelien went south to Bobo-Dioulasso, but on their way back to Ouagadougou with some Rastafarians, Evelien began to feel unwell—and the two travelers returned to the Hotel Yennenga for another period of rest and recuperation. Louisa delayed her return to Ghana for a few days to nurse Evelien, who had contracted malaria. "The hotel staff were wonderful," Evelien said. "They helped get me to the hospital, and in my absence Ibrahim ensured that my luggage was placed in safe storage. When I came back to the hotel, I thought of continuing with my original plan, which was to visit Mali and fly back to Europe from Bamako. But I was still very weak and needed time to recover, so I did some more sightseeing in Burkina. During this time, Ibrahim offered me advice and was very caring. When I finally got back to Ouagadougou, I found that he had my hotel room ready for me, and he showed me to it. It was a bit awkward for a moment. I could see he wanted to ask me something, but I didn't know what to say. Finally, he asked me out for a drink. I said I would think about it, but I didn't think about it for very long. Before even leaving the hotel, I felt comfortable and happy in his company."

Evelien and Ibrahim also discovered a common bond. When Evelien's father died, she was kept from attending his funeral and treated as if she was too young to experience grief. Coincidentally, when Ibrahim's mother died, he was also shut out of the community's grieving. During his mother's final illness, she had insisted he return to his job in Bobo-Dioulasso. Reluctantly,

he did her bidding, but she died the day after he left. Though he was twenty-one, Ibrahim's relatives only informed him of his mother's passing several weeks after the funeral. Knowing how close he was to his mother, they feared he would not be able to handle the loss. Little did they know that missing the funeral would haunt Ibrahim for many years, as he sought more information about his mother's last illness and tried to locate her grave to perform a ritual to settle his spirit and hers. He also wanted some object that had belonged to her or a photo to remember her by, hoping he might thereby alleviate the dreams that disturbed his sleep.

After Evelien returned to Europe, she stayed in touch with Ibrahim by e-mail and by phone. As their friendship deepened, Evelien realized that the only way she could be sure of her feelings for Ibrahim was to make a return visit to Burkina. Six months after leaving Ougadougou, Evelien returned. Ibrahim was astonished. He wanted to know what had brought her back. When Evelien said she had returned for him, he couldn't believe it. "For me?" he said. "You came back just to see me?" Following their happy reunion, and their decision to make a life together, the question for Evelien and Ibrahim was now whether Ibrahim could give up his job, and his life, in Burkina Faso and find fulfillment in the Netherlands. It took almost a year for the couple to work out the logistics of this radical move, which occurred a year before I first met Evelien in September 2010.

That August I had received an e-mail from Evelien in which she introduced herself as a friend of Louisa's and explained that she planned to come to Boston for a conference. I invited her to stay with my family, and during these few days together she recounted the details of her life with Ibrahim in Amsterdam. But it wasn't until I began work with Emmanuel Mulamila that I conceived the idea of asking Ibrahim, via Evelien, if he would consider including his story in the book I was writing about migrant experience. Though hesitant at first, Ibrahim gradually warmed to the idea, and in April 2012, with money I had earned from lectures at two Swedish universities, I flew to Amsterdam to meet Ibrahim and hopefully make a start on recording his story.

AMSTERDAM

It was an overcast day. Evelien, Ibrahim, and their eight-month-old daughter, Karfo, had come out to the airport at Schiphol to meet me. Undeterred

by the forecast of rain, Evelien said she had borrowed a bicycle for me so we could all cycle into the city and do some sightseeing. I was curious to know how far it was to the city center. I wasn't too keen on cycling through busy streets, dodging showers, or being a tourist. Evelien and Ibrahim assured me we would not have to go far; it was only ten minutes from the airport to their apartment and another ten to the city. Most of the journey would be through a park. Besides, the city itself was small and compact, very easy to get around. I apologized for seeming so reluctant to venture out and explained that even ethnographers—who yearn to explore new horizons— sometimes experience considerable anxiety before plunging into the unknown. Ibrahim understood perfectly. Two months after coming to live in Amsterdam, he found work with the post office as a mail carrier. But finding his way around the city was a nightmare, and he did not know how to read a map. He had seen tourists with maps in Ouagadougou and been mystified as to why they didn't ask local people where the mosque was or how best to find their way back to their hotel. Evelien had explained that Amsterdam was too big to navigate in this way. She bought a map and showed him how to use it. She explained that every street in the city had a name. "Every street!" Ibrahim exclaimed. "Yes, every street. In fact, every street in every town in Holland has a name *and* every house has a number." Ibrahim confessed that he had seen the numbers on houses and apartments but had not known what they were for. Evelien sent Ibrahim to an arbitrary address in the suburbs, telling him which bus routes would get him there and back. She made him use his cell phone to take a photo of the place, as evidence that he had actually located it.

"How long did you work for the post office?" I asked. It was the first time I had used French in many years, and I stumbled over my phrasing and had to cast around for certain words. I could already see that I was going to have to rely on Evelien, whose French was excellent, to mediate any serious conversations I might have with Ibrahim. Consequently, we often switched from French to English, with Evelien helping me out when I got into difficulties, and a tape recorder allowing me to take time later to review our more formal conversations.

"Two years," Ibrahim said in response to my question. "I never missed a single day. In every kind of weather. Snow, ice, bitter cold. One day, when I came home, my hands were so cold, so swollen, so painful, I placed them on the radiator. I could not feel a thing and burned myself badly."

"Did people accept you?"

"Not everyone, of course. One day, an elderly woman accused me of delivering her mail to the wrong address. She told me to go back where I belonged. I explained that this was not my regular mail round. I was covering for someone else. It wasn't my fault that her mail had gone missing. And I told her I didn't want to be spoken to in that way."

"I think that was the first time Ibrahim used Dutch outside a classroom," Evelien said in English. "He's very sensitive about discrimination. And work is very important to him. His pride and dignity are in his work."

After parking in the street, Evelien led the way into her apartment building. I set my suitcase down in the guest bedroom and drew the curtains to take in the view: a small balcony with flower boxes, three floors below a willow coming into leaf, a stainless steel slide and climbing equipment for children, bird feeders attached to the branches of various trees.

Within an hour, we were off again. Cycling over rain-smeared cobblestones under a lowering sky, on through Vondelpark, with Karfo riding with Evelien and Ibrahim and me close behind.

We went as far as vehicle traffic was permitted to go, locked our bicycles to a railing, and walked through the narrow seventeenth-century streets of the old city, crossing canals, wending our way past tourists, heading toward one of Evelien's favorite coffeehouses in an old house by a canal.

As we waited for our coffee, I scribbled some notes. "Anthropologists must seem like voyeurs," I said apologetically, as I pocketed my notebook. Evelien agreed. "But we all have our work to do," she said. "And Amsterdam has always been an open city, a welcoming city." As if to prove her point, we later made our way to Begijnhof. After passing through a narrow portal, we entered a large grassed courtyard surrounded by tall four-story townhouses. Evelien explained that the Beguines were, from the thirteenth century, a semimonastic community of unmarried Catholic women dedicated to doing good work. Even today, the community offered refuge to single Catholic women unable to fend for themselves. "But Amsterdam itself has always had this reputation for being open to outsiders, taking in Sephardic Jews in the early sixteenth century, Huguenots in the late seventeenth century, Flemish Protestants during the Eighty Years War, and Indonesians in the 1940s and '50s. We still say 'Leef en laat leven' [Live and let live]. More than half the people in Amsterdam are migrants."

"Like Ibrahim," I said, glancing his way.

"Well, not all of them are like Ibrahim," Evelien said. "And not all Dutch are tolerant of outsiders, especially Muslims, as you probably know."

That evening, after Karfo had gone to sleep, we watched interviews with Nicolas Sarkozy and François Hollande on TV Monde. Ibrahim explained that the Netherlands had its own elections coming up. Geert Wilders, the Islamaphobic leader of the Dutch Party for Freedom, was running on an anti-immigrant, anti-EU ticket, but he would not win. Hate would not win. And the socialists were riding high in the opinion polls.

WATER AND DRY LAND

For six months, Ibrahim had been working in the kitchens of the Royal Dutch Concert Hall. But today he was free, and we could begin recording. I began by reminding him of the houses in Dutch Renaissance style that we had seen yesterday on our stroll through the city and along the canals. Evelien had told me that the houses were built on wooden piles. As the piles rotted, the houses slumped, floors tilted, walls leaned this way and that, and the house owners often had to install false floors over the old warped ones. Even so, it was sometimes difficult to overcome a sense of vertigo as you moved about in these distorted spaces or climbed the rickety staircases from one floor to another. I asked Ibrahim if he had felt this same kind of vertigo and disorientation when he first arrived in the Netherlands from Burkina Faso.

Either because of my poor French or because the metaphor was incomprehensible, Ibrahim appealed to Evelien for help in understanding my question.

After listening attentively to Evelien's simpler version of what I had asked, Ibrahim said one of the things he found difficult to get used to in Amsterdam was the omnipresence of water. "I hadn't ever seen the sea, and the canals were new to me," Ibrahim said, explaining that he came from a country where it seldom rained and there was never enough water, and from a region, moreover, where drought and desertification had rendered life unsustainable over vast areas, including the area where he was born and raised.

Ibrahim's natal village was called Damesma. Evelien later fetched a book from my room that contained details of the village, which was established in the seventeenth or eighteenth century by Mossi migrants from Ouagadougou.[1] There was also a photograph of a Mossi village, showing innumerable conical thatched houses with mud walls, clustered into several neighborhoods (saghse), each one of which contained several compounds (zaghse). When the American anthropologist Della McMillan first visited

Damesma in 1977, villagers were suffering the effects of declining crop yields, low income, and impoverished soils, and many were leaving the village to resettle in river basins where "some of the most debilitating diseases known to humanity—malaria, schistosomiasis, sleeping sickness (trypanosomiasis) and river blindness (onchocerciasis)"—had been partially brought under control.[2] One of the most arresting comments in Della McMillan's ethnography concerned the unpredictable effects of migration. Like migrants everywhere, she writes, the "brave families who voluntarily immigrated to the AVV [Autorité des Aménagements des Vallées des Volta] went in pursuit of . . . a better life for themselves and their children."[3] But their visions changed. At first their goal was simply to survive. Then, as the years passed, some households (called *les millionaires*) succeeded where others failed. But all developed new expectations that were not only different from their original expectations but "did not always coincide with those envisioned by the project planners."[4]

For those who remained in Damesma, life also unfolded in ways that could not have been envisaged. "My father was the *tenga naba* [village chief]," Ibrahim said. "Our family had always been in the village. We could not move as others did. There were times when I thought about it, but I knew my father's importance in that place and why we had to stay."

"Why did you want to move? Was it because of the drought, the famine?"

"Not really. From age seven, I wanted to go elsewhere. You feel it inside. You can't put words to it, but it's a strong feeling, to go to a big town, to move elsewhere. When visitors came, I always wanted to be present, to hear the stories about where they came from. I was always being chased away! When I saw people who lived in bigger villages or towns, I was curious to know what life was like in those places. There was no school in my village, so I was curious to know what school was like. I wanted to discover things on the other side, though I could also see that people in towns had more to eat than in the village."

I was surprised that Ibrahim would downplay climate change and hunger when talking about why his thoughts turned to places beyond the horizon as offering the chance of a more fulfilling life. And I was intrigued that he should mention vague yearnings to explore the wider world in explaining his restiveness. I had encountered the same sentiments when talking with Roberto—sentiments that echoed Salman Rushdie's meditation on *The Wizard of Oz*, in which the imagined world becomes the real world "as it

does for us all, because the truth is that once we have left our childhood places and started out to make up our own lives, armed only with what we have and are, we understand that the real secret of the ruby slippers is not that 'there's no place like home' but rather that there is no longer any such place *as* home: except, of course, for the home we make, or the homes that are made for us, in Oz, which is anywhere, and everywhere, except the place from which we began."[5]

"Did you want to go far away?" I asked Ibrahim.

"No, I didn't think of going far. I thought mainly of going to Kaya, which was about ten kilometers from my village."[6]

"Did you know Della McMillan?" I asked.

"Of course. She and my father had an exceptionally strong friendship. I was aware of her from when I was five years old."

"She writes in her book of 'succumbing to your father's charm.' She says that your father probably saw her as an overeducated and somewhat naïve daughter, which is why he looked after her so well."

"That is so."

"How old were you when you first left your village?"

"I was twelve. I went to Kaya. Up to that time, my father was afraid to let us go to Kaya. He wanted us to know our traditions, to be strong in our customary way of life. Even now, I hear my father's voice saying, 'You must be a good example. You must honor the traditions.' But I did not want to spend all my life in Damesma. It was too limited *[limité]* for me."

"Can you tell me about your first impressions of Kaya?"

"It was the first time in my life that I saw ice."

I instantly recalled Aureliano Buendia's last memory in Gabriel García Márquez's *One Hundred Years of Solitude*—of a distant afternoon when his father took him to see a block of ice.

"I had never seen ice before," Ibrahim said. "I asked myself how it was possible. Was it magic or what? It wasn't water. Water could not be solid. I could not believe it was real. But they were selling wooden sticks with ice formed around them. There was a long line to buy one. I asked what was going on. When they told me, I joined the line."

"Were there other things that you found surprising?"

"Yes, everything!"

"For example?"

"The houses, the cars . . ."

"Had you never seen a car?"

"I had seen one, two or three years before, but not up close. Now we could run up to it and look at it, look at the tires, the places where people sat. We could walk around it and look at it properly."

"When you returned home to Damesma, what did you remember about Kaya?"

"I knew that my life would be better in a bigger place. I thought, 'Maybe one day I will go far,' but I had no way of doing this. I could not move without my family, and my family had to stay in Damesma. So I stayed too."

"How did you pass your days when you were a child in Damesma?"

"We had to go to the highlands to find firewood to give to our mother, and we also had to look after the horses, goats, and sheep. The animals were not penned. Every one had a cord around its neck. You had to catch the cord as they were running all over the place, one going to the left, another going to the right. I remember all that very well."

"Did your father also farm?"

"Yes."

"What crops did he grow?"

"We had millet, which was widely cultivated. We grew some corn, rice, beans, cotton, potatoes, and sesame. But millet was the staple. That's what we cultivated most."

"When did you begin to have problems growing enough food to live on?"

"The problems started in the north and in the nearby highlands. In the lower-lying areas the yields were all right, but the rocky soils in the highlands could not retain water, and there was not enough rain anyway. We would enrich the poorer, sandy soils by covering the ground with compost and manure, and we would leave a field fallow for ten years, so it would become productive again. But as the drought got worse, and the good land became more and more scarce, we had to cultivate the fields continually, and the yields fell off as the soils became exhausted."[7]

"When did you first experience hunger?"

"It was not only me. It was a whole generation. I grew up with hunger. It was only my older brother who knew what it was like to eat two or three times a day. By the time I was a child, we were already living with famine."

"How did you cope with such hunger?"

"Honestly, it was painful. You're hungry, and there is no food. You are like a sick person, because your stomach is constantly churning and making growling noises, and you feel very weak. Even when people say, 'Let's go,' you can't move, you can't do anything—you don't have the physical strength."

"Did you eat anything at all?"

"We ate leaves."

"What kind of leaves?"

"Our mother collected leaves from the baobab tree to make a sauce. Sometimes she boiled the leaves, sometimes she dried them in the sun and kept them. If she had maize flour she would mix the leaves with the flour and water and add a little salt. We ate leaves. No condiments. Nothing extra. We ate these leaves to fill our bellies."

"Only baobab leaves?"

"We gathered leaves from several trees—*tueiga* (baobab), *kegelega, zilega,* and two vines called *lélungo* and *bulvaka.*"

"Did you kill livestock for food?"

"No. That would have been only a short-term solution. If you killed the animals, you would not be able to replace them. We drank the milk, but the only time we ate meat was when an animal was going to die, not when we were hungry."

"Were there times when you had real food?"

"Three months a year we would have real food—tomatoes, wild eggplant, okra, green beans, chickpeas, corn on the cob, and three kinds of millet, red, white, and small. The other nine months we would eat leaves. The adults could eat leaves, but the children could not always do so. They grew weak, they were sick for a while, and they died."

"As a child, you must have seen a lot of death."

"Yes, but you did not see the bodies. It is our custom, when someone dies, not to allow strangers to see the body. You will be told, 'So-and-so died,' that's all. The elders take care of that business. In their opinion, children don't have the mental strength to see a dead body. It would keep them from sleeping, and they would grow weak."

"Did you imagine that you might die of hunger?"

"Yes, of course. We didn't have anything to eat. I remember one year that was really, really bad. No one had anything. The animals were dying, people ate meat that was bad, and even the trees that produced those leaves were not there."

"You said before that many people were migrating south, but your family stayed in Damesma."

"Yes. Some people knew that now was the time to leave. Others knew this but did not have the means to move. Others stayed, thinking things would get better. There was an organization that helped villagers move, taking them

in big trucks to better areas. It was when I was very young. I heard people talking about moving to Bitto or Bobo,[8] but I don't remember all the names of the places people moved to or the name of the organization that moved them."[9]

"But you stayed because your father was chief, and he was obliged to remain in the village?"

"Yes. His father and his father's father before him, going back hundreds of years—they had been *tenga naba* in Damesma. My father did think of sending some of the family away, but he would have to stay. If he left, the village would have to be abandoned. There would be no leadership, no government. Nothing would have been organized, because he was the one who organized everything, who saw that things were working, that certain tasks were done. If he left, injustice would have followed. The strong would have exploited the weak. People would have been hurt. He had to protect everyone and keep the peace."

"But you did leave Damesma, didn't you, to go to school? Did your father consider this a risk, thinking you might not respect local customs if you got an education?"

"No, because I came home every day. Even though the school was in Delaga, eight kilometers away, we were still together. My father wanted it that way—the family close, the kids all in one place."

"Did your father value education?"

"Yes. My father was really an intellectual. He never went to school, but he had a sharp mind. His younger brother went to school. My father would take him every morning and bring him home every afternoon, because in those days there were lions along the road, and the lions sometimes attacked people. When he was a boy, my father didn't realize the importance of education, but later he wondered why he had to walk his younger brother to and from school every day but did not attend school himself. If he wanted to write a letter, he had to rely on his younger brother to write it. If he needed to read a letter, he would have to ask his younger brother to read it to him. So when he had his first son, he sent him to school. But my older brother didn't like it. It didn't work out. So my father sent his four younger sons, saying, 'Well, I am going to send you to school because I know it will help you in the future. It won't help me, but it will help you.' It was a complete joy to us to attend school, to learn how to read and write. People in the village would come to our father and say, 'I want your son to write a letter for me.' In the beginning, my father always said, 'Sure, it's not a

problem,' but after a while he began to say, 'No, you don't send your children to school, so why should my children write letters for you?' It was his way of encouraging other parents to send their kids to school. You know, in the village at that time, there was no telephone, no telegraph. You could only communicate by letter. So there was a problem with privacy. If you got someone from outside your family to write a letter for you, that person would know everything that was in the letter, and he could go and tell other people about your personal business. If it is your own son or you who is writing the letter, the contents remain a secret. But we also saw the advantages of being able to read and write for getting a job away from the village. We could escape."

"Do you remember your first day at school?"

"It rained a lot that day, and we had to walk a great distance through the rising floodwater. The water could pull you off your feet, and my older brother, who accompanied us, had to hold on to his four younger brothers so we wouldn't be swept away."

"Did your mother approve of you going to school?"

"Yes."

"Had she ever gone to school?"

"No, but she was really, really happy that I was able to go to school."

"Can you tell me something about your school days?"

"I had always wanted to go to school. I would see other kids going off to school and want to go with them. But when I finally went to school, I was disappointed. I was sad that we didn't have good teachers, and that the law allowed teachers to beat their students. They could treat us any way they wanted, and we had no right to complain. Not even our parents had a right to complain about our harsh treatment. So it was difficult for every student, not only me, to go to school knowing you would be beaten. Only now are the schools beginning to listen to us and make changes. But before, if you didn't know the answer to a question, you would be beaten. If you made a small mistake, you would be beaten."

I was thinking of Emmanuel's ordeal at primary school in Uganda, and I asked Ibrahim to explain more about the use of corporal punishment in his school.

"They would beat you with a long plastic pipe. I remember well that we would go to school in the heaviest clothing we could find, but the teachers soon noticed that many of us were wearing this heavy clothing, so they stripped us and forced us to the ground and beat us there."

"Why did you continue at school under these conditions? What did you hope to gain from going to school?"

"We had no choice. When we returned home and told our parents that we were being beaten at school, they would say, 'You were beaten? You want to stay at home? No, you have to go to school.' We could not explain what it was like there. They did not think the situation was too serious. And we wanted to go to school, even though we were scared of being beaten."

"Was it the same at secondary school?"

"I did not get to secondary school. To go to secondary school, you had to pass an exam. If you failed to pass the exam [examen d'entrée en sixième], you would get a certificate, but without excellent grades you would not get a scholarship to pay your tuition. So I got the certificate but not the scholarship, the entrée en sixième. Because my parents didn't have the means to pay for a place for me in a secondary school, I automatically had to quit school."

"Were the fees very high?"

"No one in the village had that kind of money. This was also a period when my parents had nothing. Around harvest time, it's possible to sell some corn or rice or millet, but this was the time before harvest [which is in September–October], and they had no money and no means of earning or borrowing any money. Only by selling their crops on the market could they get money to pay their children's school fees."

"That must have been hard for you, not being able to continue with your schooling."

"It was very sad. I almost lost my mind. I had hoped to be like the others, to win a scholarship and continue with my education. Suddenly, it had to be abandoned. It was as though I had been abandoned. I lost hope completely, because I saw that nothing would change. My one thought was that someone might offer to pay my school fees and that I could finish secondary school and get a job. My dream had been to become a doctor. That, or to gain the technical skills to build a big house or start a business. Those were my dreams, but at that moment, without the means to pay for my schooling, I saw no future for me at all."

"Did you pray at this time?"

"No, honestly, I did not think of God."

"You were not angry with God?"

"No, I didn't feel that God could help me. The whole thing upset me so much that I let it go. It was something that simply befell me. I didn't have any more hope. I thought I was finished."

"What did you do?"

"I looked after my father's animals. I tended the crops."

"Did you see this as a worthwhile life?"

"No, because there is nothing you can learn from doing that. When we are with the cows, we learn nothing except how to feed them and bring them home. It's not like here, in Holland, where you learn what to do if an animal is sick, how you should treat it, what nutrients they need to produce a lot of milk, what the best conditions are for the cows to grow. We had none of those opportunities to learn. All we knew was that we had to provide enough water and nourishment for the animal. That was all."

"Were cows valued in your grandfather's day?"

"The [seminomadic] Peul had large herds, but we would only raise two or three, four or five cows. We did not raise large herds, because that would have meant leaving the village and finding places for the cows to graze. And it was difficult to keep the cows from spoiling the gardens. We kept cows until they were big enough to sell."

"For additional income?"

"Yes. But we raised crops—corn, rice, millet, beans. The Peul raised cows."

Since Evelien was now preparing lunch, I suggested we stop recording and return to our conversation later. Ibrahim was grateful for the break. He picked Karfo up and held her high, beaming at her, pulling her close to his face and rubbing kisses into her tummy. Karfo shrieked with delight.

QUR'ANIC SCHOOL

When we resumed, I asked Ibrahim if we could go back to the despair he experienced when his school days were brought abruptly to an end.

"I was blocked *[bloqué],*" Ibrahim said. "I could do nothing about it."

"Have you felt this way often in your life?"

"Once. When my mother died. My mother's death also completely changed my life. When my father died, it was difficult, but I was present at his funeral. But I was kept from attending my mother's funeral, and when I think of that, even now, it hurts me. It hurts me because of the way they treated me. I was not a child, not even an adolescent. They thought it best not to tell me the truth. But I needed to be told, so that I could express all my emotions. I needed to express everything I felt. Now I cannot. I am blocked."

I did not want to press Ibrahim further on the traumatic circumstances of his mother's death, so I turned the conversation back to something he had mentioned in passing during lunch, about having always found the courage to improve his situation. I suppose I was hoping that Ibrahim would speak, however obliquely, of the interplay between the external circumstances that closed off possibilities to him and his inner determination to take advantage of whatever small window of opportunity opened up for him. I was curious to know what margin of freedom existed for someone in an environment that appeared to offer so little room to maneuver.

"When I left school, I felt lost," Ibrahim said. "I had lost my school friends, and the only friends I now had were the village kids who wanted to go somewhere else, to go to one of the big cities. But one of these new friends, who had not gone to school, said that he was thinking of going to Bobo to study in a Qur'anic school there. I said to myself, 'Why not try this, too?' So we asked our fathers for permission to go to this school where you didn't have to pay fees, and they agreed. It was a huge adventure for me to leave the village. I thought my nightmares were going to end. It would be a joy not to be in the village anymore. I would escape. I would leave behind all the difficult things that had been weighing on my mind. I would discover life."

"Was this your first time in Bobo?"

"Yes, my first time. And it was also the first time I had taken a train. I still have the train ticket."

"How long did you stay at Qur'anic school?"

"Almost three years."

"Was it a madrassa?"

"No, I wasn't interested in a madrassa. You only learned the Qur'an there, and how to become a bandit. You could not do any serious study."

"Was Qur'anic school like the school at Delaga?"

"Honestly, no. I won't say that I was discouraged, but the behavior there was discouraging. I was happy I had left the village and moved to another place. I was happy to have discovered another life and changed as a person. But the studies were a disappointment. We were not treated well. We were like slaves. But it was a stage that brought me to another stage. And I am proud that I was not taken there by force. It was I who thought of going there, to explore, to discover. But there were other parents who took their little children by force. They could not escape. As for me, I was older, and I made the choice myself, so when I was there, despite the maltreatment, I decided that I would escape by finishing quickly and earning the right to leave. So I

told myself, 'Well, I am now in a situation where it is my choice. Either I work slowly and stay here a long time, or I complete my studies quickly and leave.' When I thought of this, it gave me courage. I said, 'Let's go,' and before three years had passed, I was done, I could leave, and I left."

ACTING AND BEING ACTED UPON

I felt a quiet sense of gratification as Ibrahim spoke of his struggle to determine his own destiny and not succumb to external pressures or the dictates of others, for this "existential imperative" was a theme that had run through my work for many years: "In spite of being aware that eternity is infinite and human life finite, that the cosmos is great and the human world small, and that nothing anyone says or does can immunize him or her from the contingencies of history, the tyranny of circumstance, the finality of death, and the accidents of fate, every human being needs some modicum of choice, craves some degree of understanding, demands some say, and expects some sense of control over the course of his or her own life."[10] But what becomes of a person who is blocked or thwarted at every turn—doors closed, hopes dashed, potential unrealized, dreams deferred? How can one persevere in life when every decision that bears on one's destiny is made by others or appears to be made by beings or forces beyond one's control or comprehension? If an ethical existence means, at the very least, *feeling* free to embrace the givenness of existence on our own terms, what kind of humanity remains to us when our words fall on deaf ears, our actions count for nothing, our needs go unrecognized, and we become, as Ibrahim put it, "like slaves"?

The anthropology in which I was first tutored reduced people's lives to the roles they occupied. Social structure defined the real, and human beings moved through it as anonymous and replaceable functionaries. At the same time, collective representations, unconscious structures of the mind, or economic infrastructures were accorded a power over human consciousness that those who described the lifeworlds of "primitive" or "peasant" populations in these reductionist terms clearly considered themselves exceptions to. And so I asked Ibrahim whether he thought there was a radical difference between his world and the world of his fathers and grandfathers, or did they, or some of them, dream in their own manner of moving, of enlarging their horizons, of seeking to strike some kind of balance between ancestral obligations and personal ambitions—a process that I had already begun to theorize, on the

basis of my conversations with Emmanuel and Roberto, as one of ethical struggle?

"Well," Ibrahim said, "you should know that my father loved to travel.[11] Moreover, in my family, there are many who migrated, not to Europe but to other places in Africa where life was easier than in Burkina.[12] But it wasn't because of them that I wanted to leave Damesma. I knew that even when people did leave, things didn't always work out for them. They would lose their lives in the course of their travels, or they would return to the village with empty hands. There were good stories, but there were many tragic ones. As for me, ever since I was very young, I wanted to be free. I wanted to have a chance at a good education, to make progress, to evolve."

"What did you do after you finished Qur'anic school?"

"I was still young, at an age when you don't pay much attention to the money you have or don't have. We did not have money at Qur'anic school, but I found work two months after leaving school. When I started earning money, I forgot all about school. I wanted to continue, but the opportunity never came. Even now, my lack of a high school education fills me with shame [honte]. I no longer aspire to being a doctor, but I often think of moving to a French-speaking country for a few years so that I can complete my high school diploma. I don't want my children asking me to help them with their homework, and having to confess that I don't understand anything in the books they are reading."

"What was the job you found?"

"It was cleaning rooms in a hotel. I remember the day I began work and the first day I got my pay. Ah, that was wonderful. I found the job 'via via'— through an acquaintance. I had to keep going back to the hotel to tell them I was interested. 'I hope you haven't forgotten me.' I did this for two months, until they hired me. I thought, 'Ah, this is such a great opportunity.' It wasn't the money that was important. It was having a job. Having something to show for myself. And it wasn't the kind of job where 'you have to do this, you have to do that, you have to finish this before you do that.' No, it wasn't like the village, where you worked very, very hard but without anything to show for it, nothing to eat. And it wasn't like school, where you also worked very hard but for nothing. No, with the hotel you knew that you'd have your pay at the end of each month, even though it was small. In the village and at school, you worked hard for no result. It was like slavery."

Over the next few years, Ibrahim steadily worked his way up the hotel hierarchy; then he moved to Ouagadougou and took the position of manager

at the Hotel Yennenga. As he recounted his progress, I once more found myself pondering the interplay of personal resourcefulness and external circumstances in shaping a life course. And so I mentioned to Ibrahim how, in my conversations with Emmanuel and Roberto, I had been struck by the pivotal role of mentors, intercessories, and patrons in their lives. Were there certain people in his life who had had a similar influence?

"Well, I remember that my father's brother always encouraged me to continue with my schooling, and the person who hired me at the hotel in Bobo always wanted me to get ahead. He never said, 'Well, he doesn't have what it takes to get to a high level, so I will leave him where he is.' He always tried to help me move forward. There were also people who had had the chance to get a higher education, who also encouraged me: 'You have to do better, you always have to look for something better.' So I had encouragement from many people."

"Did your mother encourage you?"

"Yes. My mother was a truly exceptional woman, though she never went to school. She came from a Christian family in a village not far from my father's village. Her parents died when she was three or four years old. She didn't know her father or her mother and was looked after by her grandparents, I think, or one of her father's cowives. It was within the family, though I don't know exactly who it was. No one explained that to me."

"How did your mother and father meet?"

"My mum married my father when he became chief. It happened because of a fire in my mother's village. The fire was so big that no one knew how to tackle it. There were many houses—you know, those traditional ones with thatched roofs. No sooner had the fire taken one house than it spread to another and another. People could only stand and stare. But word reached my father's father, who was chief in Damesma at that time. 'There is a fire, but we don't know what to do.' Everyone was too frightened to intervene, but my grandfather took his horse and quickly reached the village. Everyone was panicking and in shock, but he rode to where the houses had not yet caught fire and ordered people to demolish some of them. When the fire reached that place, it went no further, because there was nothing for it to burn. It was incredible, because everyone was panicking. They had lost their minds, not knowing what to do to stop the fire. So this family was very proud and said to him. 'We don't have anything to pay you or any gift to give you, but we will give you our daughter.' That was my mum. Where I come from, even today, to give a young girl to someone is the greatest gift.[13] So my mother was given, like that. She bore many

children, but after a year or two the child would die. This went on until my elder brother was born. He was a twin, but his brother died. Then I was born and also lived, and after me there was another son who died. So of the ten or more children my mother brought into the world, only two survived—myself and my older brother, Ousseni. Apart from Ousseni and my younger brother who died, I never knew my siblings. Ousseni told me what had happened to them, and other people confirmed what he said. My mother did not forget the ones who had passed away. She wasn't as strong as the other women, who fought with their husbands. My mother was always sweet. She accepted everything. If people asked, 'Who did that? Did you do that?' she would say 'I am sorry, it was me,' even though she had done nothing wrong. She always accepted everything and never argued. She never reprimanded us, saying, 'No, why did you do that?' She loved children. Children used to have fun with her because she was like a child too. Every night, all the children would fill her house to play there, until it came time for them to go home. The only thing that troubled her, I think, was some kind of sore in her mouth that she had since I was born. It never healed. Perhaps it was cancer or an abscess from a diseased tooth. It caused a swelling and a hole from her cheek to the inside of her mouth."

"Did she seek treatment for the problem?"

"Della helped my mother and father. She arranged for them to go to the hospital and have it treated. But it didn't heal. And we didn't have the money to take her back to the hospital. She lived with that problem all her life. We were afraid she would die from this problem. She was so physically strong that she thought she would never get sick, but when she got sick we thought this thing was going to kill her. In fact, she died of something else entirely."

"It must have been terribly painful for your mother to lose so many children. How did she endure such loss?"

"It was very, very difficult for her. The only thing she could do was to talk to older women who had suffered similar loss. But to lose so many children was very, very painful. And nothing really diminished that pain for her. It remained with her always. It made her afraid that she would lose Ousseni and me, too. When there was hardly any food, she would give us her food, even though it wasn't much. She would say, 'I am an adult, take this.' She did a lot for us so that we would survive."

"What kind of things did you learn from your father and mother? How are you like them?"

"Well, my father loved to travel. He loved to discover new things. I am like that too. As for my mother, she never wanted to go to a party, go

dancing, or watch a film. She always stayed at home, working, working. I'm like that too. And my father also loved children, until they turned two, when he hated them!" Ibrahim laughed. "But my mother always loved children and worked and worked without stopping. She was very respectful. She respected everyone, whether they were old people or children. She respected her husband in the same way. Maybe she respected him too much! She never said, 'That's enough, I'm not going to do that.' She always agreed with him. One of my father's strong points was his mind. He had a sharp mind. He was very intelligent, and he was a really great chief. He could sort things out when there was tension between one person and another, always finding a solid middle ground. He was much loved. He visited every family in the village. Even when he was traveling to remote places, he would make sure that he visited everyone who had ties to Damesma."

"I have the impression that if your parents were alive they would be enormously proud of what you have achieved."

"Yes. I think that too. In fact, whenever I returned to Damesma to visit my father, he was always proud that I was so like him, that I helped others and was concerned for their well-being. He even told me once, 'Ibrahim, you are my son, you are a good man.' If he were alive now he would be concerned that I was so far away. He would be concerned whether everything was working out for me."

"Among the Kuranko people in Sierra Leone, it is said that blessings come from your paternal ancestors but through your mother. If she works well and respects her husband, the blessings will come to you, but if she behaves badly, the blessings will be blocked and your life may be cursed."

"Yes, it is the same with us. If the mother is good to the father, happiness will reach the children, and they will do well. But if the parents do not have a good relationship, the children will suffer. So we think that the parents need to be happy for their children to be happy. This may be true or not, but I have seen from experience that in most families where the parents do not get along, the children are sad and have difficulties in life. Where there is love, the children succeed."

"Were your parents often together?"

"Well, they were not an ordinary couple because my father was chief. Also, when you reach the age of seven you have to leave the court, and children are not allowed to get too close to the chief. So I did not have many opportunities of seeing my parents together."

"Was the eldest son kept even further away?"

"Yes, he is a rival to his father, so he is sent far away. For twenty years we didn't even know where our eldest brother was."

"Did he become chief when your father died?"

"In the old days he would have become chief, but things are changing nowadays. We feel that if the eldest son has been living far away he won't know anything about the village, he will be out of touch. People might be scared of him. He might cause problems."

"In America, when kids become teenagers they often rebel against their parents. Did you ever go against your parent's wishes? Did you ever rebel?"

"Sometimes I would refuse to help my mum when she wanted me to work in the fields. I would refuse to carry the peas or the water. I'd say, 'I'm going to a party.' She would say, 'I need you to work,' but I would go to the party just the same. I'd do things she didn't approve of. For example, she would prepare some food especially for us, but I would say, 'No, this is no good, make it differently,' or I would steal some sugar or sauce, or beans or corn, and go and cook my own food on a fire in the bush. Or I would go out in the morning and come home late at night. Go hunting. Things that our parents didn't want us to do, but that we felt we had to do at that age. If you don't do what you want to do, you'll regret it later."

"How old were you at this time?"

"Around eighteen. I didn't rebel so much against my father. But with my mother it was very different. When I got older and thought about it, I realized it was something you have to do at that age to know life, to discover society. Even girls rebel, going off with boys, stealing, having sex, sometimes getting pregnant. In Burkina we try to keep these things hidden, but here it's much more out in the open. You see children on television screaming at their fathers, 'I don't want that! I'm not going to do that!' Back home you would not see that. Parents are more respected."

I was fascinated by the ethical dilemma Ibrahim faced, determined to make his own way in the world yet keenly aware of his filial obligations. At stake here is the Oedipal project—the need to sever one's exclusive attachments to parents in order to enter a phase of generalized attachment to peers, 'to know life, to discover society,' as Ibrahim put it. These extrafamilial attachments and friendships may be quite transitory and loyalties short-lived until, with marriage, a new phase of focused attachment begins.

This transition from being a child in one's parents' household to being an adult in a home of one's own also anticipates the transition that is mediated

by migration. Both involve initiatory ordeals. Both entail symbolic death and rebirth. And the ethos of filial piety is often at odds with the imperative of self-definition.[14] When I broached this matter with Ibrahim, he readily acknowledged the potential double bind.

"It's because of our culture. This responsibility to our family and to our parents is always on our minds. We think, 'Is this really what I should be doing? Do I have the right to do this?' Even if our parents are dead, we ask ourselves if it is really necessary or really right to do what we are doing. We grow up with this. We can't overcome this way of thinking. It's something we are born into. Sometimes I feel guilty about being in Europe without my parents' blessings. Or I think back to the time when I was finishing Qur'anic school, and my mother wanted me to return to Damesma. Even now, I regret not respecting her wishes. She died before I could explain to her why I could not go back. When I was working in the hotel in Ouagadougou, my father would come to visit me. He would say he had arranged for me to marry. I would tell him that it wasn't time, it wasn't good timing. I would put him off rather than do his bidding. Now I wonder whether my refusal to take his advice led to his death, and whether I am going to have bad luck in life because I went against his will."

I told Ibrahim that I had a Sierra Leonean friend in London whose father was a Muslim chief who had instilled in his son the values of sobriety and respect for elders. When Sewa's English friends came to his house to hang out and drink beer, Sewa would remove his father's photo from the living room, because he could not drink alcohol with his father watching him.

Ibrahim laughed. "It is the same mentality," he said. "You grow up seeing how your parents do things, and you try to copy them. Even when you are an adult, your parents are never far from your thoughts. When my father's mother died, she was buried in the house, and my father would talk of her as if she were still alive. Here, when someone dies, it's finished, there is no further contact or communication. But back home, when someone is dead they are still very important. It's not over. We feel that the spirit is still there even though their image has gone."

ON JUDGMENT

This question of how a person can reconcile the demands of tradition with the desire to determine his or her own destiny led me to ask Ibrahim how he

decides when it is expedient or appropriate to accept the status quo, and when it is necessary to voice dissent, to refuse to follow the crowd. I broached this question by asking whether Mossi shared the Kuranko view that a person's worth is relative to his or her status—so that if a child dies, its funeral is a perfunctory affair, unlike the funeral of a chief, which may go on for many days and involve dramatic displays of grief and mourning.

"It is the same with us," Ibrahim said. "If a man or woman dies unmarried, the funeral will be held on the day of the death, but the funeral of a married person will last several days, and there will be rituals thirty days later, and another one hundred days after that. But personally, I think that everyone has the right to the same kind of funeral, whether they are married or unmarried, a child or an adult, a man or a woman."

"How can you uphold custom while holding this view?" I asked.

"It is difficult," Ibrahim said.

"At what age did you develop your own views about human worth?"

"When I was eighteen or twenty. I saw that I could not change the way things were, but I was disturbed to see that the poor were treated badly by the rich. I thought to myself, 'Why do they act like this?' The question stays in your heart. It moves you, but you cannot share it with anyone. I thought that life would be easier if there was equality instead of differences. But when you are in that system of inequality, you are blocked. You have to participate—you have to agree with it, even though you don't."

"How does Holland compare with Burkina Faso in this regard?"

"Here, no matter what job you do, people will respect you. If you don't work, they may not respect you for that, but people would never say, 'What a dirty job, I wouldn't want to do that,' and not respect you because you are doing it. It may be typically Dutch, but I can eat with my boss, I can ask her any question I like, I can negotiate things with her even though I am her employee. Back home that would be practically impossible. When people get a good education, they use their power of knowledge to show that they are better than others. They will not share their knowledge. They will use it for themselves. When they see that you are not well educated they don't want to play with you. The same thing if they become rich. They will go and live in a wealthy neighborhood. They will have nothing to do with people who are poor. Here, you can have a friend who is a director or a minister, but back home you can only communicate with people at the same social level as yourself. What I like in Holland is that even if you are rich, your wealth does not make a big difference. If you are intelligent, your intelligence doesn't matter

socially. No matter who you are or what you do, you are treated as an equal. I love that. There is no such thing as, 'He has a good car' or 'He has a nice villa' or 'He went to university.' At school, the rich and poor are together. Apartments in every building are reserved for poorer people, so that the rich don't all cluster together in the same neighborhood."

"Do other migrants from West Africa see things the way you do?"

"Many do. All the Burkinabés that I have met have positive things to say about Holland. The only negative things are things you find everywhere in the world."

"Like what?"

"Immigration is difficult everywhere. It is hard to be a migrant. Once you are a migrant, that is who you are. It will always be that way. And that hurts."

"Can you explain a little more?"

"When I am here, I am obliged to leave behind many things that I know, that I have seen, that I love, just to participate in this society. Life is solitary here. People don't spend so much time *en famille*. Back home, when you have a problem, the whole family is involved. Here, when you have a problem, either you or the state has to solve it. You can't share things with others. On the other hand, when I am in Burkina, I have to adapt to the rhythm of life there; otherwise nothing will work out, and I'll be alone. So wherever I am I try to live like the locals."

"You are always switching between two very different ways of living?"

"Yes. I'm between the two. That's why it is difficult. All my compatriots experience this problem. Some find it easier than others. After ten or fifteen years here, they'll be one hundred percent Dutch. Their culture will be very one-sided. Others resist. They don't forget their distant culture. They can't."

"And you?"

"Well, until now I felt closest to my Burkina culture. I am not saying that the culture here is not good, but when you are born into a certain culture, it stays with you for a very long time. If you lose your culture and your customs, you lose everything, because it is those things that make you live. Without them you cannot live well."

"Is there anything in your own culture that is more important to you?"

"It is all important. Except that I want freedom and equality. I want everyone, whether rich or poor, to have the same opportunities. It is hard to bring about these changes in my own culture."

"What kind of changes would you like to see in Europe?"

"I would like people here to appreciate and be proud of what they have, but also to be aware of the difficulties of being poor and getting an education in countries like mine. I think people in Europe should be more satisfied with what they have, not always thinking how they can be better or get more. They waste too much. It is a consumer society. People consume, consume, consume. Instead of repairing things, they throw them away."

That morning, we had breakfasted on brioches and pain au chocolat that Ibrahim had brought home from the Royal Opera House. The food items had passed their use-by date, and though still edible, they would ordinarily have been thrown away. There was no way we could eat everything Ibrahim brought home, but he could not bear to let it go to waste. His economizing did not surprise me, for my father was a child of the Great Depression, and as a child I had become all too familiar with his habits of eating the leftovers from dinner and hoarding paper bags, pieces of string, jam jars, and tin cans in the belief that "you never know when they might come in handy"—not to mention his do-it-yourself philosophy, realized in his ability to single-handedly build crystal sets, repair radios, make wooden toys and furniture, create compost for his garden, and reno- vate our house.

I asked Ibrahim if he thought governments should legislate against waste or whether people should be educated to consume less and conserve more. "It is sometimes argued that human beings are not capable of governing themselves," I said, "and that we need strong leaders to hold our society together."

"Yes, but those in power should not have too much power. The system has to be democratic. The person in charge has to make things work well, but he should not have the power to dominate everyone and inhibit equality."

"Your father seems to have had that ability to organize village life without throwing his weight around."

"Yes, he understood that if you hit a child, then the child was not going to work. We are like musical instruments. If you hit the instrument hard, it will not make a nice sound. If you use moderate pressure, the sound will be good. Power is like that. If you hit people hard, they will rebel. You have to apply moderate force. That's what my father thought. It's like hunger: if a person is starving, he will do anything to survive. So with power—when there is too much force, it will have bad effects. My father's grandfather was very strict. Many people fled the village because they were frightened of him."

In *Nostalgia for the Future,* Charles Piot explores the emergence of a radically new political economy in West Africa, centered on NGOs and Pentecostal churches and future-oriented social imaginaries and modes of subjectivity, sovereignty, and storytelling.[15] Piot's title "indexes longing for a future that replaces untoward pasts, both political and cultural. Such longing is represented not only in Christian End Times narratives and the universal quest for exit visas but also in the embrace of a thousand development initiatives that hail youth and leave elders behind."[16] Utopian yearnings find expression in a passion for playing the green card lottery, fantasies of fictitious marriages with foreigners, belonging to churches that promise supernatural abundance, internet searches for exit strategies, and a turn to the transient pleasures of sex, drugs, and music for an instantaneous sense of *affective* power and presence. This emphasis on inwardness and self-fulfillment allegedly stands in dramatic contrast to the prevailing ethos of a traditional culture, where duty, forbearance, and respect for elders imply stoic acceptance of life as one finds it and suppression of thoughts and feelings that challenge the status quo. Traditionally, lip service was paid to the idea that one must sacrifice personal gratification and spontaneous self-expression to make sociality viable (the implication being that what is good for the many will prove good for the individual). Collective rituals and everyday practices of commensality, neighborliness, and mutuality reinforce the common weal. Modernity supposedly reverses these assumptions. *Personal* development through education, travel, and purchasing power becomes the royal road to *social* development, a precondition for the greater social good.

This revolutionary change in worldview does not occur adventitiously. It follows radical disruptions to the social fabric—civil war, famine, epidemic illness, mass migration or displacement, and urbanization. Piot paints a grim picture of the anomic background against which the new social imaginaries emerged in the 1990s. These changes "burst onto this socio-cosmological stage like a comet from the sky. Disconcerted by the violence against Kabre in the cities of the south, puzzled by those strange new keywords *démocratie* and *droits de l'homme,* attacked by the Pentecostal churches, stung by currency devaluation and state withdrawal, and increasingly neglected by cash-strapped diasporics, this authority system was shaken to its roots."[17] In theorizing this changed situation, Piot wrestles with the question of cause and effect. Did a collapse in the wider politico-economic sphere, caused by global

changes in the post–Cold war period, create a vacuum in which new and occult forms of the social imagination appeared—dreams of migration, fantasies of getting away from it all and starting over elsewhere, paranoid fears of witchcraft, belief in affective transcendence through love, rescue, or miraculous windfalls? Or did increased awareness of the wider world, through television and the Internet, usher in these new imaginings? And if young men rebel against their father's authority by citing human rights, is this because the human rights discourse now pervades the thinking of young people or because it serves as an available vocabulary for rationalizing a loss of interest in farming as a way of life, since farmers are ripped off by middlemen and farming cannot generate enough income to provide what are now deemed necessities of life—corrugated steel for roofing, cement, kerosene, imported cloth, cell phones? And if one is attracted to the Pentecostal church, is this because it offers the same sense of community once offered by collective rituals in a village setting or because it offers a completely different mode of fulfillment in "intensities and affects: of joy and happiness, of confidence and pride, of feelings of empowerment and importance (and, in the extreme, of narcissism)."[18]

My conversations with Ibrahim lent some support for these generalizations, but rather than an either/or situation—a "seismic shift"[19] in which tradition was radically eclipsed by modernity—I saw deep ambivalence and a determination to retain traditional values while embracing new possibilities. Thus while Ibrahim set great store by education—which could be construed as a focus on himself—he abhorred the self-preoccupation that, in his view, pervaded urban bourgeois life in Europe. Ironically, just as Piot sometimes argues for a theoretical perspective that acknowledges both continuities *and* discontinuities,[20] so too does Ibrahim. And if Piot "wages on rupture,"[21] so too, at times, does Ibrahim, whose sweeping generalizations about the differences between Western and African ways of life suggest that no balance can be struck between the demands of a career and the demands of a family, or between personal pleasure and public duty.

Consider, for example, our conversation about divination. Given the ethical difficulties Ibrahim experienced in reconciling the competing claims of Dutch and Burkina cultures, I wondered if he had ever sought guidance from a traditional diviner or if he preferred to rely on his own judgment—and his strong sense of filial duty—in making critical decisions.

"I never went to a diviner," Ibrahim said. "But once, at the hotel, we were watching television, and there was a magician who could change one thing

into another thing. I was curious and fascinated. But I didn't believe he was really changing these things. It wasn't true, but I was curious to know how it was done. When I was a child, I saw this done with playing cards. When you saw them, they were red. When you saw them again, they were black. The person with the cards would make money from doing this. He would take your five francs, you would take a red card, and if it was red when you picked it up again, you won. But it would be black, and you would lose your money. They said it was a djinn that made this happen. For example, they could take a piece of paper like this [Ibrahim picked up a scrap of paper lying on the table] and transform it into a biscuit. They would say that a djinn had made it into a biscuit. But I never accepted this. I always said, 'No, no, it's not true. How can it be a djinn? Where is the djinn?'

"When the television show was over, a guest at the hotel asked me, 'Brother, do you believe this?' I said, 'No, I don't.' This man was from Cameroon. He asked me to come to his room. He had a carpet there, which he covered. Then he had a book, like this one of Della's [*Sahel Visions* lay open on the table at the page with the photograph of Ibrahim's father]. He told me to place my hand on the book. Then he said, 'You have to repeat what I say. If I say "A" you will say "A," and if I say "B" you will say "B."' Then he took something and quickly covered it with his hands. I copied him. Then he opened his hands and told me to open mine. His hands were full of money. He said, 'Do you believe me now?' I said, 'Hmm, it is certainly real money, but people say that money quickly disappears.' He gave me two bills and told me to look after them for two days. If I lost them, that was my problem. If I didn't lose them, I could use them to buy food. I kept the money, and after two days it was still there. But I said to myself, 'Hmm, I don't want this money,' and I gave it back to him. He said, 'All right, do you know of anyone who needs money? If he gives me a million, I will make ten million for him.' So I understood that he was a crook. So I said, 'I don't know of anyone, but if I find someone I will bring him to you.' Then I escaped. I never told anyone, because he would have been arrested. In fact, the police did arrest him not long after. This was his work *[boulot]*. So I know a lot of people who have been to diviners, but I have never done so. I have never believed in their powers."

"It seems that you prefer to get results through hard work, not magic."

"Yes. That has been my belief ever since I was a small boy. When I was seven, I started raising chickens. I used to walk fifteen kilometers to visit the market and was really happy when I could get another chicken. One

time, I asked a man, 'Can I have a chicken?' The man said, 'No problem. I will give you one and see how well you look after it. But not a big one.' He gave me a chick, about a week old, to see if I was really interested and could really look after it. I grabbed it like this [Ibrahim clasped the imaginary chick between his hands, just as he had clasped the Cameroon con man's imaginary money]. I wanted people to think I had a real bird between my hands. Everyone who walked past me heard it chirping. 'Oh, look at him,' they said, and the chick kept chirping. When I got home, my mum said, 'Oh, what are you going to with it? It's so small!' I said, 'It's no problem.' I took some millet and crushed it because the chicken was too small to eat whole millet grains. Then I got a big box, punched a hole in it, and put the chicken, the crushed millet, and some water inside. I was always going to the box to check whether it was dead or alive. But slowly, slowly, slowly, it grew bigger and bigger, and I let it out into the yard where there was a rooster, and soon the whole house was full of chickens, and everyone was mad at me because of the chicken shit everywhere they walked. Every three months, I had two or three chickens to sell. And it was with these chickens that I bought goats. By the time I was ten, I was able to buy oxen to work in the fields. If it rained well, we had good crops, but the problem was that it never rained enough. So I understood from an early age that it's not a matter of asking, of taking money; it is not through taking shortcuts that we succeed. It is through hard work. When you work hard, you can see the results. And my mother also gave us an example. She was a hardworking woman—this helped her a lot. Otherwise it would have been very, very hard for us. You had to be physically fit because you farm with your hands. There are people who were lazy, especially with the famine—you don't feel like working. So I grew up with this 'work, work, work.' At first it was something I had to do, that I was forced to do, as if I was a slave, but now I find pleasure in working. And going to school really helped me. It's because I went to school that I want my children and their children to have the opportunity to go to school. I understood at school that you cannot expect the things you want to come to you. You have to put in the effort; otherwise you will never achieve what you want."

I retired early that night, to allow Ibrahim, Evelien, and Karfo to spend some time together and to collect my thoughts after a day so intensely absorbed in Ibrahim's story that my own sense of self had been partially eclipsed. As I fell asleep to the drumming of rain on the balcony, I thought vaguely of the floodwaters Ibrahim remembered from his first day at school,

listening eclipses
a sense of
self

a sign perhaps that his spiritual drought had broken and greener years now lay ahead.

NEITHER HERE NOR THERE

The morning broke clear, with birds singing and a pallid sun appearing above cloudbanks in the east. Evelien was determined that we should make the most of the fine weather, and since Ibrahim did not have to go to work, she suggested an excursion to the old fishing village of Durgerdam, some seven kilometers north of the city.

The village comprised a single row of houses lining a narrow road that ran along the dike. After parking the car, we walked through the village in the morning sunlight. Householders were busy at their weekend chores or carrying boxes of bric-a-brac from their cars, as boat owners began desultory repairs on their vessels. Evelien explained that the Zuiderzee had once been open to the North Sea. But following passage of the Zuiderzee Act on 14 June 1918, Holland began the monumental task of enclosing the Zuiderzee, protecting the central Netherlands from catastrophic tidal inundations and increasing the land available for food production. The thirty-two-kilometer-long enclosure dam *(Afsluitdijk)* was opened on 25 September 1933. It had required 23 million cubic meters of sand and 13.5 million cubic meters of till. An average of four thousand to five thousand workers had been employed in the dam's construction, relieving unemployment during the Great Depression.

Ibrahim said that this kind of thought and effort was needed in his own country. "You need to begin something to get a result," he said, echoing yesterday's comments on his personal philosophy of life. "If you don't make a start, you will end up with nothing."

Driving back to the city, I recalled a book that had enchanted me when I was a boy—*Hans Brinker; or, The Silver Skates*. Evelien had never heard of it, perhaps because the book had been written by an American author (Mary Mapes Dodge) and had not been widely circulated in the Netherlands. But she did know the other story that rounded out my childhood image of Holland—of the little boy who plugged a leak in the dike with his finger.

Ibrahim seemed mystified by this legend, and as we entered the one-way street to the apartment, I asked him if we might resume our recording with

an account of the Mossi Empire, the origins of which, I vaguely remembered, touched on the themes of migration and diaspora.

Evelien, Ibrahim, and I sat at the kitchen table, while Karfo played with pots and pans on the floor. I liked the idea that our conversation would be punctuated by the clangor of a child playing and intermittently asking one of her parents for help.

Ibrahim began by recalling the name of the first Mossi chief, Naba Nedega.[22] "He had a daughter called Nyennega whom he would not allow to marry. A girl should be married by age eighteen, but Nyennega was nineteen, twenty, twenty-two, and still her father had not spoken to her of marriage. The daughter asked her father, 'Why have you let me pass the age of marriage? What is to become of me?' The father did not reply. The mother did not reply. But the daughter had a horse she loved, on which she used to ride into battle or travel far and wide. So one day she rode out on her horse and at the end of the day did not return home. Needing a place a sleep, she found a hut that belonged to a hunter called Rialle.[23] The hunter had also been wandering about hunting, and when he returned that night he found Nyennega and her horse in his house. Rialle and Nyennega were attracted to each other and decided to sleep together. Nyennega became pregnant that night. She said to Rialle, 'I am pregnant. What name shall we give our child?' The hunter could not think of a name and asked her what she thought. She said, 'I think we should name him after my horse, Ouédraogo [Stallion] because it was Ouédraogo who brought me to this place. Without Ouédraogo, I would never have found my way here.' It was this Ouédraogo who founded the kingdom of Ouagadougou."[24]

"And that is also your name."

"My family name. That is the story. It is very old. All Mossi people know this story. And the horse is our symbol, the symbol of Burkina Faso."

I was less surprised that a people who set such store by nobility and mobility should make the horse an exemplar of their core values than that images of immobility were equally significant elements of the Ouédraogo narrative. The princess who cannot escape from her father's control and marry into another household echoed Ibrahim's recurring theme of feeling blocked—stuck in a village and dreaming of escape.

This motif of an impeded marriage is also linked to an even more universal theme—impeded succession. In societies where a man's son—usually his eldest son—is also his successor, the incumbent is often portrayed in myth as reluctant to relinquish power and, by implication, accept his mortality. He

therefore looks for ways of preventing the succession, either by delaying the birth of his son, banishing his son to a distant land, or actually killing the person who is destined to replace him. Among the Mossi, this Oedipal tension between the *mogho naba* and his eldest son was resolved historically by banishing the heir from the capital of Ouagadougou and maintaining a strict social separation between father and son.[25]

While a ruler may believe that his longevity is magically guaranteed by putting his son out of sight and out of mind, this strategy for arresting the natural flow of time has the potentially fatal consequence of preventing new blood from bringing new life into the lineage. When a ruler prevents his child from marrying, it entails the same dire risk of social entropy, for by delaying the marriage of his daughter, a father blocks the vital paths of exchange *between* families, just as preventing the succession blocks the vital paths of exchange between the generations.[26] Nyennega's flight from her father's village and her alliance with Rialle, mediated by a powerful symbol of mobility and strength—the horse—enabled the resumption of social time and the birth of an empire, just as the assumption of power by the young guarantees the continuity of a lineage even though it may presage the death of the old.

Curious to know whether Ibrahim had any claims to the chieftaincy in Damesma, I asked him if this had ever been a possibility.

"Yes, it is possible. But the son has to be well positioned as well as deserving of the position. If he doesn't have the ability or is not well positioned, another son will be chosen."

"How was your father chosen for the chieftaincy?"

"When his father died, there were many candidates.[27] And even though my father was the oldest son, he was very young at the time. So people said, 'Why would they give the chieftaincy to a child?' But those responsible for appointing a chief do not consider that. They consider the position and whether the candidate is mentally strong enough to be chief. Although my father was young, he had the potential. But still people asked, 'Why would the chieftaincy be given to a child?' They decided to vote. People thought that no one would vote for my father because he was so young. But all of a sudden, people changed their minds, and everyone voted for him. Despite his youth, everyone agreed that he should be chief."

"What changed their minds?"

"It was because he was the one closest to his father. The other candidates were not as closely related."

"For how many years was your father chief?"

"Fifty-four years. He passed away four years ago.[28] It was really sad."

I asked Ibrahim how he would characterize his father's rule.

"He ruled fairly. He always kept the peace. The story of Damesma may help you understand the background to the way he thought. Long ago, different districts were ruled by different brothers. There was often tension between the districts, and the brothers were often at war with each other, just like the monarchies in Europe. Also, there was tension between the district rulers and Ouagadougou. [The sovereign authority of the *mogho naba* in Ouagadougou was often resented, challenged, or ignored by the rulers of peripheral districts, even though some of these rulers had been appointed by the *mogho naba*.] Many people didn't want to be ruled from Ouagadougou; they wanted to be free to govern themselves. Our family was from Ouagadougou, and we did not want war. So we moved farther and farther away from the regions that were at war or did not want to be ruled over by strangers, until we came to Oualaga. It was already far from Ouagadougou, but we could still feel the tension there, so we continued farther until we came to Damesma. Our great-great-grandfather said, 'Now, anyone who comes and threatens us here will feel our strength, will feel the heat. We are now on our own land. We are strong and armed. No one will threaten us here.' We were very powerful. We took many small villages into our kingdom, but it was Damesma that was the center of power."[29]

"Yesterday, you were saying that it was very important for your father that you continue the traditions he upheld. What kind of traditions were these?"

"Mainly respect for one another. Then there is the bond between parents and children. This relationship must be strong. And the family must be solid and strong. Even if we are living apart, communication should keep us in touch with one another. We also have a custom that every year, after harvest [the two October harvest sacrifices of *Kiougou* and *Kitwaga*], we thank God and our ancestors for giving us life. Some customs are disappearing now—like fathers owning their children, but not the mothers who have to do all the household work, preparing food, looking after the children. We also prefer to solve problems among ourselves and not let them get so big that outsiders have to come in and sort things out for us. If there is tension in the family, we gather everyone and make a sacrifice to our ancestors. Our parents thought that when we moved away to the big towns, we would lose contact with them and with our ancestors. Certainly, there were some young people who thought they would be able to do everything on their own and not need help

from anyone. But psychologically, we all need contacts. We need to keep close together. Some people who have money no longer want to have their parents or their brothers and sisters and cousins living close to them; they want only the father, the mother, and their own children. But even if you have money, you have to think of your parents and look after your brothers. Money should not be the first thing on your mind. If money controls everything, life becomes horrible."

I was curious to know whether Ibrahim identified with any particular religious tradition but was unsure of how to broach the question. Finally, I asked if he attached any importance to religion. Since Della McMillan reported that the three Damesma clans closest to the chieftaincy were "exclusively Muslim," while less closely allied clans practiced a hybrid of Catholicism and animism, I was surprised by Ibrahim's somewhat evasive response.

"Religion is important, but this is part of my private life. I have no wish to force other people to follow this religion. I follow it myself, not because I was forced to, not because I was told it would be bad not to, but because it pleases me to do so. I do it when I want and when I can but not because I have to."

"Is Islam an important part of Mossi life?"

"It's important for the new generation. What was good about our parents and grandparents is that they never forced us to be Muslims or Christians. It was our choice. If you wanted to be a Muslim, you could be a Muslim. If you wanted to be a Christian, you could be a Christian. But you were never forced to adopt one or the other."

"What about the years you spent in Qur'anic school? Did you have to adopt Islam then?"

"Yes, but only bits. I have never learned to practice Islam properly. For example, you are supposed to pray every morning at an exact time. I don't do that. I don't pray every morning. I do many things that Islam prohibits. I do what I think is right."

"Do you have any ambition to go on hajj?"

"Hmm, I cannot decide just yet." Ibrahim laughed. "They say that when you go on hajj you become like a baby that has just been born. You carry no sins. Perhaps it's better to go on hajj *after* you have led a pure life, if that is possible!"

Once again, I was impressed by Ibrahim's independence of mind. He reminded me strongly of my late friend Noah Marah. When I first met Noah in a dusty market town in northern Sierra Leone in 1969, he proudly described himself as *sunike*—a Kuranko term for someone from a ruling

lineage, particularly a lineage that had never embraced either Islam or Christianity. Like Ibrahim, he kept faith with the traditions of his people without, however, becoming a mere slave to custom. Thirty-four years after our first meeting, I asked Noah if, after everything he had seen and suffered during the civil war, he was still *sunike*. Noah's reply stunned me. "I have never embraced any moral system," he said, "and I hope I never will." Three weeks later, Noah died, leaving me to wonder why some of us need to believe there is some overarching order in the world that rewards virtue, punishes evil, and reveals meaning, while others accept the arbitrariness of fate, or at least renounce the possibility of divining its hidden workings and— considering it as foolish to congratulate ourselves when fortune favors us as it is to express outrage or envy when it does not—focus on steadying ourselves in the midst of life's flux, struggling to embrace the rough and the smooth with equanimity.[30]

Ibrahim, Emmanuel, and Roberto, like Noah, seemed to have experienced from early childhood a dissonance or lack of fit between the world into which they were born and another world in which they might be reborn. In a sense, they were all migrating in their imaginations well before they became actual migrants. Were they exceptions to some sociological rule which deems that everyone shares the same modal personality, formed through enculturation, and implies that difference is a form of moral deviance? Or do these individuals simply highlight the indeterminate relationship that exists for everyone, between an identity thrust upon a person by birth or circumstance and a nascent identity that we yearn to bring fully into being? It is this uncertain and ambivalent relationship between how we are made and what we make of how we are made that calls into question many of the sweeping generalizations that academics make about global migrants. Seen as instantiations of irreversible transformations from tradition to modernity or from one discursive regime to another, the migrant becomes a stereotypical figure, bent on escaping his natal country, developing his mind, widening his horizons, acquiring wealth, or saving his soul. These utopian yearnings, and the existential dissatisfactions that give rise to them, are seen as radically new departures for Africans who, it is assumed, previously lived under the restraint of custom in "societies without history."

One of the most creative individuals I got to know during my years among the Kuranko was a storyteller, Keti Ferenke Koroma, who never expressed any desire to leave his village in search of greener pastures. Yet his stories, all of which began with the stock phrase, "Far off and long ago," were concerned

with the ethical struggle to find fulfillment and justice in a world where betrayal, backbiting, discrimination, and scarcity were all too common. In Ferenke's vision, no moral law, ancestral decree, religious belief, or legal code could adequately cover every situation in life, which may be why the main characters in Kuranko stories typically journeyed from their villages into the amoral space of the bush, away from circumscribed paths, seeking supernatural lifeworlds in which they might discover the magical means of "doing what they considered right."

WASTE NOT, WANT NOT

On my final night in Amsterdam, Evelien and Ibrahim took me to a Surinamese restaurant where they had arranged to meet several friends. Over dinner, Ibrahim confided to me that it had taken him a long time to get used to eating out. And he could still see no point in accompanying Evelien to a coffee bar and spending six euros on a cup of coffee when they could have coffee at home. I told Ibrahim that Sierra Leonean friends in London often admitted the same misgivings, preferring to spend money on food they could prepare at home rather than paying exorbitant restaurant prices for food that strangers prepared behind the scenes. Ibrahim explained that he and Evelien had an allotment outside the city where they grew vegetables in the summer. "I don't trust the food you buy. It doesn't taste like fresh food should."

"There must have many things you found difficult to get used to when you came to Amsterdam," I said.

Ibrahim was only too happy to provide examples. "I could not understand why Dutch people were always talking," he said. "Talking on the phone, gossiping, talking about themselves, all the time. In Dutch they call it 'having your heart on your tongue.'"

"And here I am, talking too much and making it impossible for you to eat!" Ibrahim smiled.

"In Burkina it's not good to be too direct," Evelien interjected from across the table. "For example, when Ibrahim and I decided to get married, we wanted to avoid any difficulties with the immigration authorities, so instead of filing for a civil marriage we explored the possibilities of a religious marriage. Ibrahim went to the imam of his mosque and said, 'I know of an African guy who is thinking of marrying a Dutch woman.' And when Ibrahim visits my sister [Evelien's sister had recently been seriously ill in the

hospital], he sits with her, holding her hand. He doesn't get emotional with her and say everything that's on his mind."

"It is the same in Sierra Leone," I said, thinking of how long it took me to adjust to a form of sociality that required sitting with someone in amicable silence rather than busily baring one's soul, making small talk, or engaging in detailed conversations about abstract matters.

Evelien said, "Ibrahim will ask my friends, 'Are you well? How is your family?' and be amazed at all the personal details they give in response."

"People are always prying into your life," Ibrahim said. "Always asking me what jobs I am doing, whether I like them, how much I earn. It is too much, really."

Feeling somewhat embarrassed by my own barrage of questions, I held my tongue, allowing the conversation to follow its own course and giving Ibrahim a chance to feed Karfo, who was sitting in a high chair to his right.

Later, however, as we were eating dessert, Ibrahim returned to the theme of excess.

"That is the problem with your society," he said. "You want things straight-away. You can't wait. You don't know the meaning of patience. You are like children. You expect endless pleasure and abundance. You do not know how to live with hardship."

"We Europeans cannot defer gratification," one of Evelien's friends said in English.

"And the waste!" Ibrahim said. "The things people throw out. There is enough old furniture thrown out on the street to furnish a small village." Ibrahim paused for a moment, as if silenced by despair. "There are many people who risk their lives to come here," he said. "It is horrible, because when they are in Africa they think of Europe as El Dorado. But it's not. One of my first jobs in Amsterdam was at a restaurant like this. I was surprised to see people ordering food, then leaving half of it uneaten on their plates. There were things they did not even touch, which were thrown away. It was really, really difficult for me to see this. The first time I saw it, I could not believe my eyes. I wanted to cry, because I knew how it was in my country. Many employees in the restaurants are migrants like me. They know if they serve too much food, much of it will be left on the plate. So they serve the minimum. They economize."

"What about the job you have now?"

"It's the same problem. If the expiry date is today, you have to throw that food away. We are not even allowed to give it to the people who work there.

Evelien suggested I ask my boss if it would be possible to donate this food to homeless people, but then we realized this might not be a good idea because, in the past, there had been problems with contaminated food. Honestly, it breaks my heart to see this waste. So, without saying anything to my boss, I decided to take the food that had not been touched and bring it home. The sugar, tea, coffee, pastries that haven't been used—all this saves a lot of money and gives us things to eat."

"It's not just food," Evelien said. "Ibrahim is intrigued by how quickly people divorce in Holland. He's shocked by how much people expect from a relationship, how little patience people have. Rather than solve their problems together, they'll abandon the relationship."

Everyone was quiet, even contrite, but Ibrahim had not finished.

"People might be well educated," he said, "but they don't use their heads to make life more efficient, to make the most of what they have."

Evelien urged Ibrahim to describe the system he came up with for delivering mail.

"When I was working at the post office, it was very hard," Ibrahim said. "You had to deliver three sacks of mail, and you were paid at a fixed rate. So you didn't want to waste time. At first, I would have to return to the post office twice every morning, to pick up the second and third sacks of mail. Then I had the idea of building a small cart out of materials that had been thrown out on the street. I could attach the cart to my bicycle, carry all three sacks of mail in it, and then detach it from the bicycle and push it along the street. I was a bit scared that the police might stop me and say it was dangerous, but they said nothing. So I continued to use this system."

The following morning, before leaving for the airport, I asked Ibrahim to talk a little about the difficulties of having a stake in two very different worlds, Burkina Faso and the Netherlands.

"Well, if you had the opportunity of a good education or good training in Africa, I don't see why you would want to come to Europe. We only come here because we can make quicker and easier progress than in Africa. Personally, I regret never having had a real opportunity to go to school. If I had achieved a real education, I would not stay in Europe for more than a year. I would be back home, helping people there. Even if you have a good job here and a good salary, you can't really help people over there. You are on your own. Even so, I still want to help form organizations that will plant trees to prevent soil erosion and hold back the desert. Everything depends on the rain. If it doesn't rain, there is a crisis. But with proper irrigation systems, it is possible to grow

corn and rice and other crops. I also want to provide lodging for students who really want to study, pay the fees of students who do not have parents, and make microcredit available for women. . . . These are the things I dream of doing. There is so much to do, but you must have the means. . . ."

"Have you ever thought of going into politics?"

"Yes, I would love to. Because there are many things the government has forgotten about. You don't help people by giving them money. They will spend it in a day. There has to be long-term investment to improve people's living conditions. Right now, people are starving. They have nothing to eat but leaves. They need to be fed. The children need to be sent to school, where they can be trained to do useful things. Unfortunately, in Africa you need to have the means to enter politics, and I don't have the means. And if you say things that the state doesn't want people to say, you'll be eliminated, you'll be killed. That's the problem."

Evelien added that Ibrahim had been in the Netherlands for only three years, yet he knew more about Dutch politics than many Dutch people.

"Yes," Ibrahim said, 'which is why I find it discouraging when politicians fail to set a good example, not only in Africa but in Europe. Few people tell the truth or fulfill their election promises. There are so many lies. And the villagers don't know very much, so every election they vote for the same person and fall for the same lies."

"What are the most positive things about Holland and Burkina?"

"Well, here there is political and individual freedom. You have opportunities to go back to school, to improve yourself, to work. You have the same legal rights as others, and the gap between the rich and the poor is not as great as in some other countries. What do I think of Burkina when I am there? Some of the positive things are not easy to see. It's the social life. I miss the social life. People here are always in a rush, never resting. We are not so individualistic in Burkina. Here, people like solitude. They live in solitude. In Burkina we like to be close together, always moving together. When I was a child, I could not sleep unless I was physically close to somebody. It's this closeness that makes a family strong, that keeps it together. If you have a problem, then everyone in your family will help you resolve the situation. Here, when you have a problem, you're on your own. You have to resolve it yourself. No one will come to your assistance, or they will send you to a psychiatrist who won't be able to help you."

"I agree," I said. "The deepest problems of life are not technical problems but ethical ones, and they cannot always be solved. We must learn to accept

[handwritten margin note: bodily proxima]

them, to live with them, and for this we need the support of family and friends."

"That is what Africa has—that culture. The minute we lose that culture it will be like it is here, with everyone wanting a mobile phone, a motorcar, a big house. But it's impossible. Our parents used to sleep in a hut, but they were proud. If we forget these things, we are lost."

I stretched out my hand and thanked Ibrahim for giving me so much of his time, opening up to me, and extending his hospitality.

"In Burkina, when we have a guest like you, we have to look after him until he leaves."

"You must come to Boston sometime and enjoy the hospitality of my house," I said.

IN FLIGHT AMSTERDAM–BOSTON

Talking with Ibrahim had taken me back to northern Sierra Leone, but it wasn't until an hour into my flight that I realized why. It was partly because Ibrahim's laconic manner of speaking had reminded me of how Kuranko villagers used to respond to my incessant questioning. It was also because his reaction to Dutch middle-class mores had helped me better understand the differences between the discursive worlds of an African village and a European city. In 2008, I visited old friends who had been living on a remote New Zealand commune for over thirty years. I was moved by how much of their energy and attention was absorbed by the tasks of day-to-day survival— fishing, gardening, cooking, repairing things that were broken. In the subdued light of their living room, it was easy to see them as pioneers. It wasn't only the surroundings that reinforced this impression—the wood-burning stove, the ironware, the tins of homemade bread, the bucket of local honey, the organic fruit from the commune orchard. It was their very appearance: their serviceable clothing from Kathmandu or Swanndri, their lack of cosmetic pretension, their ability to make do with basic amenities, their rough and ready language. There you discussed such subjects as fitting a wider diameter pipe to a stove, improvising a chimney cowl from a scrap of hammered tin, or replacing a worn wheel bearing on a truck with the same intensity and ingenuity with which a group of Harvard professors might debate the ethics of intervention in a foreign state. If you rarely touched on or inquired into the life of another mind, or a school of thought, or the nature of experience,

it was not because these things were irrelevant; rather, time did not permit such departures from the mundane and the never-ending struggle to make ends meet. As for social life, relationships were mediated more by doing things together than by sharing intimacies.

Much of what we know as middle-class existence depends on having sufficient means to get the mundane tasks of life performed for us by a tradesperson or a machine and being cushioned from the primary work of production. Having bought time in the form of leisure, we can afford to cultivate manners (rather than crops), dwell upon our own thoughts and emotions (rather than occupying ourselves with the demands of extended family), and contemplate nature as an aesthetic object (rather than as a resource whose exploitation exhausts us). Because we possess a surplus of time and money, we are free to devote our energies to décor, fashions, fine foods, and fads, none of which are, strictly speaking, necessary for our physical survival.[31] We create worlds centered on ourselves. In rituals of shopping, showing off, distracting ourselves, or taking costly holidays to "get away from it all," we magically conjure illusions of autonomy and of being "special." As Ibrahim observed, this pattern of immediate sensory gratification and personalized consumption stands in contrast to the traditional African emphasis on accepting hardship and awaiting one's due—a contrast between narcissism and stoicism. Indeed, the bourgeois cultivation of inwardness and "intravidualism"[32] implies a set of symbolic contrasts for separating self from society and drawing invidious distinctions between the civilized middle classes and peasants, primitives, and underlings:

Materiality/Spirituality
Body/Soul
Earth/Ether
Dirt/Cleanliness
Bondage/Freedom
Lust/Love
Emotionality/Rationality
Rudeness/Refinement

Not only do these distinctions disguise the degree to which so-called higher values are dependent on the toil and subservience of the "lower orders"; an ironic consequence of the rise of the European bourgeoisie and the colonial expansion that underpinned it has been that the very regions the "wretched

of the earth" would seek to leave in search of their own just portion of Europe's wealth were the same regions to which the middle class would travel, as tourists, to touch base with the authentic, and where anthropologists like myself would go to research their books.

My conversations with Emmanuel, Roberto, and Ibrahim constantly reminded me of this historical tension between societies in which people struggled for bare life and societies in which people's desires and preoccupations "surpassed the material reproduction of existence."[33] In its fetishized concepts, its specialist jargons, its loquacity and intellectual excess, the academy exemplified this "affirmative culture" of the bourgeoisie, and I sometimes imagined the conventional academic essay as an overfurnished baroque drawing room—designed to impress but hermetically sealed off from the brute realities of the outside world. Nevertheless, I did not want to exaggerate the differences between these worlds, making one the measure of the real and mocking the other for its artificiality and folly. Neither of these worlds guaranteed complete well-being. And while the cult of inwardness and the "dissociation of sensibilities"[34] that accompanied the rise of the urban bourgeoisie in eighteenth-century Europe did not preclude the possibility of community or nostalgia for the agrarian past, so-called primitive ontologies have never precluded the possibility of self-realization, reason, and critique. What is common to all cultures is the quest for life. Though intellectuals tend to emphasize the "meaning" of life as a fundamental existential imperative, "meaning" is only one form that life assumes in the human imagination, and it is no more or less significant than mobility, love, family solidarity, health, wealth, energy, or union with the divine—all of which figure in the life stories in this book as paths for attaining fulfillment.

THE ALLOTMENT

When I returned to Amsterdam in mid-July, I hoped to explore further with Ibrahim his views on European middle-class life. But rather than setting an agenda, I wanted to allow our conversations to be guided by our daily routines.

The unusually wet summer, coupled with Evelien's and Ibrahim's tight working schedules, had left them little time to tend their allotment garden on the outskirts of the city. With a break in the weather and Ibrahim due to fly to Burkina Faso later in the week, it was decided that we would spend a day weeding and digging potatoes. We would take turns looking after Karfo,

now ten months old and able to crawl, stand, and demand a minor role in whatever we were doing.

With Karfo in my arms, I watched Ibrahim as he bent over the bedraggled rows of red beet, onions, shallots, and corn, uprooting weeds. I was pondering the choices we make in life, weeding out certain things so that other things might flourish, clearing spaces in the wilderness of the world.

Ibrahim straightened up and smiled at Karfo. "Being in this garden reminds me of being in Damesma," he said, "except there it was obligatory, and here it is a pleasure."

"Because you choose to do it," I said.

Our conversation drifted, then, to the question of love—and the extent to which we choose to fall in love or love sweeps us away like a powerful tide.

Evelien was hoeing around a row of cabbages that had been gnawed and despoiled by rabbits. "There are times when Ibrahim asks me why he couldn't have fallen under the spell of a girl from Bobo. And I fire back, asking him why I couldn't have fallen in love with someone from The Hague! Our lives would have been so much less complicated!"

"But isn't this the nature of love," I said, "that it transcends boundaries, knows no borders, respects none of the categories with which we divide up humankind according to age, gender, class, and ethnicity?"

"But it never cancels those things out," Evelien said. "Love annuls the distinctions, but they return to haunt us."

"Isn't that the theme of all the great love stories?" I said. "Dante and Beatrice, Romeo and Juliet. Their passions were blind to all the barriers, but the barriers remained."

"This is why I often say, 'Ça va aller,'" Ibrahim said, "though I only say this because I don't really know what to do or whether things will work out well or not."

On the other side of a vast field of sugar beets, airplanes were coming in to land at Schipol airport.

I pointed out the planes to Karfo.

"When I was a boy," Ibrahim said, tugging at a deep-rooted weed, "we thought the airplanes that crossed the skies high above our village were as small as they appeared, like insects, or else they were mirages. I could never understand what they really were. But after two years at school I was told about the size of an airplane and the size of the moon, and how it was distance that made them look so small. When I went back to Damesma and told people this, they did not believe me. They were mystified by how people could land on the moon."

"Isn't it the same when you go to another society?" I asked. "You can't help but see everything through the eyes of the world in which you were raised?"

"When Ibrahim came to Amsterdam for the first time," Evelien said, "he kept asking me, 'When do you have time for your life? When do you find time to live?'"

"Honestly," Ibrahim said, "I was right to say that, because here we are prisoners of ourselves. We have to work long hours to pay our rent, to pay for electricity, to pay for food. We work, work, work, but we are not free. We are condemned to a situation where we *have* to do things. That is not life."

"When I was in the Congo, many years ago, whites used to say that Africans were lazy, that they wasted their time socializing and did not know how to work hard."

"That is partly true," Ibrahim said. "Sometimes we Africans ask ourselves, 'What is the use of having all these possessions when we are going to die and leave it all behind? We think it is enough to live our daily lives, and for that it is not necessary to be rich. Some of us who have travelled outside Africa realize that we do not always work as hard as Westerners. We rest more than Westerners do, but many of us adore this because it is *life,* and we are able to enjoy life to the fullest rather than work hard all the time and then have nothing to enjoy."

"Whenever I go back to Sierra Leone, I am amazed at the ebullience and vitality of people, even though there is poverty and great hardship. When I return to America, I am equally astonished by how harassed and dispirited people are, even though they have so much."

"That's what I say. When you have a little of something, you want more and more. There is no end. People here may have everything, but they may not have a life. They are so tense. Wanting to control everything. Wondering if they will lose their job or get promotion to a better position. All you hear is 'economic crisis, economic crisis.' It's like a war."

"How do you understand this vitality, this joie de vivre, you see in Africa?"

"I think it comes from culture and from God. I think it is a gift from God, because it is impossible to explain it. But life exists in the family; it doesn't exist in money and possessions. Often people who are too educated or have too much money no longer have a life. They are like the president. He is seen, but he can't go wherever he wants to go. He's cornered."

"What gives you the greatest satisfaction in life?"

"For me, education is very important. After that, freedom. I really want to be able to express myself freely, to travel freely, to be free in everything—without borders."

"Without obligations?"

"Without obligations."

"But there are always obligations in life!"

"You are right. You cannot do everything you want to do. There are always rules that will stop you crossing borders, stop you going where you want to go, stop you finding an easier path. It's papers that count, not words. No one trusts anything you say. You can't talk to people directly. You've got to have papers. Even if the papers are false, they will count more than your words. There is no more truth in words."

I remembered Ibrahim's bewilderment when he began work as a mail carrier in Amsterdam, having to depend on maps to find his way around rather than asking people for directions. And I remembered the difficulties of Sierra Leonean friends in London, encountering for the first time the impersonal complexities of a bureaucratic state. In West Africa, one's destiny was determined by a network of face-to-face relationships with people to whom you were obliged or who were under obligation to you, people you could "beg," in local parlance—from whom you could borrow money or expect a meal or a roof over your head. But in Europe, one quickly discovers that one has passed from a patrimonial to a bureaucratic regime, in which power resides less in people to whom one can appeal than in an impersonal forcefield that finds expression in a stranger's stare, a policeman's orders, a supervisor's demands, or the letter of the law. In this inscrutable and Kafkaesque world of bureaucratic protocols, indecipherable documents, abstract rules, and official forms of validation, one comes up against what Michael Herzfeld has called "the social production of indifference."[35] The "living spirit" of community has given ground to the "dead letter" of a system that recognizes no one because it is nobody.[36]

By the time we had weeded the allotment and dug the potatoes, it was late afternoon. I helped Ibrahim clean the hoes and forks under a tap by the garden shed, then cart the sacks of potatoes in a wheelbarrow to the car. It was Ramadan, and I marveled that Ibrahim could fast through these long midsummer days, yet work so hard.

From Hoofddorp, Evelien detoured toward the inland sea. She wanted me to appreciate the sky, "a sky from a Dutch old master." Dark smudges of cloud

had massed above sunlit beds of cumulus. There were patches of cerulean and slanting spears of light falling between empyrean and earth. In the distance, a church spire and half-hidden village were the sole evidence of human habitation. How insignificant and fugitive our lives seem from this perspective. Yet to enter fully into the life of any one individual is to discover a world as deep, compelling, and complex as this landscape, the light transforming its appearance before one's train of thought has reached its end.

Postscript

JOAN DIDION ONCE WROTE, "We tell ourselves stories in order to live."[1] Our stories provide us with parsimonious, coherent, and uncomplicated versions of events that have overwhelmed us. They offer the consoling illusion that even if we do not always have a hand in determining the course of our lives, a hidden hand is guiding our destiny from behind the scenes. In the opening of his autobiographical novel *Look Homeward, Angel,* Thomas Wolfe imagines a thread of fated connections that transcend time and memory: "Each of us is all the sums he has not counted: subtract us into nakedness and night again, and you shall see begin in Crete four thousand years ago the love that ended yesterday in Texas. The seed of our destruction will blossom in the desert, the alexin of our cure grows by a mountain rock, and our lives are haunted by a Georgia slattern because a London cut-purse went unhung. Each moment is the fruit of forty thousand years. The minute-winning days, like flies, buzz home to death, and every moment is a window on all time." Beautiful though this passage is, it leaves unremarked the extent to which our lives are discontinuous, accidental, and unrepeatable. That everything seems to make sense in hindsight does not bestow on us the gift of foresight. Stories, like cosmologies and scientific theories, simply "reduce the anxiety that we would experience if we allowed ourselves to fully acknowledge the uncertainties of existence."[2] They reflect our all too human resistance to the idea that "life is chaotic, a jumble of accidents, ambitions, misconceptions, bold intentions, lazy happenstances, and unintended consequences."[3]

This gap between the ways we construe our lives in retrospect and the ways we act in the here and now suggests two very different forms of experience. While the first *(erfahrung)* tends to be considered, durable, and carefully crafted, the second *(erlebnis)* is more a matter of pure sensation and gut

feeling than conscious deliberation.[4] It is ironic that though Emmanuel, Roberto, and Ibrahim spoke of searching for a more fulfilling life, all were accidental migrants—moving abroad because they fell in love with foreigners or, in Roberto's case, because his parents made this choice for him. What I also found compelling in my conversations with Emmanuel, Roberto, and Ibrahim was the tension within their stories between conscious reflection and direct description. Yet there was a difference, for while Emmanuel's and Ibrahim's narratives resist closure, remaining open to the uncertainties of the future, Roberto's religious faith entails, at least in retrospect, an emphasis on divine providence and an expectation that well-being will be finally secured. As such, these narratives point to the very different ways in which ethnography may be written—as an allegorical mode whose "expressive mission . . . is to show that human beings are exiled from the truth they wish to embrace" or as a romantic mode of world-making that assumes the world to be inherently coherent and comprehensible.[5] My own preference is for an ironic juxtaposition of these two contrasted tendencies that does not deploy necessity and contingency—or the real and the symbolic—as mutually exclusive ontologies but rather describes life as a perpetually unsettling oscillation between these modes of experiencing one's being-in-the-world. I have therefore sought a form of ethnographic writing that assigns as much value to showing as to knowing, while accepting that some of the most illuminating moments in a human life exceed our ability to grasp them cognitively or translate them into the language of the academy. By implication, a form of writing—either discursive or creative—that stirs a reader emotionally is as valuable as a form of writing that seeks to systematize or edify.

This discrepancy between a sense of life that is immediate and one that is mediated is analogous to what Daniel Kahneman speaks of as the gap between a "remembering self" and an "experiencing self."[6] The indeterminate space *between* these ways in which we see ourselves defines a site of ethical struggle, for while a person may frame his or her story in terms of abstract moral principles or social roles, these do not necessarily determine his experience or explain her actions. In *Moments of Reprieve,* Primo Levi writes of the "small causes" in one's history or biography that, in retrospect at least, appear to have had momentous effects. In Auschwitz, such small causes could mean the difference between living and dying. These "bizarre, marginal moments of reprieve," Levi writes, are as arbitrary as they are unpredictable, yet when we set down the story of our life such moments often stand out as determinative and decisive. Emmanuel's, Roberto's, and Ibrahim's stories are so replete

with small causes that they constitute an implicit critique of the teleological bias toward the bigger picture, *la longue durée,* the hidden variable, the underlying cause.[7] This is the gist of my argument against reducing ethics to "a code to which one is obligated, a set of criteria to which one assents or subscribes," and for exploring the ways in which ethics is "responsive to the surprises that regularly punctuate life."[8] It is in such "minor experiences" and spontaneous actions (Løgstrup's "sovereign expressions of life") that our humanity is redeemed. To put it another way, our humanity is often compromised by moral codifications, masked by the generalizations and abstractions of social science, and destroyed by the stereotypes and doctrines in whose name the worst violence of the twentieth century was committed. As Hannah Arendt noted in 1943, "We actually live in a world in which human beings as such have ceased to exist for quite a while; since society has discovered discrimination as the great social weapon by which one may kill men without any bloodshed; since passports or birth certificates, and sometimes even income tax receipts, are no longer formal papers but matters of social distinction."[9] The refugee and the migrant remind us that when people are "unprotected by any specific law or political convention," they are *nothing but human beings.*"[10]

It is this challenge—to address this primitive recognition that oneself and the other are of a kind, humankind, regardless of any specific morality, law, or concept of human rights—that defines the task of philosophical anthropology. This challenge implies an ethics before ethics, whose quintessential expression is love—one's capacity to set one's ego aside and enter into the situation of someone else, seeing the world from his or her standpoint. There is an uncanny parallel here between Løgstrup's notion of the "sovereign expressions of life" and Husserl's notion of the phenomenological standpoint. If the "natural standpoint" implies a world of facticity and presence "in which I find myself and which is also my world-about-me,"[11] the phenomenological standpoint implies a world of pure consciousness in which my presuppositions about fact and fiction, or truth and falsity, are bracketed out.[12] But rather than emphasizing "pure consciousness," I find it more interesting to explore the ways in which the epoché entails a movement toward the consciousness of the other—a suspension not only of one's own taken-for-granted *ideas* about the world *but of one's own customary sense of self.* The epoché thus embraces what we call empathy. Husserl's intentional "consciousness of something"[13] becomes "consciousness of another,"[14] though this "other" is *a suppressed dimension of one's own many-sided self,* occluded or held in

love as ethnography

potentia, since one inevitably inhabits a social milieu that privileges one mode of being at the expense of all other possible modes of being.

Anthropology is, in this sense, unavoidably phenomenological. It assumes the possibility of going beyond oneself and entering into the lifeworlds of others. Where anthropologists differ is in whether this project is one of knowing the other, experiencing the world as the other experiences it, achieving a modus vivendi with the other, or achieving a quasi-transcendent position that enables one to penetrate the hidden forces that explain the other's behavior, motivations, values, and consciousness. Whatever the emphasis, however, anthropology remains, for the most part, a body of theories and methods for having something interesting to say about worlds that lie outside the worlds of privilege and power to which most anthropologists belong.[15] For this reason, anthropologists struggle not only to suspend their own worldviews and enter into the life-worlds of others; they struggle with the gap between haves and have-nots, either by seeking to use their knowledge to ameliorate the conditions under which the other lives or by bearing witness, in their writings, to the humanity of the other. Unfortunately, an anthropology that is focused on the practical ingenuity and social vitality that may be found in even the most poverty-stricken societies is sometimes criticized for deflecting attention from the work that must be done to improve living conditions in these societies. One riposte is to criticize the anthropological focus on global processes and political economies that construe the poor as victims of social violence, wholly lacking the wherewithal to live, and thus reinforcing, albeit inadvertently, the implicit tendency in modern societies to write off the lives of billions of human beings as insignificant and even undeserving of life. Such a society, writes Jacques Derrida:

> *Puts to* death or . . . *allows* to die of hunger and disease tens of millions of children (those neighbors or fellow humans that ethics or the discourse of the rights of man refer to) without any moral or legal tribunal ever being considered competent to judge such a sacrifice, the sacrifice of others to avoid being sacrificed oneself. Not only is it true that such a society participates in this incalculable sacrifice, it actually organizes it. The smooth functioning of its economic, political, and legal affairs, the smooth functioning of its moral discourse and good conscience presupposes the permanent operation of this sacrifice.[16]

A balance may be struck, however, between these extremes of testimony and indignation. In his ethnography of "Vita," a "zone of social abandonment"

in southern Brazil—where the mentally ill, the sick, the homeless, and the unemployed are left by relatives, neighbors, hospitals, and the police—João Biehl steers a course between a critique of the society that condemns so many of its citizens to social death and description of the ethical struggle of the *abandonados* to "hold onto the real," to "articulate their experience," and to "transmit [their] sense of the world and of [themselves]."[17] Similarly, in her study of a slum known as Annawadi near Mumbai airport, Katherine Boo underscores the need to alleviate poverty, while testifying to the life that nonetheless finds expression in this place where, for all the evidence of hopelessness, hope springs eternal—often in minor things. Slum dwellers spoke of "better lives casually, as if fortune were a cousin arriving on Sunday, as if the future would look nothing like the past," and Boo was struck "by the ethical imaginations of young people, even those in circumstances so desperate that selfishness would be an asset."[18] "It is easy, from a safe distance, to overlook the fact that in under-cities governed by corruption, where exhausted people vie on scant terrain for very little, it is blisteringly hard to be good. The astonishment is that some people are good, and that many people try to be."[19]

In the Buddhist view, we cannot avoid pain. But suffering is another matter, since suffering arises from our desire to avoid pain. It is not death that causes us the greatest anxiety, but our fear of the pain of dying. As Shalom Auslander puts it, "It isn't the fire that kills you, it's the smoke."[20] The insight is crucial. It echoes Husserl's distinction between the natural and phenomenological standpoints and suggests that human beings have a hard time distinguishing between the emotions and moods of the moment and the stories they have learned to tell themselves about their histories and their lives. It is not easy to dump the conceptual baggage we carry and subtract our conception of pain from the pain itself. Yet in poor and affluent societies alike, people struggle to define what can and cannot be changed, accepting that life is always lived within limits, defined by our mortality, our vulnerability to illness and loss, the vicissitudes of human relationships, and the struggle for fulfillment in work or recognition from peers.

MIGRANT IMAGINARIES AND MULTIPLE SELVES

When anthropologists and social theorists write about migration, they often invoke binaries, speaking of divided selves and double binds, of halfies,

hybrids, and being in between. Subjective conflicts are said to mirror social crises, also described in binary terms and thus suggesting radical breaks between autocratic and democratic regimes, political and occult economies, an orientation toward the past and an orientation toward the future.[21] But to describe the self "as torn between self-interest and collective good, struggling over desire and responsibility, negotiating contradictory emotions"[22] may all too easily give the impression that human beings find little satisfaction in their mutability and prefer the illusion of a unitary and stable sense of self.[23] But rather than implying that people necessarily find fulfillment in being settled in one place or possessing a single core identity, I consider it imperative that we complement this view of a stable self with descriptions of human improvisation, experimentation, opportunism, and existential mobility, showing that individuals often struggle less with aligning their lives with given moral or legal norms than with finding ways of negotiating *the ethical space* between external constraints and personal imperatives. This capacity for strategic shape-shifting, both imaginative and actual, defines our very humanity.

I find it ironic, therefore, that most of the writers who invoke images of psychological division and historical discontinuity would *not* wish to make a case either for static, one-dimensional personalities or for monocultural *societies* in which nothing and no one changed. Why, then, should we hesitate to embrace the view that "a pluralistic universe"[24] applies equally to both polis and persons, to states and selves?

Recent psychoanalytical work on the self challenges the concept of the person as a seamless, stable, skin-encapsulated monad.[25] Rather than being constant, we constantly change according to our surroundings, like chameleons, and we possess an extraordinary "capacity to feel like one self while being many."[26] Indeed, our ability to shift and adjust our self-state in response to who we are with, what circumstance demands, and what our well-being seems to require is not only adaptive; our lives would be impossible without it.[27]

This conception of the self as several rather than singular has a long history. In 1580, Michel de Montaigne observed, "Anyone who turns his prime attention onto himself will hardly find himself in the same state twice." "Every sort of contradiction can be found in me," he wrote, "depending on some twist or attribute. . . . There is nothing I can say about myself as a whole simply and completely, without intermingling and admixture. . . . We are fashioned out of oddments put together. . . . We are entirely made up of bits and pieces, woven together so diversely and so shapelessly that each one of

them pulls its own way at every moment. And there is as much difference between us and ourselves as there is between us and other people."[28]

In 1857, Herman Melville wrote in a similar vein against the "fiction" of an independent, unique self that remains stable over time. "A consistent character is a *rara avis*," he said, going on to explain that a work of fiction "where every character can, by reason of its consistency, be comprehended at a glance, either exhibits but sections of character, making them appear for wholes, or else is very untrue to reality; while on the other hand, that author who draws a character, even though to common view incongruous in its parts, as the flying-squirrel, and, at different periods, as much at variance with itself as the caterpillar is with the butterfly into which it changes, may yet, in so doing, be not false but faithful to facts."[29]

In 1928, Virginia Woolf touched on the same theme, observing that the selves "of which we are built up, one on top of another, as plates are piled on a waiter's hand, have . . . little constitutions and rights of their own. . . . One will only come if it is raining, another [will emerge only] in a room with green curtains, another when Mrs. Jones is not there, another if you can promise it a glass of wine—and so on. . . . [E]verybody can multiply from his own experience the different terms which his different selves have made with him—and some are too wildly ridiculous to be mentioned in print at all."[30]

It is not impossible that at the same time Virginia Woolf wrote these lines, the heteronymous Fernando Pessoa was writing, "Each of us is several, is many, is a profusion of selves. . . . In the vast colony of our being there are many species of people who think and feel in different ways."[31]

William James also emphasized the multiplicity of the self, noting in 1890 that "*A man has as many selves as there are individuals who recognize him* and carry an image of him in their mind," and that a man's self "*is the sum total of all that he* CAN *call his,* not only his body and his psychic powers, but his clothes, and his house, his wife and children, his ancestors and friends, his reputation and works, his lands and horses, and yacht and bank account."[32] Furthermore, James notes, a person's own well-being is intimately tied to the well-being of these significant others, objects or qualities. "To wound any one of these images is to wound him."[33]

All these writers touch on what I have elsewhere called "the migrant imaginary"[34]—our human capacity for coping with changing situations by calling forth or bringing to the forefront of consciousness hitherto backgrounded aspects of ourselves. Psychological multiplicity or plasticity is not, therefore, a problem that requires therapeutic interventions which return us

to a one-dimensional, stable state that is continuous and consistent over time and in all situations; it is the creative and adaptive expression of sociality itself.

Let us consider three closely related aspects of this adaptability—adapting to other people, adapting to other societies or forms of life, and adapting to changes in our life course. While the first aspect involves being affectively moved in relation to other selves, the second involves movement from place to place, while the third aspect covers the critical transitions that mark our passage through life.

Our capacity for becoming other in relation to other selves is the basis for mutual recognition and empathy. The suppressed aspects of ourselves, seldom fully acknowledged and often actively abhorred, enable us to find common ground with people who initially appear so radically different from us that we sometimes hesitate to call them human. Indeed, this capacity to see others in the light of normally occluded aspects of ourselves may, under certain circumstances, help us recognize animals and objects as sharing in the being we ordinarily attribute solely to ourselves. Thus recent researchers have identified symptoms of posttraumatic stress disorder in African elephants whose herds have been decimated by culls, illegal poaching, and habitat loss. Calves that have witnessed the killing of their mothers and female caretakers or have lacked male socialization show abnormal startle responses, depression, unpredictable asocial behavior, and hyperaggression.[35]

The psychoanalytic anthropologist George Devereux has argued for the psychic unity of humankind in just these terms—that every individual contains the potential of Everyman, creative as well as destructive, and that what is foregrounded in one person or made normative in one society exists in a subdominant, repressed, or potential form in another person or another society.[36]

Our capacity for becoming other in relation to other selves also explains the persistence with which human beings have from time immemorial moved, migrated, and mutated, adjusting to radically new circumstances, despite the risks involved, the losses incurred, and the suffering undergone.

One of the commonest experiences of encountering a complete stranger or moving from a familiar to an unfamiliar environment or passing from one phase of life to another is disorientation. This cognitive bewilderment is variously and viscerally experienced as vertigo, nausea, nostalgia, and exhaustion. "I'm the empty stage where various actors act out various plays, living the lives of various people—both on the outside, seeing them, and on the inside,

feeling them," writes Fernando Pessoa, who appears to have lost all sense of a core self.[37]

In this dissociated state, selves that were previously foregrounded are no longer affirmed by others as normal or even as natural, or they no longer serve one's immediate interests. The person you once reviled may now be the person on whom you depend for recognition and succor. You may have become an adult, but the child in you cries out for comfort. You have arrived in Rome and are trying to do as the Romans do, but you crave, if only for a moment, eating your own food in your own home with your own kith and kin. No shift in self-states is straightforward. To be in transition is to be in doubt and adrift and to experience dissociation—to suddenly discover that one has become a stranger to oneself. As Ibrahim put it, reflecting on his first bewildered days in Amsterdam, "You cannot do everything you want to do. There are always rules that will stop you crossing borders, stop you going where you want to go, stop you finding an easier path. It's papers that count, not words. No one trusts anything you say. You can't talk to people directly. You've got to have papers. Even if the papers are false, they will count more than your words. There is no more truth in words."

This is not a matter of being between two worlds, but of being dis-membered—no longer being fully integrated into a familiar community. And so the migrant is obliged to re-member himself, to constantly piece together, like a bricoleur, new *assemblages* from the various aspects of his past and present selves.[38] Thus Ibrahim's focus oscillates among his father's expectations, his mother's wishes, obligation to his wife and daughter in Holland, and his personal ambition to become better educated—moving continually among these self-states, each associated with a different country, a different period in his life, a different kind of loyalty, and a different person. In London, my friend Sewa found himself of two minds about alcohol use. Out of respect for his beloved father, Sewa preferred not to drink, although this seriously compromised his English social life. How could he drink beer with friends in his apartment when his father's photograph on the wall was a stern reminder of his lack of filial respect? "There's one thing [my father] never wants any of his kids to do, and that is drink alcohol. When I go out and drink alcohol, as soon as I come home and step into my room and see that picture, I have to run out of the room again. I want to go and take the picture and put it away, like in my cupboard or box, but I know I have alcohol in my system so I cannot touch the picture. I have to wait for days, days, to take that picture and put it somewhere, so I can walk into my room and not see it

straightaway. I know it's just a picture, but it's like it's him seeing me—what I'm doing, you know. You see, I've got all these beliefs. And when I stop drinking, pray to him, ask him for forgiveness, I know that's the only thing I'm doing that my dad's unhappy about."

Sewa's English girlfriend suggested that Sewa hang the photo of his father in the living room, now bare except for a small lacquered plywood map of Sierra Leone in which different seeds—sesame, millet, mustard, chili, and several species of rice—had been glued to mark the different provinces. "But I can't put pictures in the sitting room. I can't imagine myself sitting here holding a beer, drinking, when my dad's picture is looking at me. So that's what's stopping me putting the picture up. I can't live in a house where friends will come and want to drink, and my dad is seeing me—I just can't do that. I feel I'm doing the wrong thing, which he doesn't want me to do. Even though he's not alive in the real world, I just don't want to do that."

"But you have made so many changes in your life, since coming to England," I said. "Big changes."

"It's true, Mr. Michael. Sometimes I can't believe myself."

Despite the anguish Sewa often felt as he tried to work out new configurations and compromises in his lifestyle, he did not "fall apart." This is because, as Philip Bromberg points out, a multiple self is not incompatible with normal mental functioning because "a person can access simultaneously a range of discrete self-states that, despite their contrasting and even opposing perspectives on personal reality, are able to engage in internal dialogue. It is this capacity that permits oppositional aspects of self to coexist in consciousness as potentially resolvable intrapsychic conflict." It might be more accurate, however, to speak of multitasking rather than multiple selves, since possessing a repertoire of social or practical skill sets does not necessarily imply that we are composed of discrete identities. Techniques and stratagems that mobilize us to act or interact more effectively do not necessarily spring from any conception we have of ourselves or any worldview we may have embraced. Epistemological or ontological categories are more often than not post-facto rationalizations of practices that have proved useful. The limit is not simply where we fall apart and the perennial possibility arises of being born again; it is where we are driven to intense experimentation, searching for a strategy, skill, object, or ally that will help us overcome an obstacle, regain a sense of agency, or perform a daunting task.[39]

The migrant exemplifies, therefore, a vital aspect of each person's passage through life—an ability to change with changing situations, conjuring

different mindsets and calling upon different means for addressing different challenges. "This view of self as multiple and discontinuous," writes Stephen Mitchell, "is grounded in a temporal rather than spatial metaphor: Selves are what people do and experience over time rather than something that exists someplace."[40] This notion of topological time captures the perpetual oscillation in human consciousness between memories of past events or images of remote places, and complete absorption in the here and now. It also reminds us that we can actively foreground or background people, places, and times in assembling self-states best suited to the exigencies of our changing life situations. Thus, despite his encounters with racism in Denmark, Emmanuel made a conscious choice not to see *himself* as African, but to redouble his efforts to apply for work on the strength of his academic qualifications and personal qualities. As for Roberto's recourse to religion, this occurred at those *moments* when he found himself at the limit of what he could endure—thrown into a prison cell among drunks and derelicts or facing another day of thankless labor in the fields. Though the police and field bosses treated him like dirt because he was Mexican, Roberto negotiated his situation *in his own terms,* as a Christian, though sometimes made no reference at all to God.

A contrast may be drawn here between agonistic and submissive attitudes. The agonistic attitude involves active resistance. We seize the initiative, determined to contest and change our situation. The submissive mode suggests passive resistance. We withdraw to lick our wounds, to figure out some way of enduring the situation, suffering and surviving it rather than willfully confronting it. In the modern West, we tend to extol the agonistic mode, deeming it heroic or noble. When someone dies of cancer, we speak of him or her as having lost a battle with the disease, as if fighting were ethically superior to submission. At the same time, we disparage the submissive mode by calling it defeatist or fatalist. This has long been one way men distinguish themselves from women and the West contrasts itself with the East; while westerners supposedly take active responsibility for ourselves, people east of the Bosphorus allegedly blame others for their misfortunes before they blame themselves, shifting personal responsibility to God or fate and remaining resigned to their lot rather than determining their own destinies. An empirically more accurate view of life in the West or the East reveals constant shifting between activity and passivity. Except in extreme cases, no individual and no culture, Western or Eastern, is permanently stuck in one mode to the exclusion of the other. Human beings move constantly between activity and

passivity, engagement and retreat, ego-centered and other-centered modes of being-in-the-world, depending on circumstance.[41]

Even when a person abstains from action and appears to have relinquished agency, doing nothing—as we say—and placing his or her hope, trust, or faith in others or in higher powers, he or she may be actively imagining or thinking a great deal. Accordingly, behavioral passivity does not mean that the mind has ceased to seek ways of coming to grips with the problem that brought the body to a standstill. Indeed, it may be more useful to speak of an oscillation between being physically still and mentally active rather than an oscillation between passivity and activity, for in all but exceptional cases— such as when a person attains a mystical state of absolute physical and mental calmness—we are constantly moving between very different modes of consciousness and engaging in very different modes of acting. Human existence implies continual readjustment and revision, in our memories and imaginations as well as in our lived relationships with others and our environments. Roberto suppresses his Mexican past to better focus on the exigencies of his present American situation. Emmanuel represses the anger that still boils up in him when he thinks of the abuse he suffered as a child, the better to meet the needs of his daughter. In many ways, this mobility and mutability of self-awareness is both phylogenetically and ontogenetically crucial to what we call adaptability. "To live is to be other," wrote Fernando Pessoa. "What moves lives."[42] No wonder, then, that I found in the experiences of the migrants I met in Europe and America dramatic analogues of my experience as an ethnographer, where an ability to improvise and play with new possibilities of action and thought, experimenting with alternative modes of consciousness, not only defines the condition of possibility for knowing others but, perhaps more pertinently, offers a key to achieving viable coexistence in a pluralistic world.

HIERARCHY AND HUMANITY

Whereas morality implies the clarity and certainty of an either/or logic, ethics suggests the doubt and consternation of both/and. Where the moralist might dignify an action by invoking concepts of free will, sound judgment, and conscious choice, the ethics of everyday life reminds us of how difficult it is to overcome bad habits, to know exactly what we are doing, to practice what we preach, or to reconcile what is good for us with what is good for

others. As such, the tension between ethics and morality implies a tension between immanence and transcendence, as well as particular and universal conceptions of the human. On the one hand, we are conscious of what makes us different from others. Not only is every individual unique, but we tend to draw sharp contrasts between ourselves and those who do not resemble us or share our values, respect our laws, belong to our soil, or speak our language. On the other hand, there is an ineradicable sense that despite such differences, we share with all other human beings a sense of species being or common humanity. This is what the Cynics meant by nature *(phusis)*, which they contrasted with the socially constructed rules and regulations *(nomos)* that defined the polis, which differed from place to place and applied unequally to different social classes. Yet the notion of the human often flows into the realm of animals and objects, which, under certain circumstances, take on the attributes of will, consciousness, and moral reasoning that define humanness, while human beings may lose these attributes and become, at least metaphorically, mere animals or inert objects.[43]

This sense that the other is myself in other circumstances and that anyone may transcend differences and circulate in other worlds as if they were his or her own underpins the ethic of hospitality, the concept of *cosmopolites,* finds expression in bonds with animals and material possessions, and is evident from time immemorial in patterns of human migration, intermingling, and interaction across the globe. Equally timeless, however, is the tension between these competing notions of singularity *(ipse)* and similarity *(idem)*. Emphasizing distinction implies that a person's worth is relative to birth, nationality, ability, or social status, while emphasizing sameness suggests that one's worth is conditional on nothing more or less than the fact that one is human. This *minima moralia,* which is suggested by such phrases as "the right to life," "a fair deal," or "a just society,"[44] inevitably comes up against the distributive moralities[45] associated with hierarchical social formations. All too often, this distributive morality, based on our particular identities as male or female, poor or rich, black or white, old or young, citizen or alien, overrides our awareness of what we owe others, leading us to carelessly write off large portions of humanity as essentially unlike us, having no claims on us, and in extreme cases, not deserving to survive. Yet a sense of our common humanity continues to haunt us, as though it were impossible to fully divorce categories from persons, rules from lives.[46] This was vividly shown when I asked Ibrahim whether Mossi shared the Kuranko view that a person's worth is relative to his or her status. Though Ibrahim said that this was, indeed, the

case among the Mossi, he immediately stated his own position on the matter—that every human being, whatever his or her status, gender, age, or ethnicity, was owed a decent life and a decent burial.

THE OEDIPAL PROJECT

Existentially, the tension between hierarchy and humanity reflects the two-fold character of our being-in-the-world. Though we are bound by the rules and roles visited upon us by being born in a particular place, at a particular time, and into a particular family, we also seek to reconfigure our lives within and sometimes without these circumscriptions and constraints, *particularly at times of crisis and transition.* There is a profound connection between the unsettling experiences of limitation that marked the early lives of Emmanuel, Roberto, and Ibrahim and their yearning to escape and begin a wholly different life for themselves elsewhere.

Norman O. Brown calls this the oedipal project[47]—the existential imperative to discover and create one's own ground, objectifying oneself in a form other than the form first defined by parents, tradition, or circumstance. This process of becoming a person in one's own right is, however, characterized by a tension that is never fully resolved, for the desire to become autonomous is countermanded by a yearning to be dependent. The desire to do what one wants is no less urgent than the desire for limits, and the dream of a more fulfilling life comes up against one's sense of responsibility for and indebtedness to others. This was vividly shown in Ibrahim's remarks about the difficulty of respecting his parents' wishes when his heart was set on a life beyond the horizons of his natal village. Every independent step away from their world increased his burden of guilt, the feeling that he was betraying his father and mother and that this betrayal would bring ill fortune upon him. The same dilemma sometimes oppressed Roberto, who once confided, "Our stories are not success stories. They are overshadowed by guilt. Survivor guilt." And I was reminded of those passages in Primo Levi's *The Drowned and the Saved* where he repudiates the idea of providence, speaking of the blind luck that distinguishes drowning from being saved, and reminds us of the terrible burden every survivor bears—that he "might be alive in the place of another, at the expense of another," and that he must for as long as he lives atone for this injustice.[48]

For more than forty years, my fieldwork among the Kuranko of northeast Sierra Leone has provided me with culturally specific examples of how this

dialectic between home and away plays out in everyday life. While social identity is determined patrilineally (and physiological essence stems solely from the father's semen), one's destiny may depend as much upon one's mother and mother's brother as on one's father and his brothers. This counterpoint between a space dominated by rules and a space of greater informality, affection, and playfulness finds expression in the contrast between the father's place (*fa ware*)—the place where one was born and raised—and the mother's place (*na ware,* the home of one's mother's brothers).[49] This tension between the patriarchal law of the father and the loving care of the mother not only informs the intersubjective life of the family but finds expression in images of the polis, since rulers, whether local or national, are expected to embody the power to administer the law of the land as well as the power to protect and care for their subjects.[50] When Kuranko say they are "in the hands of" a chief or power holder, the metaphor is double-edged, since they are at once under his protection and subject to his whims, recipients of his bounty and in his debt.

Among the Kuranko, the dialectic of obligation and choice is evident in the interplay between village and bush. The village is often associated—particularly by the youth of today—with oppressive limitations, whereas "the bush" signifies an encompassing, dangerous, yet potentially liberating space in which social norms are placed in abeyance, social boundaries transgressed, and miraculous transformations undergone. The bush is an imagined elsewhere, a transitional space, in which the socio-moral ties of the town can be loosened, and a person experiences his relations with others in transcendental terms, mediated by music, palm wine, money, friendship, spirit possession, laughter, love, magical mobility, and even the promise of eternity. But just as achieving independence carries the responsibility to provide for those who brought one into the world, so any gains won in the wilderness must be shared with the community from which one originally set forth.

A corollary of the Oedipal project is that it is, paradoxically, by suffering the actions of others that one realizes one's own capacity for action. Only the dutiful and subservient son can hope to receive his father's blessings and eventually take his place. And in traditional initiation, it is the neophyte's unflinching response to the ordeals visited upon him by his elders that proves his right to be given the power to act in kind, as an autonomous subject. In this sense, migration is a kind of initiation, for in both cases suffering is the price paid for the privilege of fully realizing the right to possess a life worth living.

To be subdued by circumstances one cannot change, acted upon yet powerless to act, may be bearable if there is the hope or promise of some reward, a return on one's suffering. If, despite one's patience, no amelioration in the situation is forthcoming, it is all too easy to believe that one's life has been unfairly taken away and that one is therefore owed a new lease of life in lieu of the life that has been lost. This is true of people whose social circumstances condemn them to passivity and degradation, their voices unheard, their agency denied. It is even more painfully evident when historical events such as war, famine, poverty, dispossession, and epidemic illness strip people of the wherewithal of life, leaving them with little option but to search for well-being elsewhere.

Migrants effectively place their lives in parentheses. They suspend their ties to one world in order to open themselves to another. It is for this reason that both migration and initiation may be seen as expressions of the Oedipal project, whereby one severs ties with one lifeworld in order to forge quite different ties with another. The <u>logic of sacrifice</u> is also entailed here.[51] Without sacrificing what one has, one cannot hope to be filled with what one does not yet have, though this "something missing"[52] remains an "abstract utopia" of which one can only dream. This sense of hope as possibility or potentiality, this sense that more lies in store for us, is central to human existence and defines the field of ethical struggle. Ethics explores the strategies, both real and imaginary, whereby we seek to augment our sense of life as forthcoming, promising, and renewable. It is vital, however, that our ethnographies of migrant lives do justice to the complex mix of motives and imperatives that influence the decision—which is not always a conscious decision—to migrate. One might agree with Ernst Bloch that "something is missing" in a person's life, making him or her feel empty, dissatisfied, unfulfilled, and incomplete; but it is seldom clear to the person exactly *what* will satisfy this inchoate need.[53] Amorphous and volatile, one's will-to-exist fastens or focuses opportunistically on various objects, some actually at hand, some absent, some wholly fantastic, in a search to objectify or consummate oneself in the world. But unlike reality testing, the imagination always goes beyond what the world actually is or what any person can actually be.[54]

Money begins, Philippe Rospabé argues, as "a substitute for life."[55] But many other things beside money can give momentary form to the vague sense of what will make good the lack in one's life. When a migrant speaks of a quest for a better life, we cannot presume to know what this "life" may be. Utopia, need we remind ourselves, means no-place *(ou-topos)*. The narratives

in this book disclose the ever-changing variety of things that have been lost, or have gone missing, or have yet to be found, and without which one's life is profoundly impaired—an absent parent, a lost home, a lack of food, money, mobility, or companionship—while at the same time suggesting that dreams are seldom realized. All this was vividly borne home to me one morning, as Roberto Franco and I talked about our childhood longings to go beyond the physical and social horizons that circumscribed our lives. "For as long as I can remember," Roberto said, "the world presented itself to me as a question."

One unusually clear morning in Mexico, when he was a small child, Roberto saw a volcano on the distant horizon. By the time he shared his vision with his family, the volcano could no longer be seen, and he was told that he must have seen something else or made a mistake. "What makes some of us so fascinated with what lies beyond us?" I asked. When Roberto described how his mother had always yearned for a better life, I realized that my own yearnings were, in many ways, born of my mother's thwarted dreams to receive an education, travel, and enlarge her horizons. The same continuity of a vision of elsewhere informed Emmanuel's story and were summed up in Ibrahim's comment, "From age seven, I wanted to go elsewhere. You feel it inside. You can't give words to it, but it's a strong feeling, to go to a big town, to move elsewhere." This view that the world as given is not enough or is too confining, and its corollary—that one must chose another world, cultivating one's own garden rather than working on one's father's farm—entails a double bind that every migrant experiences in some measure, and which speaks to us all, caught as we inevitably are between the circumstances that shape our lives and the lives we project and hope to create for ourselves.

AN ETHICS OF SMALL THINGS

Hannah Arendt observes that phenomenology involves turning our attention back to "the little things" of life in which "the secret of reality lies hidden."[56] Similarly, in his summons "to the things themselves," Husserl echoes Hugo von Hofmannsthal's celebration of the homely, fugitive, and minor experiences that "awaken in us again the old fondness for the world."[57] Traveling through Greece with a companion, following Oedipus's fateful footsteps toward Thebes, Hofmannsthal captures, albeit in a vivid memory of close friends, this luminary power of small things, when "Life flares up in us—the revealer of the unrevealed."[58]

While they were standing before us and looking at us, the smallest circumstances and things, through which our union with them had come to pass,
were present. A twitching, a softening glance, a moistening of the inner hand
in an agitated hour, a perplexed faltering, a gliding away, an estrangement,
again a drawing near—all these very small delicate things were in us, and
with the strangest vividness; yet we hardly knew whether what we remembered were the stirrings of our own inner selves or those of the others whose
faces were looking at us; *only that it was lived life and life that somehow continued to live on, because everything appeared to be the present.*[59]

The "wonder of minor experiences"[60] alludes not only to the small gestures
that lift our spirits or bring enchantment to our lives; they include such
dispiriting experiences as being refused help, publicly humiliated, or subject
to a racist slur. Such experiences can make our day or cast an instant pall over
it. But can we confidently say that such episodes are informed by an ethics?

In an essay on the moral ambiguity of foreign aid to Africa, a Moroccan
student of mine, Soumia Aitelhaj, turned from speaking of the ways in which
economic aid camouflaged "the real problems" caused by government-owned
mining companies in her village to recount a relatively minor incident during
her childhood when a neighbor gave her a few Moroccan cents (dirham) with
which to buy food, so that her body was no longer aching with fatigue and
she could finish her schoolwork. This small gesture not only restored Soumia's
sense of agency; it showed her that humanity may sometimes transcend hierarchy. "To have someone who does not have to care stop and not have a look
of pity but rather a look of compassion—or, rather, taking on another's
suffering—to me that is the 'otherness' or 'something' in humanity that is
not religiously based and motivates humanitarianism."[61]

In 1963, Douglas Lockwood accompanied a patrol into the Western
Desert by members of the Welfare Branch of Australia's Northern Territory
Administration. The goal was to bring Pintupi people in from the Gibson
Desert and relocate them on missions or government settlements to "save
them from dying out altogether."[62] The expedition leader, Jeremy Long, told
Lockwood of an incident during an expedition in 1957, when an Aboriginal
man with an amputated leg was brought into the settlement at Yuendumu.
Long discovered that this man, known as Peg-Leg Mick, had sustained a
spear wound in a fight, and his leg had become gangrenous. Because food and
water were in short supply, the group was obliged to continue moving or
perish. Normally, Mick would have been abandoned. But his prospective
father-in-law carried him for four months, sometimes covering thirty or forty

miles a day. From one point of view, Japanangka, the father-in-law, had a moral obligation to Jampijinpa, the son-in-law, but from another, the exigencies of survival would have suspended that obligation had Japanangka chosen to give mere physical survival greater weight.[63]

Perhaps the paradigmatic example of the power of a simple or spontaneous act is the parable of the Good Samaritan (Luke 10:25–37).[64] Here, an apparently unpremeditated act of neighborliness transcends what we often regard as the "big things" of life, namely our religious or social identity. In being asked, "Who is my neighbor?" Jesus does not preach a sermon (invoking a moral norm) but tells a story that provokes thought.

> A man was going down from Jerusalem to Jericho, when he was attacked by robbers. They stripped him of his clothes, beat him and went away, leaving him half dead. A priest happened to be going down the same road, and when he saw the man, he passed by on the other side. So too, a Levite, when he came to the place and saw him, passed by on the other side. But a Samaritan, as he traveled, came where the man was; and when he saw him, he took pity on him. He went to him and bandaged his wounds, pouring on oil and wine. Then he put the man on his own donkey, brought him to an inn and took care of him. The next day he took out two denarii and gave them to the innkeeper. "Look after him," he said, "and when I return, I will reimburse you for any extra expense you may have."

When I discussed this theme with Roberto, he recalled a trip he made back home to California at the end of his first year at Harvard. "As I passed through Tejon Ranch and descended into the San Joaquin Valley, I took note of the fields, packing companies, and restaurants where I had labored as a migrant worker. I had taken these jobs as I searched for my life's purpose, just as migrants move through the thick winter fog, which reduces visibility in the valley to a hundred feet, in search of their work site, step by step, taking each corner carefully and ready to break at any time. It is when this fog dissipates that one realizes how far one has traveled, and that it is due to kind acts by other human beings that we actually move safely ahead in life. I immediately thought of all those people in Apaxco who had helped me save my mother during her sickness, of the border patrol officer who gave us food and fifteen dollars before deporting us, of my college president who paid my tuition, and of a man called Chava who gave my mother refuge during her journey to the U.S. I thanked God for these individuals as I drove home to where my mother awaited me with warm tamales, sopes, and enchiladas, and I kept thinking about all these people during the days before Christmas,

when I suddenly remembered that I had a green card and could go to Mexico to see Chava. Furthermore, I had learned that President Wilson was living near San Diego, so I resolved to go visit these two individuals, who had been instrumental in my life's journey. I borrowed my father's pickup truck, packed some food and clothes, and took the road rarely traveled. I reached Santa Ana early in the evening and met my longtime mentor, patron, and friend for dinner. Without delay I thanked him for all his support during those financially troubling years in college. 'I knew you needed that opportunity,' he said. After a long conversation on my plans for the dissertation, on Latin American politics, and the spread of Pentecostalism in the so-called Third World, he invited me and my fiancée to spend the night at his house, which we did. Next morning, he was already up at seven o'clock and had breakfast ready for us. After a brief conversation, I thanked him again, gave him a hug, and took Interstate 5 to Mexico.

"On our way to Mexico, my fiancée inquired about Chava and what exactly he had done for us. I explained to her that soon after our first deportation from San Clemente, we attempted to cross through Nogales around noon. It so happened that a baseball field was located right next to the border fence, and we cut right through it in the middle of a game. At this moment, I could not tell whether the fans were enraged because we were crossing illegally or because we were disrupting their game, though I suspect it was the latter. Around three in the afternoon, we finally made our way to California and around six we finally reached the Arizona-California border. Unfortunately, we encountered an inspection point, and some of the officers remembered my mother from previous detentions. 'María, is that you again?' We were deported to Mexico around midnight and roamed the streets without a set direction, or so I thought. We ate dinner, and then my mother made a phone call to a guy called Salvador (literally 'Savior'). Soon, were on our way to La Misión, a place an hour south of Tijuana, between Rosarito and Enseñada, in Baja California.

"On our way to Chava's house, my mother explained that she had met him at a critical moment during her own journey to the U.S. The coyote that was supposed to help her cross wanted to take advantage of her and my two little sisters. In fact, he kidnapped them and kept them in a secluded location near Rosarito. To instill fear in them and ensure they would not attempt to escape, the coyote would burn puppies or cats at night. Fortunately, his daughter felt compassion for my mother and younger sisters, and one early evening, after the coyote had gone to Tijuana, she released my mother and asked to come

with her and her daughters wherever they were going. My mother thanked her but refused on grounds that the coyote would never cease looking for them. After walking several miles and fearing that the coyote might appear at any time, they finally reached the main road in Rosarito, not knowing where to go next. Was going to the police an option? No, the police could not be trusted. Everybody knew they were often in the pay of cartels and human-trafficking gangs. My mother stood by a group of people who seemed to be waiting for the bus, merging with them. Finally, a van arrived, and my mother boarded it with my siblings. Once the door was closed, the driver interrogated my mom, saying, 'Señora, where are you going?' Overwhelmed with anxiety, my mom said, 'Please, señor, we are in danger, take us wherever you are going.' It turned out that the people waiting for the van were Chava's relatives, and they were all attending his wife's birthday party. When they arrived, Chava's daughter recognized everyone in the cohort except my mother and two sisters. 'Y ellas quienes son? [Who are these people?],' she asked. Cleverly, Chava replied, 'This is my other wife and children—give them a hug!' The family allowed my mom to live in an old RV truck parked in their backyard. They also procured a job for her at the company where they worked and helped her and my siblings until they were all able to join my father in the U.S.

"When the bus arrived at La Misión, my siblings and I felt as if we were in a familiar place and had traveled that road before. However, Chava would always remind us that the road south to La Misión was rarely traveled because everyone was going north to the U.S. As soon as we stepped off the bus, Chava and his daughter were there to welcome us. They made breakfast for us and then took us to the RV, which they had cleaned in anticipation of our arrival. Soon, my mother started working with them, and between her salary and my dad's they had enough money to attempt another crossing. When I started meeting other people in La Misión, I was surprised to find out they were all from central and southern Mexico. They all wanted to cross into the U.S. but had found a good alternative at La Misión, which had been the site of a Spanish mission and part of the larger California mission system in colonial times. But I was shocked by the number of Anglos living in the area. Since their money was worth more in Mexico, they had come to retire here and live the good life they could not afford in America. This two-way traffic baffled me but gave me hope that perhaps someday I would return to retire in Mexico and live the good life, and that one day I could take that rarely traveled road to Apaxco.

"My fiancée had listened attentively to my story but wondered if I would remember the way back to Chava's house. After all, it had been nearly twelve years since I passed through there. 'We'll soon find out,' I said. We crossed into Tijuana, and the memories of my crossing became all the more clear, as if the place itself contained journals that could only be accessed by revisiting it. After some confusion with traffic signals, I finally reached the main highway to Rosarito. There we had lunch and I explained to Noemi the ordeal my mom had lived through there. In the crowd of people waiting for the bus, I could see a woman with her two daughters anxiously waiting to go everywhere and nowhere, as long as it was far away from Rosarito and safe. During this time, I also tried to remember key turns and exits to Chava's house, but all my brain could muster was the town's name, La Misión. So we got on the road again for La Misión and were relieved when after thirty minutes we encountered the sign. Again, I began to remember the landscape and, above all, the streets. In a manner of minutes I made my way through the town and reached Salvador's house.

"From a distance, the house looked decrepit and abandoned, and it appeared as if Chava and his family had moved away. When I reached the entrance, he came to greet us but didn't recognize me. 'I'm Roberto, María's son.' 'Oh, yes,' he said, 'I remember!' He began to recount how he had met my mother, and the jokes he played on his family that night. He was sad to tell me that his wife had died, his daughter had moved away, and he didn't spend much time at home. After catching up, I expressed my gratitude for all he had done for me and my family. He had tears in his eyes, and so did I, for seldom does one meet people as compassionate and caring as Salvador, who, for no other reason except a belief that we ought to help one another, decided to lend us a hand. My family was able to be reunited in California thanks to this man's hospitality and kindness, and I will be forever indebted to him. There is no way of paying for what he did for us. He asked me to greet my parents, and after exchanging numbers, we set off back to California. It has been a long journey, with many bumps and stops, but I live convinced that God leads us as we pass through the fog."

The theme of small things or minor miracles is linked to a second theme that migrant stories compel us to consider—the role of chance and contingency in our lives. In the last lines of the postscript to his Gifford Lectures on Natural Religion, William James cites Edmund Gurney's observation that

chance is what makes the difference between "a life of which the keynote is resignation and a life of which the keynote is hope."[65] As we have seen, the timely or fortuitous intervention of a significant other may change a person's destiny—Ibrahim's father insisting he go to school, Emmanuel's stepfather helping him at a critical stage in his schooling, the college president offering to cover Roberto's fees at a time when all options seemed to have been exhausted, and Chava coming to the assistance of Roberto's mother. These small but crucial interventions recall not only the role of luck—good and bad—in our lives but the yearning for life, the will to life, that drives us to move to where life seems more abundant and accessible, that makes us persevere when the going gets rough, that bolsters our hopes and lifts our spirits, and that draws us back to life when we have lost our hold upon it. This is the basis of my argument that the ethical struggle for well-being only partially and incidentally reflects extant moral codes, legal constraints, and social circumstances. That Emmanuel, Roberto, and Ibrahim all sought a lifeworld beyond the one they were born into, which so many around them accepted as inevitable, destined, or right, suggests that a gap always exists between what is given and what is imagined, and that, for some of us, this gap is never fully closed, leaving us both fulfilled in what we have achieved "against all odds" and frustrated that we can never reconcile the person we have become with the person we might have been had we never left our native shores.

This brings me back to the vexed and irreconcilable relationship between the *human* striving for a more fulfilling life and the particular laws and mores in a given society that determine who has the right to live in that society and under what conditions. Consider Emmanuel's revealing comment, "My mother taught us one thing: the ability to wait, to be patient, and to do what is right. *Not always what is legal, but if you break the law, then do it for the right reasons.*" This notion that there is a higher law than the law of a particular land and an ethics of life that transcends the ethics of any particular faith or culture is captured by the pro-immigration poster that appeared in San Francisco's Mission District in 2010, proclaiming in Spanish, "No human being can be illegal."[66] This idea was basic to Jose Antonio Vargas's argument for "coming out" and publicly declaring himself to be an undocumented immigrant in the United States. Responding to the question, "Do you think you belong to a special class of people who can break any laws they please?" Vargas replied, "I don't think I belong to a special class of people—not at all. I didn't get a [driver's] license to spite you or disrespect you or because I think I'm better than you. I got the license because, like you,

I needed to go to work. People like me get licenses because we need to drop kids off at school and because we need to pick up groceries. I am sorry for what I did, but I did it *because I had to live and survive.*"[67]

Many migrants experience recurring anxiety because they entered a foreign country based on forged papers, fake IDs, fake names, and a tissue of lies. Even for those who subsequently become citizens, a fear remains of being found out—of the past catching up with them, and their new lives coming to an abrupt end.[68] They suffer the curse of all liars, as they are compelled to continue lying, cover their tracks, evade detection, and hold onto the hope that their errors will be forgotten, if not forgiven. Just as the law recognizes a statute of limitations for the prosecution of some crimes and the Biblical jubilee provides for liberating slaves and writing off debts, so the migrant dreams of a new beginning. Arguably, this is the ethical summons that we in the affluent North must meet as we address the question with which human beings have lived from the Biblical dawn of time: to what extent are we our brothers' keepers, and how can we reconcile the fact that while we are all different, possessing different laws, different moralities, and different notions of human rights, we are at the same time all human? The reality is, however, that despite the globalization of trade and government in the twenty-first century, it appears to be all but impossible to pass laws, implement policies, or decide actions based on a universalized notion of the human. No sooner is the concept of the human introduced into the realm of economic and political affairs than it splinters, giving rise to definitions of humanity that simply mask local interests.

As I write (11 September 2012), American consulates are under siege throughout the Islamic world, and American flags are being trampled and burned by crowds of outraged youth. I am reminded that there is a dark side to the stories I have recorded in this book—stories of resentment and frustration, acted out rather than recounted, that speak violently against closed doors and unbridgeable gulfs, and suggest that those who fail to find paradise on earth will sometimes seek to symbolically turn it into hell.

YOU CAN'T GO HOME AGAIN

A third thread that runs through the life stories in this book is the impossibility of reconciling one's life abroad with the life one has left behind.

Toward the end of Thomas Wolfe's *You Can't Go Home Again,* the protagonist, George Webber, comes to realize that "you can't go back home to

your family, back home to your childhood, . . . back home to a young man's dreams of glory and of fame . . . back home to places in the country, back home to the old forms and systems of things which once seemed everlasting but which are changing all the time—back home to the escapes of Time and Memory." The irreversibility of time is intimately connected with the irretrievability of one's place of origin, and this entwined movement *through time* and *across space* proves perplexing to many migrants, who, in imagining themselves one day returning to the place from where they started out, forget that there is no transport which will convey them back into the past. This point of no return often passes without being noticed. Ties to the homeland atrophy or are deliberately severed, as in the case of the Mossi migrant who said, when asked why he had never returned home, "In Ghana I am something. So why should I go where I am nothing?"[69] Often it is only by going home that it becomes starkly and disconcertingly clear that one's natal village is no longer the same and *that one has also changed*. One of the greatest fictional renditions of this surreal blurring of the boundaries between absence and presence is Juan Rulfo's *Pedro Páramo*. A dying woman beseeches her son to seek out his father in the Mexican town of Comala, her birthplace, which she fled many years ago. The town proves to be a place of unstable memories, uncanny silences, and fugitive voices. Is the town a mirage? And is he a ghost or a living person whose reality has been undermined by the spectral images that surround him? "The town is filled with echoes. It's like they were trapped behind the walls, or beneath the cobblestones. When you walk you feel like someone's behind you, stepping in your footsteps. You hear rustlings. And people laughing. Laughter that sounds used up. And voices worn away by the years. Sounds like that. But I think the day will come when those sounds fade away."[70]

In 2002, after eleven years in the U.S., Roberto went back to his natal village. People looked through him or past him. He recognized no one, though everyone seemed vaguely familiar. He bought a taco in a local shop, where the owner admitted a vague recollection of Roberto's family. When Roberto explained who he was and mentioned the names of his parents, the owner said he had thought they were dead.

So it is that migrants travel abroad in pursuit of utopia, but having found that place, which is also no-place (*ou-topos*), they are haunted by the thought that utopia actually lies in the past. It is the family they left behind. That is where they properly belong. Though the family broke up long ago and is now scattered to the four winds, they imagine a reunion in which they are together

again. And so, my friend Sewa Koroma, now living in London, builds a grand house in his natal village in northern Sierra Leone. The house adjoins the ruins of his father's house and his father's grave. But Sewa may never live in this house, and every return visit to his village leaves him with a sense of emptiness and disconnectedness. Perhaps it will be the same for Ibrahim, who is using his earnings in Amsterdam to build some townhouses in Ouagadougou. He will rent these houses out. Whether he will live in one of them is another matter. "I am blocked," he told me. "I want to be there but I need to be here."

The indeterminate status and ambivalent emotions of the migrant places him, in effect, in a "state of exception." This state more or less obtained for Emmanuel, Roberto, and Ibrahim, reminding me often of Giorgio Agamben's figure of Homo Sacer, whose life is reduced to "bare" or merely "biological" life *(zoe)* and excluded from the life *(bios)* of the polis.[71] Although modern democratic states, at least since the French Revolution, have sought to make life itself *(zoe)* the foundation of basic human rights within the polis ("Men are born and remain free and equal in rights"),[72] the line between natality and nationality is never fully erased. As Hannah Arendt observed, the "same essential rights that were claimed as the inalienable possession of all human beings" are also claimed as the "specific heritage of specific nations."[73] The notion that we enjoy certain human rights simply by virtue of being born into this world is thus compromised by the assumption that the citizens of a state have priority over people who are not citizens. For Arendt, the refugee, who is not a citizen of any sovereign state, embodies a form of life that has not only forfeited the Rights of Man but, as a stateless person, is seen as intrinsically foreign and potentially threatening to the life of the state *(bios politikos)* on whose margins he or she dwells.[74] Ironically, this perception springs partly from the fact that the stateless person is by definition outside the pale of the law. "That stateless person, without right to residence and without the right to work, had of course constantly to transgress the law. He was liable to jail sentences without ever committing a crime. More than that, the entire hierarchy of values which pertain in civilized countries was reversed in his case. Since he was an anomaly for whom the general law did not provide, it was better for him to become an anomaly for which it did provide, that of the criminal."[75]

Even naturalization, repatriation, and deportation to a neighboring country do not solve the problem. Not only is the bureaucratic task of assimilation beyond the means of the state, but citizens fear that they will be overwhelmed

by vast numbers of foreigners, while the foreigners themselves resist the assumption that they can be accepted as citizens only by repudiating their own language and heritage. In other words, human rights always reflect the interests of the dominant class in any society, which universalizes its own hierarchical model of what is appropriate and healthy for the *bios politikos*.[76] Though such discrimination is seldom spelled out in the charter myths of the state, it finds expression in the shadows—in countless gestures of disdain, indifference, and condescension, and in recurrent eruptions of hatred and persecution. Most importantly, these exclusionary acts are directly experienced by those on the margins of the state (though they dwell within it as disempowered, infantilized, voiceless, and despised minorities). Though Homo Sacer *may be killed and yet not sacrificed,* to quote Agamben,[77] we must remember that exclusion is experienced as social death, and that under such conditions of degradation and invisibility, actual death may be considered a release.

Though displacement, homelessness, and statelessness are often seen as tragic symptoms of the twentieth century, in which totalitarian regimes "consciously attacked and partially destroyed the very structure of European civilization,"[78] there is a kinship between the experience of the refugee and the experience of the migrant that is more compelling than the legal distinctions between the two categories. A common experience is the impossibility of ever bridging the gap between one's natal ties to the place one left because life was insupportable there, and the demands of the nation to which one has traveled, legally or illegally, in search of a better life. And this tension between belonging and not belonging, between a place where one has rights and a place where one does not, implies an unresolved relationship between one's natural identity as a human being and one's social identity as an "undocumented migrant," a "resident alien," an "ethnic minority," or "the wretched of the earth," whose plight remains a stigma of radical alterity even though it inspires our compassion and moves us to political action.

SUFFERING, ACTING, AND ENDURING

Finally, these life stories bring home to us the subtle interplay between what we accept or submit to and what we cannot accept and seek to change. For Hannah Arendt, we are all caught up in an existential dialectic between suffering—in which we are subjected to the actions of others—and agency,

in which we appear to be the authors of our own lives. "Because the actor always moves among and in relation to other acting beings, he is never merely a 'doer' but always and at the same time a sufferer. To do and to suffer are like opposite sides of the same coin."[79] Paradoxically, therefore, action is often contingent upon yielding conscious control over one's life, as in that desperate moment in the vineyard when Roberto prayed for a chance to go to college. Though God gave him no sign, Roberto's anxiety went away. He learned that while one's fate is often in the hands of others, there are times when each person must take life into his or her own hands. Yet there are no guarantees, either that the gods will smile benignly upon us or that our efforts will be rewarded. Hence one's very existence sometimes feels like a gift that cannot be repaid, or a miracle, or simply absurd.

In November 2011, I was participating in an ethnographic workshop in Melbourne, Australia, when I received an e-mail invitation to give a lecture at the University of Uppsala on the theme of life and death. Despite the daunting theme, I thought meeting this challenge might help me bring into focus my thoughts on migratory experience, and the promised honorarium would enable me to revisit Emmanuel and Ibrahim. Having accepted the invitation, I put the matter from my mind, trusting that some ideas would emerge if I did not force the issue.

I had planned, that morning, to visit the National Gallery of Victoria, and after leaving my hotel I headed down Swanston Street toward the Yarra River. Suddenly and unaccountably, I was filled with a quiet yet overwhelming joy at simply being alive. Was it because I had lived for a year in this city almost fifty years ago, painfully alone and unsure of my direction, and now, returning, I realized that, unlike the old codgers I glimpsed in the pubs or side streets, weather-beaten and disoriented, I had found fulfillment in life and truly come into my own? Almost all the downtown buildings had been demolished and replaced, yet here I was, still standing, in good health, with a wife and children that I loved, deeply absorbed in my research and writing. It seemed at that moment nothing short of a miracle that I existed, let alone that I was happy. Yet I felt no sense of having earned this state of well-being. Nor did I see my good fortune as the result of happenstance. Rather, I simply felt that life had increased for me over the years rather than diminished, and this caused me to remember those passages in Spinoza's *Ethics* where he proposes that life and death are never absolute poles of being and nothingness, but questions of being more or less alive.

Paul Ricoeur observes, however, that Spinoza's conception of *conatus* "excludes all initiative that would break with the determinism of nature and that persevering in being does not involve going beyond this being in the direction of something else, in accordance with some intention that could be held to be the end of that effort."[80] Ricoeur's insight is crucial, for it implies a critique of the widespread contemporary assumption that our lives can be evaluated in terms of our success in transcending external circumstances and freeing ourselves from environmental constraints. Though Emmanuel, Roberto, and Ibrahim traveled far from their humble beginnings, their struggle was to accept events as they transpired, in all their complexity, pain, and contradiction. Their stories are not stories of heroic triumph; they are chronicles of separation and loss. As such, they are expressions of "the work of mourning, understood as the acceptance of the irreparable."[81]

At times, my interlocutors appeared perplexed that they should be alive when others were not. Their stories might hint at an unfolding design or the fulfillment of a desire, but for the most part they suggest that life is an improvisation, and one moves through it by trial and error, by guess and by God. As for most of us, the struggle for being plays out in small ways, in everyday life, as a matter of gaining a slight edge over the forces that threaten to deplete, disparage, and degrade. Life is never a secure possession. Life is lived, as so many adages point out, between Scylla and Charybdis, between a rock and a hard place, between the devil and the deep blue sea. Life is a matter of compromises, not perfect solutions. Every gain entails a loss, and the denouements, happy endings, and resolutions that are contrived in literature, spelled out by policy makers, promised by politicians, envisioned by religious prophets, and conjured in the discursive work of academics are, in a sense, all opiates that enable us to gain momentary respite from the aporias of existence. I like to think that if life and death are not absolute states or ultimate destinations, then life is always ebbing and flowing, waxing and waning, making interminable demands on our resourcefulness but yielding as many joys as sorrows, so that when our stories are told, they are not full of sound and fury, signifying nothing, but echo the note of Dilsey Gibson, the black maid in William Faulkner's *The Sound and the Fury* whose two words, "They endured,"[82] are a sharp reminder that for most people in the world, "endurance is fundamentally far more important than happiness."[83]

APPENDIX: EXISTENTIAL MOBILITY

Paleoarchaeological evidence suggests that for our Plio-Pleistocene hominid ancestors, tactical mobility in responding to changes in resource quality and availability was as crucial as flexible forms of social organization and the possession of stone tools in competing with predatory carnivores for scarce and scattered faunal resources. The physical ability to cover great distances at great speed and the social intelligence to organize and mobilize—for hunting, pilfering, and carrying meat, or for locating lava and quartzite for tool making—gave these hominids an adaptive edge in the struggle for survival.[1] This *behavioral* mobility implied *mental* agility, particularly an ability to communicate effectively with others, negotiate critical decisions, adapt to changing circumstances, assess risk, and creatively use past experience in forming future plans. Particularly advantageous for *Homo sapiens* was an emerging pattern of "cross-community migration" that kept dispersed groups in contact with one another.[2]

Evidence of continuity with our hominid past is compelling. Every infant carries in its genes a propensity to be soothed by being rocked at sixty cycles a minute or above—the same rhythm at which our plains-dwelling ancestors walked—while patterns of courtship, attachment, maternal care, and mourning are much the same in all human societies, suggesting a common phylogenetic source.[3] However, one must be wary of assuming that identical behaviors betoken identical meanings, motives, or emotions. At the same time, a distinction must be made between scientific and existential truth. The truths we live by—cultural, religious, moral, experiential—are seldom congruent with the truths with which science explains the human condition. To put these different truths in competition (or combine them in order to achieve a unity of knowledge) is to overlook the variety of situations in which human

beings find themselves, the variety of means whereby they make their lives worthwhile, and the multiple models *we* may draw on to illuminate any one of these situations.[4] To invoke adaptation as a universal measure of success in life is as intellectually limiting as claiming one worldview to be superior to all others.[5] One does not have to embrace the sociobiological view that contemporary human preferences reflect "ancient needs"—so that we instinctively gravitate "toward savanna forest (parkland), [where we can look] out safely over a distance toward reliable sources of food and water"[6]—to make the case for mobility as giving us an edge in environments our ancestors could not have dreamed of and where genetic selection is seldom the sole determinant of adaptive advantage. Nor does foraging alone favor mobility. Even 100,000 years ago, the exigencies of trade, marriage, ceremony, and political alliances were as significant as food gathering in determining patterns of human movement and settlement.[7] For thousands of years, transhumant pastoralists have moved with the seasons, seeking verdant pastures. Nomads have traversed arid lands in search of water, game, wild seeds, and fruit. Swidden farmers have periodically moved to new farm sites where the soil is nutrient rich. And children in most societies have circulated among caregivers in response to the differential distribution of scarce resources. Conscious choice, not genetic selection, determined the implementation of these ways of life, as well as their abandonment when changing environmental conditions rendered them obsolete.

This struggle for being unfolds in our relations with others, the gods we worship, and the scarce resources, both within ourselves and without, on which we draw in sustaining our lives. Existence is never simply a Darwinian struggle for survival, for what is at stake for human beings are existential imperatives, such as striking a balance between our commitment to others and our duty to ourselves, or transforming the world into which we are thrown into a world we have a hand in making—so that we are actors and not merely acted upon. Life is never simply bare survival, but rather a matter of realizing one's humanity in relation to others, and death is never physical extinction but only the nullification of the relationships that sustain one's life among others.

When we consider the conscious and affective dimensions of human life, survival is less a question of the continuity of the species than the continuity of families, the fate of souls, and the management of symbolic goods. The question of life after death may have figured in the thinking of our ancestors 35,000 years ago as much as questions relating to the sustenance of physical

life and the integrity of social groupings.[8] Moreover, escaping danger was both a physical and existential matter. Certainly, the plight of *Homo neanderthalenis* fleeing the depredations of the first members of our own species in southern Europe[9] presages the tragic displacements of entire populations throughout human history, in which people were forced to flee for their lives from singularly human forms of hatred and intolerance—religious persecution, predatory warfare, and genocide. Migration, therefore, is but one expression of mobility as a survival strategy. And while mobility may cover activities that range from transhumance, nomadism, asylum seeking, and physical exercise to the movement of labor, capital, knowledge, stories, commodities, viruses, and medicines across the face of the earth, it also applies to phenomena like "social mobility" and those forms of the imagination in which we entertain such notions as the transmigration of souls, karmic rebirth, religious conversion, the cybernetic fusion of bodies and machines, or escape from a stultifying situation. Even when people agree on the minimal requisites for life—water, food, and shelter—these basic elements are conceptualized in widely divergent ways. No one lives by bread alone, and human beings will risk or even sacrifice their lives in pursuit of *symbolic* goods whose meaning cannot be reduced to the kinds of adaptive behaviors that enabled survival 200,000 years ago.

Mobility must, therefore, be understood existentially as well as phylogenetically. It is a metaphor for freedom as much as a means for accessing life-giving resources,[10] and we learn from the conversations in this book that respect, recognition, honor, trust, prestige, autonomy, agency, love, and the ability to share one's experience with others all emerge as vital sources of life. Equally compelling are the minor, fugitive, and often unremarked events that momentarily change a person's experience of being-in-the world—an expression of care or concern, an offer of sympathy, a small gift, or time spent "with people you love and who love you."[11] Clearly, human consciousness itself is fluid, which is why we associate emotion with mood shifts, states of affective agitation, and sudden changes in our environment.[12] While telling migrant stories stirs deep emotions in the teller, we are also moved, for such stories unsettle and problematize many of the discursive conventions with which we render the world intelligible, as well as broaching critical questions concerning the political, moral, and legal orders we customarily invoke in laying down the conditions under which *our* pursuit of life, liberty, and happiness is best guaranteed.

ACKNOWLEDGMENTS

To the three individuals who shared their life stories with me, convinced that their testimonies and opinions might contribute to an improved understanding of the lived realities and ethical dilemmas of migrant life, I owe an enormous debt. I hope that my determination to document migrant narratives in depth, with minimal interpretive interruption, will justify the faith Emmanuel M. Mulamila, Roberto M. Franco, and Ibrahim Ouédraogo placed in me and in this project. My gratitude extends to Emmanuel's wife, Nanna Olsen, and Ibrahim's's wife, Evelien Kuipers, whose timely mediations, unstinting help, and warm hospitality was vital to my work. Taped conversations in Copenhagen and Amsterdam were meticulously transcribed—and, in the case of my conversations with Ibrahim, translated—by Lulie El-Ashry, whose capable assistance I acknowledge once again.

In Copenhagen, Hans Lucht and his wife, Anne, provided a haven, as well as thoughtful conversations that bore directly on my work-in-progress. At Harvard, Nathan Dorman and Daniel Herron gave me critical feedback on ethics, Sarah Brady and Tyler Zoanni introduced me to relevant books, Devaka Premawardhana provided invaluable comments, and Soumia Aitelhaj permitted me to cite an essay written for my course, *The Politics of Storytelling*. Despite my failure to find funds for fieldwork, a small grant from the Center for the Study of World Religions at Harvard Divinity School enabled me to make return visits to Copenhagen and Amsterdam in the early summer of 2012 to check details, review my draft manuscript, and add new sections. My thanks are due to Professor Frank Clooney, director of the Center for the Study of World Religions, and to his staff—particularly Charles Anderson and Jane Anna Chapman—for their help and advice in arranging my air travel and managing my reimbursements.

NOTES

PREAMBLE

1. See the appendix for a more detailed and critical account of movement and migration from an evolutionary point of view.

2. Sewa's story is recounted in Michael Jackson, *Excursions* (Durham, NC: Duke University Press, 2007), 102–34; and Michael Jackson, *The Palm at the End of the Mind: Religiosity, Relatedness and the Real* (Durham, NC: Duke University Press, 2009), 14–51.

3. Michael Jackson, *Life within Limits: Well-Being in a World of Want* (Durham, NC: Duke University Press, 2011).

4. Albert Camus, *The Myth of Sisyphus*, trans. Justin O'Brien (London: Hamish Hamilton, 1955), 11. This section's title, "The Journeying Self," is borrowed from a book by Maurice Natanson, who defines individuation as a process involving mobility and becoming, in which a person projects himself or herself into the world rather than living reactively, as if all were decided from without or from above. *The Journeying Self: A Study in Philosophy and Social Role* (Menlo Park, CA: Addison-Wesley, 1970), 6–7.

5. Cited by Olivier Todd, *Albert Camus: A Life,* trans. Benjamin Ivry (London: Vintage, 1998), 23.

6. On *anthropos* as defined by morphism, see Bruno Latour, *We Have Never Been Modern* (Cambridge, MA: Harvard University Press, 1993), 137. Unfortunately, Latour's comprehensive account of boundary blurring and hybridity is so emphatically objectivist that it fails to consider the subjective, rather than merely discursive, thresholds of tolerance for crossing the boundaries between conventionally separated categories. See Michael Jackson, "Biotechnology and the Critique of Globalization," in *Existential Anthropology: Events, Exigencies and Effects* (New York: Berghahn, 2005), 111–25.

7. Fyodor Vasilyuk makes this point very well in his discussion of lifeworlds and the means whereby human beings cope with critical situations in life—processes that are captured by the Russian word *perezhivaniye*. "Experiencing, taken in the

most abstract sense, is a struggle against the impossibility of living, in a certain sense it is a struggle against death in life." *The Psychology of Experiencing,* trans. Ruth English (Moscow: Progress Publishers, 1988), 95.

8. Clara Han argues for a position midway between movement and stasis, in which "the possible" is revealed through becoming alert to what has not yet been seen. This implies a "more laterally oriented than forward moving" conception of how people work to improve their life chances. "Symptoms of Another Life: Time, Possibility, and Domestic Relations in Chile's Credit Economy," *Current Anthropology* 26, no. 1 (2011): 7–32, 8.

9. Elizabeth Hill Boone, "The House of the Eagle," in *Cave, City, and Eagle's Nest: An Interpretive Journey through the Mapa de Cuauhtinchan No. 2,* ed. Davíd Carrasco and Scott Sessions (Albuquerque: University of New Mexico Press, 2007), 27–47.

10. Davíd Carrasco and Scott Sessions, "Introduction," in *Cave, City, and Eagle's Nest,* 1.

11. Davíd Carrasco, *City of Sacrifice: The Aztec Empire and the Role of Violence in Civilization* (Boston: Beacon Press, 1999), 179, 148.

12. "Prayer for My Daughter," in *The Collected Poems of W. B. Yeats* (New York: Collier MacMillan, 1989), 188.

13. Michael Jackson, *At Home in the World* (Durham, NC: Duke University Press, 1995).

14. This "phenomenological turn" in migration studies is exemplified by Knut Graw and Samuli Schielke, eds., *The Global Horizon: Expectations of Migration in Africa and the Middle East* (Leuven: Leuven University Press, 2012). As I note in the afterword to this volume (194–99), anthropological studies of migration have hitherto reflected an interest in globalization processes, as well as "transnational social fields" and social networks based on new technologies of international communication, new forms of social mobility, economic opportunity, and fluid or hybrid identities. This perspective reflects the public preoccupations, governmental policies, and media-driven discourse of the receiving countries, and has often left the lived experiences of migrants unexplored. The late 1990s saw greater interest in the personal expectations, moral dilemmas, and changing worldviews of migrants. This "transnationalism from below" focused on geographic, social, and existential mobility and the changing modes of subjectivity and intersubjectivity, both fantasized and realized, among young migrants moving in the shadows of the global village, testing the limits of what is possible and endurable, and doing things their forefathers could only have dreamed of. To some extent, Arjun Appadurai registers this shift from a Euro-American statist discourse to a phenomenology of African modes of being-in-the-world in *Fear of Small Numbers,* where he remarks that his earlier work, *Modernity at Large,* had painted a somewhat too rosy picture of globalization and neglected to explore the violence, exclusion, and inequality that characterized the poor and dispossessed who sought to improve their life chances by migrating to the global North. The shift is also noted by James Ferguson, who writes of the need to center discussions of the global "less on transnational flows and images of unfettered

connection than on the social relations that selectively constitute global society." Arjun Appadurai, *Modernity at Large: Cultural Dimensions of Globalization* (Minneapolis: University of Minnesota Press 1996); Arjun Appadurai, *Fear of Small Numbers: An Essay on the Geography of Anger* (Durham, NC: Duke University Press, 2006), ix; James Ferguson, *Global Shadows: Africa in the Neo-liberal World Order* (Durham, NC: Duke University Press 2006), 23; Michael Peter Smith and Luis Eduardo Guarnizo, eds., *Transnationalism from Below* (New Brunswick, NJ: Transaction Publishers, 1998).

15. Jean-François Bayart, *Global Subjects: A Political Critique of Globalization* (Cambridge: Polity, 2007), 105, 277–80. John Chernoff makes the same critique, questioning the social scientist's talk of "floating" or "marginal" populations, "subcultures" and "dis" people (disadvantaged, displaced, disoriented), and pointing out the irreducibility of human experience to politico-economic infrastructures, either local or global. John M. Chernoff, *Hustling Is Not Stealing: Stories of an African Bar Girl* (Chicago: University of Chicago Press, 2003), 39–42.

16. Roberto Franco and Ibrahim Ouédraogo are pseudonyms.

17. John M. Chernoff, *Exchange Is Not Robbery: More Stories from an African Bar Girl* (Chicago: University of Chicago Press, 2005), 6.

18. Ibid., 2.

19. Ruth Behar, *Translated Woman: Crossing the Border with Esperanza's Story* (Boston: Beacon Press, 1993).

20. Joseph Conrad, "Author's Note," in *Youth, Heart of Darkness, The End of the Tether: Three Stories* (London: J. M. Dent and Sons, 1946), vi–vii.

21. It is both tragic and ironic, as Sarah Willen points out, that despite "moral obligations that may cling to (or exude from) imperial histories, lingering postcolonial ties, or contemporary neocolonial imbrications, countries in the Global North—especially Western Europe, North America, Australia, and now Israel—have been loath to accept or integrate refugees from the Global South." "Darfur through a Shoah Lens: Sudanese Asylum Seekers, Unruly Biopolitical Dramas, and the Politics of Humanitarian Compassion in Israel," in *A Reader in Medical Anthropology: Theoretical Trajectories, Emergent Realities,* ed. Bryon J. Good, Michael M. J. Fischer, Sarah S. Willen, and Mary-Jo DelVecchio Good (New York: Wiley-Blackwell, 2010), 505–21, 506.

22. Baruch Spinoza, *Ethics,* trans. Samuel Shirley (Indianapolis, IN: Hackett, 1982), 109–12, III:6. I have elsewhere spelled out the fascinating parallels between Spinoza's view and Kuranko notions of life as a matter of being filled and contained, Warlpiri notions of life as a dialectic of being-in-presentia *(palka)* and being-in-potentia *(lawa),* and Maori notions of waxing *(tupu)* and waning *(mate).* Michael Jackson, *Existential Anthropology,* xvi–xvii, xxxi, 186–87.

23. Paul Ricoeur, *Critique and Conviction: Conversations with François Azouvi and Marc de Launay* (New York: Columbia University Press, 1998), 94.

24. This view is anticipated in Montaigne's turn from the question of what we *should* do to what we *actually* do in striving for a "fully human, satisfying, flourishing" life. Sarah Bakewell, *How to Live; Or, A Life of Montaigne in One Question and*

Twenty Attempts at an Answer (London: Chatto and Windus, 2010), 4. Writing about those German citizens who did not comply with Nazi decrees, Hannah Arendt observes that these individuals "never went though anything like a great moral conflict or a crisis of conscience . . . but acted according to something which was self-evident to them even though it was no longer self-evident to those around them. Hence their conscience, if that is what it was, had no obligatory character, it said, 'This I *can't* do,' rather than, 'This I *ought* not to do.'" Hannah Arendt, "Some Questions of Moral Philosophy," in *Responsibility and Judgment,* ed. Jerome Kohn (New York: Schocken Books, 2003), 49–146, 78 (emphasis in text).

25. See Jackson, *Life within Limits*, 68–70, for a detailed discussion of this perspective of the "proto-ethical" that bears comparison with Michael Lambek's notion of "ordinary ethics." See Lambek's introduction to *Ordinary Ethics: Anthropology, Language and Action* (New York: Fordham University Press, 2010), 1–36. Arthur Kleinman has also written persuasively of the sense of fairness, justice, rightness that pervades ethical experience without, however, being identical to prevailing legal or moral codifications of value. This is why it is possible for people to develop a critical awareness that their social and political worlds are "wrong" and protest or act against the established order of things. Arthur Kleinman, *What Really Matters: Living a Moral Life amidst Uncertainty and Danger* (New York: Oxford University Press, 2006), 1–4.

26. Jarrett Zigon notes that it is precisely at these moments of rupture, crisis, or breakdown that the ethical comes into play. These are the moments "in which ethics must be performed. In this way, then, I make a distinction between morality as the unreflective mode of being-in-the-world and ethics as a tactic performed in the moment of the breakdown of the ethical dilemma." Jarrett Zigon, "Moral Breakdown and the Ethical Demand: A Theoretical Framework for an Anthropology of Moralities," *Anthropological Theory* 7, no. 2 (2007): 131–50, 137. Cf. Alain Badiou, *Ethics* (London: Verso, 2001).

27. Georg Simmel, "The Stranger," in *The Sociology of Georg Simmel,* trans. Kurt H. Wolff (New York: Free Press, 1950), 402–8, 402.

28. Michel Foucault makes a distinction between moralities, which are clearly codified, and ethics (strictly speaking, "ethics-oriented moralities"), which cover "practices of the self." "Here the emphasis is on the forms of relations with the self, on the methods and techniques by which he works them out, on the exercises by which he makes of himself an object to be known, and on the practices that enable him to transform his own mode of being." Foucault, *The Use of Pleasure,* vol. 2 of *The History of Sexuality,* trans. Robert Hurley (New York: Vintage, 1990), 30.

29. Jean-Paul Sartre, "The Itinerary of a Thought," in *Between Existentialism and Marxism,* trans. John Matthews (London: Verso, 1983), 35.

30. Émile Durkheim, *The Elementary Forms of the Religious Life,* trans. Joseph Ward Swain (New York: Free Press, 1965), 258.

31. Clifford Geertz, "Religion as a Cultural System," in *Anthropological Approaches to the Study of Religion* (London: Tavistock, 1966), 1–46, 2.

32. Paul Ricoeur, *Critique and Conviction: Conversations with François Azouvi and Marc de Launay,* trans. Kathleen Blamey (New York: Columbia University

Press, 1998), 92; Paul Ricoeur, *Oneself as Another,* trans. Kathleen Blaimey (Chicago: University of Chicago Press, 1992), 173–75. James Faubion coins the term "paranomic" (beside or parallel to the law) to suggest that ethical praxis often bypasses or bends rules without necessarily breaking them. In reinforcing this point, he notes that virtue is better understood in many practical contexts as a matter of virtuosity—skill in getting around difficulties, playing with possibilities, rather than slavishly following set rules or respecting conventional protocols. James D. Faubion, "Paranomics: On the Semiotics of Sacral Action," in *The Limits of Meaning: Case Studies in the Anthropology of Christianity,* ed. Matthew Engelke and Matt Tomlinson (New York: Berghahn, 2006), 189–209, 205.

33. Emmanuel Levinas, *Time and the Other,* trans. Richard A. Cohen (Pittsburg, PA: Duquesne University Press, 1987), 82–84.

34. Jean-Paul Sartre and Benny Levi, *Hope Now: The 1980 Interviews,* trans. Adrian van der Hoven (Chicago: University of Chicago Press, 1996), 68, 71. As Ricoeur puts it, this means retaining from Aristotle "only the ethics of reciprocity, of sharing, of living together." Ricoeur, *Oneself as Another,* 187. It is possible that Sartre and Merleau-Ponty preferred a situated ethics on the grounds that Kant's ethics was "too well-ordered to be true; to be, alas, too removed from human life— and death—and probably even culpably remote, morally speaking, given the shattering realities of postwar Europe." Forrest Williams, preface to *An Investigation of Jean-Paul Sartre's Posthumously Published Notebooks for an Ethics,* by Gail Evelyn Linsenbard (Lampeter, Wales: Edwin Mellen Press, 2000), viii. Thomas Schwarz Wentzer has also pointed out to me that both Sartre and Ricoeur follow Hegel's discovery of the priority of an ethics inscribed in custom and shared routines, contrasting it with Kant's rationalist ethics and terming it *sittlichkeit* rather than "morality."

35. Sartre, "The Itinerary of a Thought," 70.

36. Maurice Merleau-Ponty, *The Phenomenology of Perception,* trans. Colin Smith (London: Routledge and Kegan Paul, 1962), 362.

37. Maurice Merleau-Ponty, *The Structure of Behaviour,* trans. A. L. Fisher (London: Methuen, 1965), 222.

38. As Webb Keane puts it, "The sociological imagination would put the bare fact of life with others at the heart of ethics." Keane also points out that many other ethnographers have arrived at a similar conclusion, particularly in analyses of children's conversations and interactions that reveal "collaborative acts of framing" and "the subtle acts of evaluation and judgment [that] linguistic anthropologists categorize as stance." Webb Keane, "Minds, Surfaces, and Reasons," in Lambek, ed., *Ordinary Ethics,* 64–83, 82, 74.

39. Ed Tronick, *The Neurobehavioral and Social-Emotional Development of Infants and Children* (New York, W. W. Norton, 2007), 292. See also Allan Schore, *Affect Regulation and the Repair of the Self* (New York: W. W. Norton, 2003), 37–41. Daniel Stern notes that "interaffective sharing" is absent in psychotics. Stern, *The Interpersonal World of the Infant: A View from Psychoanalysis and Developmental Psychology* (New York: Basic Books, 1985), 204.

40. Tronick, *Neurobehavioral and Social-Emotional Development*, 262–73. Physical abuse or psychological trauma during childhood seriously impairs social-cognitive development, as well as associated skills of moral reasoning, affect regulation, and the ability to discriminate between right and wrong. J. G. Smetana, M. Kelly, and C. Twentyman, "Abused, Neglected, and Nonmaltreated Children's Judgments of Moral and Social Transgression," *Child Development* 55 (1984): 277–87.

41. Lambek, *Ordinary Ethics*, 14.

42. Veena Das, *Life and Words: Violence and the Descent into the Ordinary* (Berkeley: University of California Press, 2007), 15.

43. David Graeber, *Debt: The First* 5,000 *Years* (New York: Melville House, 2011), 89.

44. Michael Jackson, *Allegories of the Wilderness: Ethics and Ambiguity in Kuranko Narratives* (Bloomington: Indiana University Press, 1982).

45. Ibid., 59.

46. In contemporary Anglophone Cameroon, "any place where there is money can be called 'bush'" (i.e., the West or *white man kontri*), and the dream of migration is known as "bushfalling." Maybritt Jill Alpes, "Bushfalling: The Making of Migratory Expectations in Anglophone Cameroon," in Graw and Schielke, eds., *The Global Horizon*, 43–58, 43.

47. Jackson, *Life within Limits*.

48. Darrell J. Fasching, Dell Dechant, and David M. Lantigua, "Religion, Ethics, and Storytelling," in *Comparative Religious Ethics: A Narrative Approach to Global Ethics* (Chichester: Wiley-Blackwell, 2011), 5, 6, 5.

49. Ibid., 5.

50. For examples of "straight" and "crooked" in Kuranko, see Jackson, *Allegories of the Wilderness*, 28. In Warlpiri, see Jackson, *At Home in the World* (Durham, NC: Duke University Press, 1995), 175. See also Western Apache metaphors of smoothness and steadiness of mind in Keith Basso, "Wisdom Sits in Places: Notes on a Western Apache Landscape," in *Senses of Place*, ed. Steven Feld and Keith Basso (Sante Fe, NM: School of American Research Press, 1996), 74–75.

EMMANUEL

1. Peter Geschiere, *The Perils of Belonging: Autochthony, Citizenship, and Exclusion in Africa and Europe* (Chicago: Chicago University Press, 2009).

2. James C. Scott, *The Art of Not Being Governed: An Anarchist History of Upland Southeast Asia* (New Haven, CT: Yale University Press, 2009).

3. "Cameroonian Farmers in Anti-rape Protest," BBC.com, Nov. 15, 2011, available at www.bbc.co.uk/news/world-africa-15737141.

4. Liisa H. Malkki, *Purity and Exile: Violence, Memory, and National Cosmology among Hutu Refugees in Tanzania* (Chicago: University of Chicago Press, 1995), 68–71.

5. Even though the Iteso regarded themselves as possessing absolute rights in this region of eastern Uganda, they themselves came to the area from elsewhere. Originally members of the Karimojong tribal cluster, they migrated south (according to legend) in search of a "promised land." Ivan Karp, *Fields of Change among the Iteso of Kenya* (London: Routledge and Kegan Paul, 1978), 15–16.

6. Ibid., 13.

7. Susan Reynolds Whyte and Michael A. Whyte, "Children's Children: Time and Relatedness in Eastern Uganda," *Africa* 74, no. 1 (2004): 76–94, 77.

8. Susette Heald, *Controlling Anger: The Anthropology of Gisu Violence* (Oxford: James Currey, 1998), 211.

9. Amelie Oksenberg Rorty, "The Vanishing Subject: The Many Faces of Subjectivity," in *Subjectivity: Ethnographic Perspectives,* ed. Joao Biehl, Byron Good, and Arthur Kleinman (Berkeley: University of California Press, 2007), 34–51.

10. Erick Otieno Nyambedha, "Sharing Food: Grandmothers and 'the Children of Today' in Western Kenya," in *Generations in Africa: Connections and Conflicts,* ed. Erdmute Alber, Sjaak van der Geest, and Susan Reynolds Whyte (Berlin: Lit Verlag, 2008), 71–88, 86.

11. Suzette Heald, *Manhood and Morality: Sex, Violence and Ritual in Gisu Society* (London: Routledge, 1999), 11.

12. Ibid., 24–25.

13. Ibid., 28.

14. Ibid., 14.

15. I had assumed that in Bugiso, as in many African societies with agnatic descent, the mother's brother would be an accessible, benevolent figure and possibly offer refuge to a fatherless sister's son. Heald writes that this is not necessarily the case. "Although he has a special relationship with his sister's son, he is at the same time closely identified with the father, as his brother-in-law, as a member of the senior generation and in terms of his obligations to his sister's son. The relationship is one of restraint," though the mother's brother "may be called upon to ensure that his sister's son is treated fairly." Heald, *Controlling Anger,* 149. A similar ambiguity exists in Bunyole, where the mother's brother commands both respect and prestations because he is a "wife-giver," yet is expected to share his sister's love and concern for her child. "Thus the sister's children have to show the somewhat stiff formality which Nyole express by the verb *ohutya,* to fear and respect; yet they can look to their mother's brothers for support and even affection." Susan Reynolds-Whyte, *Questioning Misfortune: The Pragmatics of Uncertainty in Eastern Uganda* (Cambridge: Cambridge University Press, 1997), 157.

16. Michael Jackson, *Allegories of the Wilderness: Ethics and Ambiguity in Kuranko Narratives* (Bloomington: Indiana University Press, 1982), 93–116.

17. "The History of Jack and the Bean-Stalk," in *The Classic Fairy Tales,* ed. Iona Opie and Peter Opie (New York: Oxford University Press, 1980), 216–18.

18. Jean-Paul Sartre, *The Family Idiot: Gustave Flaubert 1821–1857,* vol. 2, trans. Carol Cosman (Chicago: University of Chicago Press, 1987), 174.

19. Paul Auster, *The Book of Illusions* (New York: Picador, 2002), 5.

20. Henri Bergson, *Laughter: An Essay on the Meaning of the Comic* (London: MacMillan, 1911).

21. In Mande societies, silence is not necessarily regarded as a psychologically negative strategy for avoiding coming to terms with a traumatic experience; rather, it may be viewed as stoic virtue that is more conducive than speech to the recovery of social bonds and the affirmation of social solidarity. "Such silence may be . . . a way of healing and reconciliation, and not a way of evading or repressing an issue." Michael Jackson, "The Prose of Suffering and the Practice of Silence," *Spiritus* 4, no. 1 (2004): 44–59, 56.

22. This image of a gilded cage also recurs in the discourse of illegal migrants in the United States. As a popular song puts it, "What good is money if I am like a prisoner in this great nation? When I think about it, I cry. Even if the cage is made of gold, it doesn't make it less a prison." Leo Chavez, *Shadowed Lives: Undocumented Immigrants in American Society* (Orlando, FL: Harcourt Brace), 160.

23. Charles "Mase" Onyango-Obbo (born in Mbale in 1958) became a well-known Ugandan author, journalist, and political commentator.

24. René Girard, *The Scapegoat,* trans. Yvonne Freccero (Baltimore, MD: Johns Hopkins University Press, 1986), 22.

25. Heald, *Controlling Anger,* 102–3, 107. Sorcery accusations in Bunyole also tend to reflect population pressures on the land. Reynolds Whyte, *Questioning Misfortune,* 184.

26. R. J. Biellik and P. L. Henderson, "Mortality, Nutritional Status, and Diet during the Famine in Karaomoja, Uganda, 1980," *Lancet* 2, no. 8259 (1981): 1330–33.

27. In times of drought, crop failure, cattle disease, and famine, the Gogo pastoralists of Tanzania speak of a reversal in the ideal state of things *(mbeho).* Since everything is upside down (Gogo say, "The years have turned about"), it seems logical that by creating a social simulacrum of the environmental condition and ritually manipulating this man-made disorder, a re-reversal of time and a return to the previous ritual state can be induced. "For a set period of time," therefore, "a certain number of married women, acting in concert, dress like men, and ceremonially carry out male tasks performed in 'normal' circumstances exclusively by men, or even 'prohibited' *(mwiko)* to women." The women, acting as men, "dance away" the forces that have contaminated the land, moving steadily in a westerly direction until they reach a low-lying area or swamp, where they "throw down" the bad ritual state *(ibeho).* Peter Rigby, "Gogo Rituals of Purification," in *Dialectic in Practical Religion,* ed. Edmund Leach (Cambridge: Cambridge University Press, 1968), 153–78, 159.

28. Kees van Kooten summarizes Løgstrup's view in these words: "We do not become aware of the sovereign expressions of life until a failure or conflict or crisis disrupts our immediate preoccupation with the needs of the other." Kees van Kooten Niekerk, introduction to Løgstrup, *Beyond the Ethical Demand,* xx, xviii.

29. This echoes a distinction the Israeli state makes between Palestinian citizens and unauthorized migrant workers from West Africa, South America, Eastern Europe, the former Soviet Union, and Southeast Asia, who were arrested, detained, and deported between 2002 and 2005. While the Palestinians are "real others," the migrant workers are "other others"—an invidious discrimination that Sarah Willen describes as symptomatic of a "complex, ongoing strategic game of biopolitical regulation and statecraft." "Citizens, 'Real' Others, and 'Other' Others: The Biopolitics of Otherness and the Deportation of Unauthorized Migrant Workers from Tel Aviv, Israel," in *The Deportation Regime: Sovereignty, Space, and the Freedom of Movement,* ed. Nicholas de Genova and Nathalie Peutz (Durham, NC: Duke University Press, 2010), 262–94, 264.

30. Mikkel Rytter, "'The Family in Denmark' and 'the Aliens': Kinship Images in Danish Integration Policies," *Ethnos* 75, no. 3 (2010): 301–22, 303. Peter Geschiere has documented a similar shift in Dutch immigration policies toward "more forceful integration," following the murders of the populist politician Pim Fortuyn (in 2002) and the filmmaker Theo van Gogh (in 2004), both of whom had given voice to widespread Dutch fears of rising criminality and Islamic fundamentalism among second-generation *allochtonen*. As Geshiere points out, the increasing use of the contrasted terms *allochtonen* and *autochtonen* is a measure of the widening gap between primary and secondary modes of citizenship and national belonging. *The Perils of Belonging: Autochthony, Citizenship, and Exclusion in Africa and Europe* (Chicago: University of Chicago Press, 2009), 130–68.

31. Michael Jackson, *In Sierra Leone* (Durham, NC: Duke University Press, 2004), 57.

32. Stephen Jackson, "'It Seems to Be Going': The Genius of Survival in Wartime DR Congo," in *Hard Work, Hard Times: Global Volatility and African Subjectivities,* ed. Anne-Maria Makhulu, Beth A. Buggenhagen, and Stephen Jackson (Berkeley: University of California Press, 2010), 48–68, 48.

33. I am echoing Marx's elaboration on a remark of Hegel's at the beginning of the latter's *The Eighteenth Brumaire of Louis Bonaparte* (Moscow: Progress Publishers, 1934).

34. Hannah Arendt, *The Human Condition* (Chicago: University of Chicago, 1958), 178.

35. Baruch Spinoza, *Ethics,* trans. Samuel Shirley (Indianapolis, IN: Hackett, 1982), 109–12, especially propositions 6, 12, and 13. In a similar vein, Alain Badiou notes that hope does not necessarily encompass an expectation of improvement or justice; it is, in its most ontologically basic form, a kind of obstinacy, patience, or perseverance, warranted by the sense that one's subjectivity is ongoing rather than about to come to an end. Alan Badiou, *Saint Paul: The Foundation of Universalism,* trans. Ray Brassier (Stanford, CA: Stanford University Press, 2003), 93.

36. "Before the relevant requirements on agency are requirements imposed by principles, they are requirements imposed by the specific and concrete situation, which latter enjoin us to act in ways answering to ethical predicates with descriptive

content ... including especially requirements prescribing communicative acts whose descriptions involve such predicates—a sovereign expression of life, the showing of trust, the offering of help, veracity, and the like." Knud Løgstrup, cited in Kees van Kooten Niekerk, introduction to Løgstrup, *Beyond the Ethical Demand*, xxiii.

37. As Kees van Kooten Niekerk puts it, Løgstrup "does not deny that reference to general principles or norms may play a part in ethical argumentation. But he stresses that norms and principles are subordinate to moral experience." Ibid.

38. Løgstrup, *Beyond the Ethical Demand*, 68.

39. Emmanuel Levinas, "Ethics of the Infinite," in Richard Kearney, *Debates in Continental Philosophy: Conversations with Contemporary Thinkers* (New York: Fordham University Press, 2004), 65–84.

40. Filip de Boeck, "City on the Move: How Urban Dwellers in Central Africa Manage the Siren's Call of Migration," in *The Global Horizon: Expectations of Migration in Africa and the Middle East*, ed. Knut Graw and Samuli Schielke (Leuven: Leuven University Press, 2012), 59–85, 63.

41. Ibid.

42. Hans Lucht, *Darkness before Daybreak: African Migrants Living on the Margins in Southern Italy Today* (Berkeley: University of California Press, 2012), xii, 83.

43. Ibid., 78.

44. Ibid., 33.

45. Ibid., xiii.

46. Ibid., 107.

47. Michel Serres, *The Natural Contract*, trans. Elizabeth MacArthur and William Paulson (Ann Arbor: University of Michigan Press, 1995), 38.

48. *Homini sacri*—lives excluded from the polis. Giorgio Agamben, *Homo Sacer: Sovereign Power and Bare Life*, trans. Daniel Heller-Roazen (Stanford, CA: Stanford University Press, 1998).

49. Serres, *The Natural Contract*, 38.

50. I borrow a phrase from Claude Lanzmann here. When working on a film, Lanzmann says, he distanced himself, forgot himself, entering into the "reasons and the madness, the lies and the silences of those I wished to portray or those I was questioning, until I reach a precise, hallucinatory state of hyper-alertness, a state that, to me, is the essence of the imagination." Claude Lanzmann, *The Patagonia Hare* (New York: Farrar, Straus and Giroux, 2012), 271.

51. Veit Bader, "The Ethics of Immigration," *Constellations* 12, no. 3 (2005): 331–61, 331.

52. David Grossman, *The Yellow Wind*, trans. Haim Watzman (London: Picador, 1989), 5–8.

53. *The Ethical Demand*, trans. Theodore I. Jensen (Philadelphia: Fortress Press, 1971), 8.

54. Judith Butler, "Violence, Mourning, Politics," *Studies in Gender and Sexuality* 4, no. 1 (2003): 9–37, 10, 36.

1. The original site of Mexico City was known as Mexico-Tenochtitlan, after the Nahua Aztec people, the Mexica. The name of the city, Mexico-Tenochtitlan, means "the place of the Mexica among the stone cactuses"—an allusion to the image of an eagle perched on a cactus that grew from a stone in the middle of Lake Texcoco.

2. Zygmunt Bauman, *Wasted Lives: Modernity and Its Outcasts* (Cambridge: Polity, 2004).

3. Tracy Kidder, *Strength in What Remains* (New York: Random House, 2009), 126–30.

4. Paul Ricoeur, "The Power of the Possible," in *Debates in Continental Philosophy: Conversations with Contemporary Thinkers,* by Richard Kearney (New York: Fordham University Press, 2004), 42–46.

5. Ricoeur, "The Power of the Possible," 44.

6. Paul Ricoeur, *Oneself as Another,* trans. Kathleen Blamey (Chicago: University of Chicago Press, 1992), 314.

7. Every day, 300,000 people pass between Tijuana and San Ysidro, making this the busiest land border crossing in the world.

8. Gloria Anzaldúa, *Borderlands / La Frontera: The New Mestiza* (San Francisco: Aunt Lute Press, 1999).

9. Equally dehumanizing is the reduction of the migrant to a hegemonic, racialized identity—"a collection of 'cultural' elements and sustained essentialist constructions of the presumed values, beliefs, and everyday practices purportedly shared by members of all Latin American nationality groups." Nicholas De Genova and Ana Y. Ramos-Zayas, *Latino Crossings: Mexicans, Puerto Ricans, and the Politics of Race and Citizenship* (New York: Routledge, 2003), 18.

10. Primo Levi, *The Drowned and the Saved,* trans. Raymond Rosenthal (New York: Vintage, 1989), 12. Writing about the experiences of refugees, Hannah Arendt makes a similar observation: that refugees were exhorted to forget their past, to put it behind them. "Apparently nobody wants to know that contemporary history has created a new kind of human being—the kind that are put in concentration camps by their foes and in internment camps by their friends." "We Refugees," *Menorah Journal* 31, no. 1 (1943): 69–77, 70.

11. Emmanuel Levinas, "Ethics of the Infinite," in *Debates in Continental Philosophy: Conversations with Contemporary Thinkers,* by Richard Kearney (New York: Fordham University Press, 2004), 65–84, 75.

12. Vladimir Solokiev, *The Justification of the Good* (London: Constable, 1918), cited in Neville Symington, *Emotions and Spirit: Questioning the Claims of Psychoanalysis and Religion* (London: Cassell, 1994), 115.

13. On the relevance of Michael Oakshott's notion of conversation to ethnographic method, see Michael Jackson, *Excursions* (Durham, NC: Duke University Press, 2007), x.

14. Symington, *Emotions and Spirit,* 121.

15. Ruth Behar, *Translated Woman: Crossing the Border with Esperanza's Story* (Boston: Beacon Press, 1993), 320.

16. Claude Lanzmann, *The Patagonia Hare,* trans. Frank Wynn (New York: Farrar, Straus and Giroux, 2012), 231.

17. Jaspers contrasts *grenzsituationen* with *altagssituationen* ("everyday situations"). While we are able to "gain an overview" of our everyday situations and get beyond them, border situations "possess finality"; "they are like a wall against which we butt, against which we founder." Karl Jaspers, *Philosophie*, vol. 2, *Existenzerhellung* (Berlin: Springer Verlag, 1932), 178–79. For an account of *grenzsituationen* in English, see *Karl Jaspers: Basic Philosophical Writings,* ed. and trans. Edith Ehrlich, Leonard H. Ehrlich, and George B. Pepper (New York: Humanity Books, 2000), 97. Though Adorno treats the term "frontier-situations" as part of a jargon of authenticity—on a par with "being-in-the-world," "individual existence," and "heroic endurance"—a way of "usurping religious-authoritarian pathos without the least religious content," I see it as a way of escaping the two dominant discourses of our time, the first reducing all meaning to political economy, the second to religious belief or doctrine. In my view, it is precisely this tendency to politicize or intellectualize religious experience that the existential concept of *situation* helps us overcome. Theodor Adorno, *Minima Moralia: Reflections from Damaged Life,* trans. E. F. N. Jephcott (London: Verso, 1978), 152.

18. David Carrasco, "Desire and the Frontier: Apparitions from the Unconscious in *The Old Gringo*," in *The Novel in the Americas,* ed. Raymond Leslie Williams (Boulder: University of Colorado Press, 1992), 102.

19. Ibid., 106

20. Anzaldúa, *Borderlands / La Frontera,* 101.

21. Nicholas De Genova, *Working the Boundaries: Race, Space, and "Illegality" in Mexican Chicago* (Durham, NC: Duke University Press, 2005), 26.

22. Primo Levi, *Moments of Reprieve,* trans. Ruth Feldman (London: Abacus, 1987), 149.

23. Ibid.

24. Ibid., 160.

25. Carolyn Moxley Rouse, *Engaged Surrender: African American Women and Islam* (Berkeley: University of California Press, 2004). For significant ethnographies on the meaning of submission and devotionalism, see R. Marie Griffith, *God's Daughters: Evangelical Women and the Power of Submission* (Berkeley: University of California Press, 1997); Rouse, *Engaged Surrender*; Saba Mahmood, *Politics of Piety: The Islamic Revival and the Feminist Subject* (Princeton, NJ: Princeton University Press, 2005).

26. Daniel G. Groody, *Border of Death, Valley of Life: An Immigrant Journey of Heart and Spirit* (Lanham, MD: Rowman and Littlefield, 2002), 104.

27. Arthur D. Nock, *Conversion: The Old and the New in Religion from Alexander the Great to Augustine of Hippo* (Baltimore, MD: Johns Hopkins University Press, 1998), 7.

28. In their comments on "migration as horizon," Knut Graw and Samuli Schilke point out that Edmund Husserl "described objects and acts of perception

as defined not just by the properties of the act or object itself but by their horizon *(Horizont)* or *Hof* (halo, a term describing a circle or circular space around something, derived from the Greek *halos,* originally a threshing floor), that is defined by the objects and perceptions that precede, come after or surround it." Introduction to *The Global Horizon: Expectation of Migration in Africa and the Middle East,* ed. Knut Graw and Samuli Schielke (Leuven: Leuven University Press, 2012), 7–22, 14.

29. Hans Lucht, *Darkness before Daybreak: African Migrants Living on the Margins of Southern Italy Today* (Berkeley: University of California Press, 2012), 103.

30. Ibid.

31. Marianne Søndergaard Winther, "Cleaning in a Gold Cage: Social and Physical (Im)mobility in the Lives of Undocumented *Latinas* in California," master's thesis, University of Copenhagen, 2012, 2–3.

32. The image seems to have originated with a popular song, "Jaula de Oro." Leo Chavez, *Shadowed Lives: Undocumented Immigrants in American Society* (Orlando, FL: Harcourt Brace, 1992), 159–60.

33. In Mexico, the passage from girlhood to womanhood is marked by the celebration of the *quinceañera,* or fifteenth birthday. From a north-of-the-border viewpoint, it may be seen as a cross between sweet sixteen and a debutante's coming-out party. The celebration is a way to acknowledge that a young woman has reached maturity and is thus of marriageable age.

34. Ricoeur, *Oneself as Another,* 315. Cf. William James: "Does God really exist? How does he exist? What is He? are so many irrelevant questions. Not God, but life, more life, a larger, richer, more satisfying life is, in the last analysis, the end of religion." *The Varieties of Religious Experience: A Study in Human Nature* (New York: Signet, 1958), 382.

35. Ricoeur, *Oneself as Another,* 316.

36. "What I find intriguing about Spinoza's notion of *conatus,*" Ricoeur writes, "is that it refuses the alternative between act and potency. . . . For Spinoza, each concrete thing or event is always a mélange of act and possibility." And this defines the field of ethics. Ricoeur, *The Power of the Possible,* 44

37. William James, *The Varieties of Religious Experience,* 383–84 (emphasis in original).

38. Primo Levi, "The Force of Amber," in *Other People's Trades,* trans. Raymond Rosenthal (London: Michael Joseph, 1989), 126–30, 126.

IBRAHIM

1. Della E. McMillan, *Sahel Visions: Planned Settlement and River Blindness Control in Burkina Faso* (Tucson: University of Arizona Press, 1995).

2. Ibid., 1.

3. Ibid., xxx.

4. Ibid.

5. Salman Rushdie, *The Wizard of Oz,* 2nd ed. (London: Palgrave Macmillan, 2012), 58.

6. Kaya is a provincial capital on the Mossi Plateau, a center for weaving and tanning. When Ibrahim first visited the city, it had a population of about thirty thousand.

7. Della McMillan provides details of the six major categories of arable land in and around Damesma, noting, "Land types differ not only in natural soil fertility but in their vulnerability to flooding and drought, suitability for different crops, and ease of cultivation. Given the erratic rainfall, water retention is generally the most valued characteristic of a field." McMillan, *Sahel Visions,* 177.

8. People in Damesma often used Bitto, a town near the Ghana border, and Bobo Dioulassa, a city inhabited by large numbers of Mossi migrants, as general terms for the new settlements in the south-central and southwest areas, respectively. Ibid., 21.

9. The organization was the Volta Valley Authority (Autorité des Aménagements des Vallées des Volta), or AVV, which moved people from the densely populated Mossi Plateau and resettled them in new villages in the sparsely settled river basins to the south.

10. Michael Jackson, *The Politics of Storytelling: Violence, Transgression and Intersubjectivity* (Copenhagen: Museum Tusculanum Press, 2002), 14.

11. Della McMillan observes that in 1979, Ibrahim's father—the Damesma chief *(tenga naba)*—was "an active man in his mid-forties who had extensive dealings throughout the central plateau as well as in Ougadougou, Bobo Dialasso, Côte d'Ivoire, and now the AVV." His extensive relations with the national administration and other far-flung regions reflected traditional Mossi precedents and "were routed through the thousands of Damesma immigrants and their descendants," who lived in southwestern Burkina and Côte d'Ivoire. *Sahel Visions,* 66.

12. In the 1950s and '60s, thousands of Mossi moved into southern and central Ghana seeking seasonal work in industry or cocoa farming. Many became permanent residents. In 1960, the Mossi were the largest group of immigrants in Ghana, and 28 percent of the Mossi had been born in Ghana. Enid Schildkrout, *People of the Zongo: The Transformations of Ethnic Identities in Ghana* (Cambridge: Cambridge University Press, 1978), 40.

13. "Most Mossi marriages were based on an exchange of women between two lineages linked by a long-term series of reciprocal exchanges of goods and services. Women were regarded as the most valuable part of this system." Elliott Skinner, *The Mossi of the Upper Volta: The Political Development of a Sudanese People* (Stanford, CA: Stanford University Press, 1964), 22.

14. Among the Tallensi of northern Ghana, the tension between being an actor and being acted upon finds expression in the dialectic between chosen and preordained destinies. "Life—symbolized for the Tallensi in the breath *(novor)*—is only the raw material for living," writes Meyer Fortes. "What one makes of it depends on other spiritual agencies." These "other spiritual agencies" include the influences of one's mother, father, or other kin (strictly speaking, "the Prenatal Destiny" of such

significant others) and the influence of the Prenatal Destiny that one chooses for oneself before being born. This prenatal decision may be made against having a spouse, bearing children, or being a farmer—in effect, rejecting a normal moral life. Fortes refers to this as "Oedipal fate," contrasting it with the "Jobian fulfillment" that comes from recognizing the superior powers of the ancestors and seeking redemption through them. But just as a bad prenatal choice can be revoked by setting up a shrine and making sacrifices to one's ancestors—ritually submitting to and complying with "the norms and customs instituted by them," a person's positive dispositions may be undermined should he or she neglect or ignore the lineage ancestors. Meyer Fortes, *Oedipus and Job in West African Religion* (Cambridge: Cambridge University Press, 1983), 15, 23.

15. Charles Piot, *Nostalgia for the Future: West Africa after the Cold War* (Chicago: University of Chicago Press, 2010).

16. Ibid., 20.

17. Ibid., 99.

18. Ibid., 68.

19. Ibid., 13–14.

20. Ibid., 14.

21. Ibid., 13–14.

22. "According to the most widespread Mossi belief, some forty generations ago a ruler called Naba Nedega . . . who lived at Gambaga in present-day Ghana, reigned over the Dagomba, Mamprusi, and Nankana." Skinner, *The Mossi of the Upper Volta*, 7.

23. According to some traditions, Rialle was the son of a Mali chief; according to others, he was a Busansi hunter. Ibid., 7.

24. Probably in the mid-fourteenth century. Ibid., 8.

25. "The relations between the Mogho Naba and his children, including his heir, were characterized by formality—at least in public the Mogho Naba was not expected to enjoy seeing his son and heir, because of the Mossi father's traditional anxiety regarding those individuals who would profit most from his death." Ibid., 48.

26. "A reluctance to surrender or assume a position of authority in the family or lineage has the same social consequences as a reluctance to surrender sisters and daughters to another lineage in marriage. The latter is, of course, a widespread theme in myth and folklore (Acrisius and Danae; Aleos and Auge)." Michael Jackson, "Prevented Successions: A Commentary on a Kuranko Narrative," in *Fantasy and Symbol: Studies in Anthropological Interpretation,* ed. R. J. H. Hook (London: Academic Press, 1979), 95–131, 118.

27. Competition for the position of *tenga naba* "was very keen because of the greater number of lineage members eligible for the nam [the God-given power first possessed by the original founders, which enables one man to control another] and the shallow genealogical depth. Every man who had the ability or desire to rule was encouraged to seek the post." Skinner, *The Mossi of the Upper Volta,* 57–58.

28. Ibrahim's father became *tenga naba* in 1954.

29. Della McMillan provides a rather different account of the origins of Damesma. In this account, groups of Mossi from Ouagadougou moved north in the eighteenth century and acquired the right to cultivate land from the indigenous people of the region. When the settlers requested that the *mogho naba* give them a chief, the *mogho naba* sent one of his sons, who was club-footed and lame. After living for short periods in several villages, Naba Piko (the lame-footed chief) made Damesma his headquarters. McMillan, *Sahel Visions*, 28.

30. Michael Jackson, *In Sierra Leone* (Durham, NC: Duke University Press, 2004), 10.

31. Norbert Elias, *The Civilizing Process: The History of Manners and State Formation and Civilization,* trans. Edmund Jephcott (Oxford: Blackwell, 1994); Jonas Frykman and Orvar Löfgren, *Culture Builders: A Historical Anthropology of Middle-Class Life,* trans. Alan Crozier (New Brunswick, NJ: Rutgers University Press, 1987), 126–53.

32. Elisabeth Lasch-Quinn, "From Inwardness to Intravidualism," *Hedgehog Review* 13, no. 1 (2011).

33. Herbert Marcuse, "The Affirmative Character of Culture," in *Negations: Essays in Critical Theory,* trans. Jeremy J. Shapiro (Boston: Beacon Press, 1968), 88–133, 120.

34. T. S. Eliot argued that while metaphysical poets like John Donne sought to unify sensations and ideas, feelings and thoughts, the early seventeenth century saw these modalities of experience become increasingly separated, creating an increasing division between ratiocination and emotionality and giving rise to genres of writing that defined their identities in mutually exclusive terms.

35. Michael Herzfeld, *The Social Production of Indifference: Exploring the Roots of Western Bureaucracy* (New York: Berg, 1992).

36. Hannah Arendt, *The Human Condition* (Chicago: University of Chicago Press, 1958), 95, 169.

POSTSCRIPT

1. Joan Didion, *The White Album* (Harmondsworth: Penguin, 1979), 11.

2. Daniel Kahneman, *Thinking, Fast and Slow* (London: Allen Lane, 2011), 205.

3. Jill Lepore, "Obama, The Prequel: An Origin Story," *New Yorker,* June 25, 2012, 70–74, 70.

4. Walter Benjamin. *Selected Writings II,* 1927–1934, trans. Rodney Livingstone et al., ed. Michael W. Jennings, Howard Eiland, and Gary Smith (Cambridge, MA: Harvard University Press, 1999), 266.

5. Mattijs van de Port, *Ecstatic Encounters: Bahian Candomblé and the Quest for the Really Real* (Amsterdam: Amsterdam University Press, 2011), 164–65.

6. Kahneman, *Thinking, Fast and Slow,* 408–9. Kahneman's distinction echoes the contrast in contemporary psychoanalytical theory between "core self" and

"multiple self"—and the paradoxical copresence of experiences of oneself as both discontinuous and continuous over time. See Ghislaine Boulanger, *Wounded by Reality: Understanding and Treating Adult Onset Trauma* (London: Analytical Press, 2007), 69–75.

7. Citing Deleuze, Biehl and Locke make a similar point, calling for a cartography rather than an "oedipal archaeology" of the subject as moving through a variety of milieus rather than being moved by past events and hidden histories— becoming rather than merely being. João Biehl and Peter Locke, "Deleuze and the Anthropology of Becoming," *Current Anthropology* 51, no. 3 (2010). See Gilles Deleuze, *Essays Critical and Clinical* (Minneapolis: University of Minnesota Press, 1997), 61.

8. Jane Bennett, *The Enchantment of Modern Life: Attachments, Crossings, and Ethics* (Princeton, NJ: Princeton University Press, 2001), 3.

9. Hannah Arendt, "We Refugees," *Menorah Journal* 31, no. 1 (1943): 69–77, 77.

10. Ibid., 76 (emphasis added).

11. Edmund Husserl, *Ideas: General Introduction to Pure Phenomenology,* trans. W. R. Boyce Gibson (New York: Collier Macmillan, 1962), 93.

12. Ibid., 99–100.

13. Ibid., 103.

14. This is precisely where Levinas parted company with Husserl.

15. Pierre Clastres conceived this relation as one between (primitive) society and the state—where "primitive society" serves as a summary metaphor for the human variety of languages and lifeways that are written off, suppressed, or disguised by whoever has the power to determine the dominant discourse, the prevailing ethos, and the approved behaviors of the status quo.

16. Jacques Derrida, *The Gift of Death,* trans. David Wills (Chicago: University of Chicago Press, 1995), 86.

17. João Biehl, *Vita: Life in a Zone of Social Abandonment* (Berkeley: University of California Press, 2005), 88, 90, 24.

18. Katherine Boo, *Behind the Beautiful Forevers* (New York: Random House, 2012), 253–54.

19. Ibid., 254.

20. Shalom Auslander, *Hope: A Tragedy* (New York: Riverhead Books, 2012), 1.

21. Charles Piot, *Nostalgia for the Future: West Africa after the Cold War* (Durham, NC: Duke University Press, 2010).

22. Arthur Kleinman, Yunxiang Yan, Jing Jun, Sing Lee, Everett Zhang, Pan Tianshu, Wu Fei, and Guo Jinhua, *Deep China: The Moral Life of the Person* (Berkeley: University of California Press, 2011), 5.

23. This bias is characteristic of the so-called ontological turn in anthropology, in which single aspects of self-experience are essentialized and reified to characterize the psychology of entire cultures, much as the culture and personality school did in the 1940s and '50s.

24. William James, *A Pluralistic Universe* (Cambridge, MA: Harvard University Press, 1977).

25. Stephen A. Mitchell, *Hope and Dread in Psychoanalysis* (New York: Basic Books, 1993).

26. Philip M. Bromberg, *Standing in the Spaces: Essays on Clinical Process, Trauma, and Dissociation* (Hillsdale, NJ: Analytical Press, 1993), 186.

27. This model of multiple selfhood is not to be confused, however, with multiple personality disorder, when, as Philip Bromberg puts it, the normally "flexible multiplicity of relatively harmonious self-states . . . becomes a rigid multiplicity of adversarial self-states" (now known as dissociative identity disorder). Philip M. Bromberg, *Awakening the Dreamer: Clinical Journeys* (Hillsdale, NJ: Analytical Press, 2006), 191.

28. Michel de Montaigne, "On the Inconstancy of Our Actions," in *The Essays: A Selection,* trans. M. A. Screech (Harmondsworth: Penguin, 1993), 128, 129, 131.

29. Herman Melville, *The Confidence Man: His Masquerade* (Harmondsworth: Penguin, 1990), 84–85.

30. Virginia Woolf, *Orlando* (New York: Harcourt Brace, 1928), 308–9, cited in Philip M. Bromberg, *Awakening the Dreamer,* 52.

31. Fernando Pessoa, *The Book of Disquiet* (Harmondsworth: Penguin, 2003), 327–28.

32. William James, *Principles of Psychology,* vol. 1 (New York: Dover, 1950), 294, 291 (emphasis in text).

33. Ibid., 294.

34. Michael Jackson, *Excursions* (Durham, NC: Duke University Press, 2007), 102.

35. G. A. Bradshaw, Allan N. Schore, Janine L. Brown, Joyce H. Poole, and Cynthia J. Moss, "Elephant Breakdown: Social Trauma," *Nature* 433 (2005): 807.

36. George Devereux, *Ethnopsychoanalysis: Psychoanalysis and Anthropology as Complementary Frames of Reference* (Berkeley: University of California Press, 1978), 74–77.

37. Pessoa, *The Book of Disquiet,* 254.

38. I am riffing here on Barbara Myerhoff's theme of "re-membering" as a strategic means whereby a person re-aggregates and reorders the self by summoning prior and prospective selves and collaborating with significant others in generating new forms of selfhood. "Life History among the Elderly: Performance, Visibility, and Remembering," in *A Crack in the Mirror: Reflexive Perspectives in Anthropology,* ed. J. Ruby (Philadelphia: University of Pennsylvania Press, 1982), 99–117. More recently, Michael White has used Myerhoff's work on re-membering in the context of narrative therapy, mediating a client's creative construction of alternative "multivoiced" modes of self-identity. *Maps of Narrative Practice* (New York: W. W. Norton, 2007), 136–39.

39. In Arendt's terms, this is an expression of natality—the "startling unexpectedness" that is "inherent in all beginnings and in all origins" and that occurs "against the overwhelming odds of statistical laws and their probability." This is why "the new . . . always appears in the guise of a miracle." Hannah Arendt, *The Human Condition* (Chicago: University of Chicago Press, 1958), 177–78. Etymologically,

"experimentation" and its cognates "experience" and "empirical" derive from the Indo-European base "per" (to attempt, venture, try out) and imply that testing is never without risk but rather involves perils, peregrinations, and trials, in which a person may be taken to the limit of what he or she can endure, physically or conceptually.

40. Mitchell, *Hope and Dread in Psychoanalysis,* 101.

41. This kind of opportunistic switching between direct action and strategic inaction brings to mind Aristotle's distinction between "active" and "passive" agency (*Metaphysics,* book V, ch. 12), the first referring to a subject's action on the world that changes it in some way, the second referring to being subject to the actions of others—suffering, receiving, being moved or transformed by external forces. Hannah Arendt speaks of this contrast between being an actor and being acted upon as a difference between being a "who" and a "what." *The Human Condition* (Chicago: University of Chicago Press, 1958), 181–86.

42. Pessoa, *The Book of Disquiet,* 91, 30.

43. Among the Kuranko, for example, "being is not necessarily limited to human being," and the qualities of personhood *(morgoye)* "may be found in relations between man and ancestor, man and totemic animal, man and God, and so on. . . . Since personhood is distributed into the natural world rather than concentrated or fixed, it is readily conceivable that an animal can be a kind of ancestor, that God can become a person, that a fetish can speak, and that a man can change into an animal." Michael Jackson, *Allegories of the Wilderness: Ethics and Ambiguity in Kuranko Narratives* (Bloomington: Indiana University Press, 1982), 17.

44. David Graeber argues that the idea of life value finds consummate expression in the "baseline communism" of Marx and Engels: "To each according to his abilities, to each according to his needs." Hierarchical societies don't work from this assumption. There is no obligation to those without. And one of the reasons human life is so complicated is that these hierarchical and humanitarian principles contradict each another. *Debt: The First* 5,000 *Years* (New York: Melville House, 2011), 95–99.

45. I borrow the term "distributive morality" from Kenneth Read, while rejecting the notion that in "traditional" or tribal societies the moral worth of a person is *wholly* dependent on his or her specific role or status—or the corollary, that ideas of human equality in the sight of God or of impartial justice are absent from such societies. Kenneth Read, "Morality and the Concept of the Person among the Gahuku-Gama," *Oceania* 25, no. 4 (1955): 233–82.

46. Giorgio Agamben calls this the "problem of the relationship between rule and life." *De la très haute pauvreté: Règles et forme de vie,* trans. Joël Gayraud (Paris: Bibliothèque Rivages, 2011), 7. In a similar vein, Alain Pottage and Martha Mundy speak of a discrepancy "between the legal constitution of the person and the natural reality of human individuality" and note that "the act of distinguishing between these two orders is itself radically contingent." Alain Pottage and Martha Mundy, eds., *Law, Anthropology, and the Constitution of the Social* (Cambridge: Cambridge University Press, 2004), 3.

47. I have adapted this term from Norman O. Brown, *Life against Death: The Psychoanalytical Meaning of History* (Middletown, CT: Wesleyan University Press, 1985).

48. Primo Levi, *The Drowned and the Saved,* trans. Raymond Rosenthal (New York: Vintage, 1989), 82. Sometimes survivor guilt finds expression in a *nostalgie de la boue.* Wealthy or successful individuals who come from humble beginnings are often beset by a sense that they do not deserve their acquired status and good fortune. Plagued by a nagging guilt that they have risen above their proper station and distanced themselves from their peers and family to achieve a better life for themselves, they sometimes commit some petty crime, effectively committing social suicide and plummeting back into the milieu from which they came, to which they irrevocably belong. Primo Levi dedicated his life after Auschwitz to testifying to the horror, keeping the names of the dead alive. But having completed the work, he no longer had any justification for being alive and killed himself. And then there are those celebrities and sports stars who come from humble origins and fund schools, hospitals, and welfare programs, seeking to "give back," to cancel the debt they feel they have incurred by rising above their class and kind.

49. A similar contrast may be drawn between the formality of relations within one's own generation and relations with grandparents, with whom, as with the mother's brother, a playful or "joking" relationship obtains.

50. George Lakoff argues that this same tension between patriarchal control and maternal care finds expression in American political ideologies. While liberals emphasize the responsibility of the state to care for its citizens, conservatives emphasize the state's responsibility to protect the country and its constitution. *Moral Politics: What Conservatives Know That Liberals Don't* (Chicago: University of Chicago Press, 1996), 62–63. See also Ghassan Hage, "The Spatial Imaginary of National Practices: Dwelling-Domesticating/Being-Exterminating." *Environment and Planning D: Society and Space* 14 (1996): 463–85.

51. As Ana, a de facto single parent, explained to Marianne Søndergaard Winther, "For every benefit, a sacrifice *(de un beneficio, hay un sacrificio).* For Ana, the benefit of being in the United States is that her 3-year-old daughter gets the chance to 'become someone important,' whereas the sacrifice consists in not being together with her husband who, desperate because he was unable to find work, went back to Mexico one and a half years ago." Marianne Søndergaard Winther, "Cleaning in a Gold Cage: Social and Physical (Im)mobility in the Lives of Undocumented Latinas in California," master's thesis, University of Copenhagen, 2012, 74.

52. Ernst Bloch and Theodor W. Adorno, "Something's Missing: A Discussion between Ernst Bloch and Theodor W. Adorno on the Contradictions of Utopian Longing," in *The Utopian Function of Art and Literature,* by Ernst Bloch, trans. Jack Zipes and Frank Mecklenburg (Cambridge, MA: MIT Press, 1988), 1–17.

53. Ibid.

54. Jean-Paul Sartre, *The Imaginary: A Phenomenological Psychology of the Imagination,* trans. Jonathan Webber (London: Routledge, 2004).

55. Philippe Rospabé, "Don Archaïque et Monnaie Sauvage," in *MAUSS: Ce que donner veut dire: Don et intéret* (Paris: Éditions la Découverte, 1993), 35, cited in

David Graeber, *Debt: The First 5000 Years* (New York: Melville House, 2011), 133. Graeber points out that this substitution of money for life explains why debts are often collected in the form of "bloodwealth"—through the taking of life or pain inflicted on the body of the debtor.

56. Hannah Arendt, "Existenz Philosophy," *Partisan Review* 13, no. 1 (1946): 34–56, 36.

57. Ibid., 37.

58. Hugo von Hofmannsthal, "Moments in Greece," trans. Tania and James Stern, in *The Whole Difference: Selected Writings of Hugo von Hofmannsthal,* ed. J. D. McClatchy (Princeton, NJ: Princeton University Press, 2008), 80–100, 87. Cf. Arundhati Roy: "Little events, ordinary things, smashed and reconstituted. Imbued with new meaning. Suddenly they become the bleached bones of a story." *The God of Small Things* (New York: Random House, 1997), 32–33.

59. Von Hofmannsthal, "Moments in Greece," 87 (emphasis added).

60. Jane Bennett, *The Enchantment of Modern Life: Attachments, Crossings, and Ethics* (Princeton, NJ: Princeton University Press, 2001), 3.

61. Soumia Aitelhaj, "Aid and African Communities," unpublished essay, Harvard Divinity School, April 2012.

62. Douglas Lockwood, *The Lizard Eaters* (Melbourne: Cassell, 1964), 8.

63. Ibid., 15–16.

64. The Samaritan leitmotif also has contemporary relevance, notably the "Samaritans" who help illegal migrants in the Sonoma Desert and the "Samaritans" who run hotlines for chronically depressed or suicidal individuals. See Ananda Rose, *Showdown in the Sonoran Desert: Religion, Law, and the Immigration Controversy* (New York: Oxford University Press, 2012), 81–84.

65. Edmund Gurney, *Tertium Quid: Chapters in Various Disputed Questions* (London: Kegan Paul, Trench, 1887), 99, cited in William James, *The Varieties of Religious Experience: A Study in Human Nature* (New York: Signet, 1958), 397.

66. Søndergaard Winther, "Cleaning in a Gold Cage," 20.

67. Jose Antonio Vargas, cited in "Not Legal, Not Leaving," *Time Magazine,* June 25, 2012, 34–44, 41.

68. The existential complexities and contradictions of carrying false papers is explored in compelling detail by Karsten Paerregard in *Peruvians Dispersed: A Global Ethnography of Migration* (Lanham, MD: Lexington Books, 2008), chapter 8.

69. Enid Schildkrout, *People of the Zongo: The Transformations of Ethnic Identities in Ghana* (Cambridge: Cambridge University Press, 1978), 45.

70. Juan Rulfo, *Pedro Páramo,* trans. Margaret Sayers Peden (New York: Grove Press, 1994), 41.

71. Giorgio Agamben, *Homo Sacer: Sovereign Power and Bare Life,* trans. Daniel Heller-Roazen (Stanford, CA: Stanford University Press, 1998).

72. The Declaration of the Rights of Man and the Citizen, 1789, first article.

73. Hannah Arendt, *The Origins of Totalitarianism* (New York: Schocken Books, 2004), 297.

74. Ibid., 372.

75. Ibid., 363.

76. "Hitler's motto that 'Right is what is good for the German people' is only the vulgarized form of a conception of law which can be found everywhere. . . . A conception of law which identified what is right with the notion of what is good for—for the individual, or the family, or the people, or the largest number—becomes inevitable once the absolute and transcendent measurements of religion or the law of nature have lost their authority." Ibid., 379.

77. Agamben, *Homo Sacer,* 8.

78. Arendt, *Origins of Totalitarianism,* 342.

79. Hannah Arendt, *The Human Condition* (Chicago: University of Chicago Press, 1958), 190.

80. Paul Ricoeur, *Oneself as Another,* trans. Kathleen Blamey (Chicago: Chicago University Press, 1992), 316.

81. Paul Ricoeur, "On Life Stories," in Richard Kearney, *Debates in Continental Philosophy: Conversations with Contemporary Thinkers* (New York: Fordham University Press, 2004), 33–37, 37.

82. In 1945, Faulkner wrote an appendix to the novel to be published in the then-forthcoming anthology *The Portable Faulkner.* At Faulkner's behest, however, subsequent printings of *The Sound and the Fury* frequently contain the appendix at the end of the book, where it is sometimes referred to as the fifth part. Written sixteen years after *The Sound and the Fury,* the appendix presents some textual differences from the novel but serves to clarify the novel's opaque story. The appendix concludes by accounting for the black family who worked as servants to the Compsons. Unlike the entries for the Compsons themselves, which are lengthy, detailed, and told in an omniscient narrative, the servants' entries are simple and succinct. Dilsey's entry is the last in the appendix.

83. John Berger and Jean Mohr, *A Fortunate Man: The Story of a Country Doctor* (London: Writers and Readers Publishing Cooperative, 1976), 134.

APPENDIX

1. P. Jeffrey Brantingham, "Mobility, Competition, and Plio-Pleistocene Hominid Foraging Groups," *Journal of Archaeological Method and Theory* 5, no. 1 (1998): 57–98.

2. Patrick Manning, *Migration in World History* (New York: Routledge, 2005), 20–21.

3. John Bowlby, *Attachment and Loss,* vol. 1, *Attachment* (London: Random House, 1997), 295.

4. Darwin himself allowed that what evolves through natural selection may become an encumbrance in a cultural setting where selection is often based on "unnatural" "habits of life." "But a still more important consideration is that the chief part of the organisation of every living creature is due to inheritance; and

consequently, though each being assuredly is well fitted for its place in nature, many structures have now no very close and direct relations to present habits of life." Charles Darwin, *The Origin of Species by Means of Natural Selection* (Madison, WI: Cricket House, 2010), 135. Darwin's point is reiterated by Stephen Jay Gould in his critique of "ultra-Darwinian fundamentalism." Pluralists, Gould argues, "accept natural selection as a paramount principle" while allowing "a large role for history's unpredictable contingencies" and seeking "to identify a set of interacting explanatory models, all fully intelligible, although not reducible to a single grand principle like natural selection." Gould, "Evolution: The Pleasures of Pluralism," *New York Review of Books,* June 26, 1997.

5. I follow Devereux in suggesting that we treat all explanatory models, operationally or pragmatically, as part of a toolkit from which we may draw, depending on the exigencies of the situation we are trying to understand and the kind of outcomes we are trying to achieve. The methodological value of the phenomenological epoché is to remind the researcher of the necessity of suspending a priori assumptions in order to judge which tools offer explanatory leverage *in the task at hand,* much as a psychotherapist borrows eclectically and changes tack constantly in seeking the best course of action for treating a client. As Devereux pointed out in 1961, one cannot deploy sociologistic and psychologistic models *at the same time.* For example, Freudian and folk explanations of any symbolic complex may differ radically. This does not mean that we must choose between them on the grounds that only one can be epistemologically or logically true; rather, they yield different insights, some of which may be more relevant to our research interests than others. In Devereux's terms, the models are complementary. They cannot be integrated and deployed simultaneously; they must be applied serially in light of specific explanatory or therapeutic goals. The epoché implies an even more radical assumption: that we suspend prejudgments as to whether our scholarly models are scientific or nonscientific. Whether they mirror the nature of the world or measure up to an Aristotelian test for logical coherence is less important than whether the intellectual labor engaged is productive or destructive of life. In this vein, Devereux cites Bohr's "principle of destruction" *(Abtötungsprinzip)* in addressing the way any "study of the phenomenon 'life' which is *carried too far* destroys precisely that which it seeks to define precisely: Life." George Devereux, *Ethnopsychoanalysis: Psychoanalysis and Anthropology as Complementary Frames of Reference* (Berkeley: University of California Press, 1978), 9. Applied to anthropology, this means avoiding reification (the reduction of lived experience to interpretive schemata) and remembering that all interpretations of the world are tied to specific existential interests, including the quest for certainty and authority. George Devereux, "Two Types of Modal Personality Models," in *Studying Personality Cross-Culturally,* ed. B. Kaplan (New York: Harper and Row, 1961), 22–32.

6. Edward O. Wilson, *The Social Conquest of Earth* (New York: W. W. Norton, 2012), 272.

7. Robert L. Kelly, "Mobility/Sedentism: Concepts, Archaeological Measures, and Effects," *Annual Review of Anthropology* 21 (1992): 43–66.

8. I am thinking specifically of Neanderthal burials around fifty thousand years ago, in which the disposition of the corpse and associated grave goods have suggested to some a care for the life of the individual beyond the grave. These conclusions may, however, be wishful thinking. See Jeffrey D. Sommer, "The Shanidar IV 'Flower Burial': A Reevaluation of Neanderthal Burial Ritual," *Cambridge Archaeological Journal* 9, no. 1 (1999): 127–29.

9. Jared Diamond, *The Third Chimpanzee: The Evolution and Future of the Human Animal* (New York: HarperCollins, 1992), 52. More recent research on the Neanderthal genome suggests that *Homo sapiens* and *Homo neanderthalensis* interbred, which led to the absorption of the Neanderthals into our species, but this conclusion has also been contested and the common genetic elements explained in terms of the two species sharing a common ancestor. Alok Jha, "Study Casts Doubt on Human-Neanderthal Interbreeding Theory," *Guardian,* August 13, 2012, available at www.guardian.co.uk/science/2012/aug/14/study-doubt-human-neanderthal-interbreeding.

10. Sigurd Bergmann, "The Beauty of Speed or the Discovery of Slowness—Why Do We Need to Rethink Mobility?," in *The Ethics of Mobilities: Rethinking Place, Exclusion, Freedom and Environment,* ed. Sigurd Bergmann and Tore Sager (London: Ashgate, 2008), 13–24.

11. Daniel Kahneman synthesizes a considerable number of psychological experiments which suggest that our more abstract, considered, and remembered accounts of our lives (emphasizing such factors as our religious faith, family background, careers, or income) may be readily eclipsed by small changes in our immediate situation. A headache or a bad day at the office may affect one's general sense of well-being, and a significant "predictor of the feelings of a day is whether a person did or did not have contact with friends or relatives." *Thinking Fast and Slow* (London: Allen Lane, 2011), 395.

12. William James emphasizes the embodied or psychophysiological character of the emotions. William James, "What Is an Emotion," *Mind* 9, no. 34 (1884): 188–205. Recent researchers avoid this physiological reductionism, focusing on an individual's state of mind as interacting with biochemical (internal) and environmental (external) influences. In humans, emotion fundamentally involves "physiological arousal, expressive behaviors, and conscious experience." David G. Myers, "Theories of Emotion," in *Psychology: Seventh Edition* (New York: Worth Publishers, 2004), 500.

INDEX

Brown, Norman O., 210
Buchwald, Art, 38
Buddhism, 201
Bugisu region, Uganda, 21, 55
Bunyole region, Uganda, 239n15, 240n25
Burkina Faso: drought in, 156–57, 159; migration in, 157, 160–61; tropical diseases in, 157. *See also* Mossi people; Ouédraogo, Ibrahim, as child and young adult in Burkina Faso
Burundi, 16, 17, 97
bush, as symbolic space, 11, 12, 186, 211
Butler, Judith, 86

California, immigration to: and border crossings from Mexico, 110–21, 215–18; and immigrant community in Bakersfield, 121–44; and immigrant community in San Francisco, 131, 219. *See also* Franco, Roberto as immigrant in U.S.
Cameroon, 20
Camus, Albert, 2
capitalism, global, compared to narcissism, 117
Carrasco, Davíd, 123
Catholics, 103–4, 120, 155, 184
chance, as factor in human experience, 8, 197, 198, 210, 218–19, 225, 250n39
Chernoff, John, 5, 235n15
Chinese students, ethical dilemma faced by, 14
Christianity, 84, 86, 184, 185. *See also* Bible; Catholics; Pentecostals
citizenship, U.S., 87–89
Clastres, Pierre, 249n15
colonialism, 5, 16–17
comedy, as survival strategy, 37–40
conatus, Spinoza's concept of, 136, 225, 245n36
Conrad, Joseph, 5
consumerism, 175, 191
contingency. *See* chance
conversation, as ethnographic method, 118, 237n38, 243n13
Copenhagen Business School, 14, 60, 70
Copenhagen University, 14
coyotes (smugglers), 104, 111–15, 119–21, 216–17

culturalism, 124
Cynics, 98, 209

Damesma, Burkina Faso, 156–65, 168–71, 182–83, 246–47nn7–8, 248n29
Danish language, 14, 58, 59, 60, 63–64
Darwin, Charles, 228, 254–55n4
Das, Veena, 11
Dechant, Dell, 12–13
De Genova, Nicholas, 124, 243n9
Deleuze, Gilles, 249
Denmark, immigration legislation in, 57. *See also* Mulamila, Emmanuel, as immigrant in Denmark
Derrida, Jacques, 200
Devereux, George, 204, 255n5
Didion, Joan, 197
distributive morality, 209, 251n45
diviners, 136, 141, 177, 178
Dobbs, Lou, 90
Donne, John, 248n34
drug cartels, in Mexico, 113
Dryden, John, 38–39
Durkheim, Émile, 9
Dutch language, 155
dyadic consciousness, 10

East African Community (EAC), 16
elephants, 204
Eliot, T. S., 248n34
Emmanuel. *See* Mulamila, Emmanuel
emotion, 198, 229, 256n12
English language: Emmanuel as speaker of, 23, 25, 34, 65; Evelien as speaker of, 154, 155; Roberto as speaker of, 88, 132–33, 147
epoché, 199, 255n5
essentialism, 124, 243n9, 249n23
ethics: beyond legal or moral codification, 7, 10–13, 35, 55–56, 78, 98, 185, 186, 198–99, 208–9, 219, 236, 237; and Chinese students' dilemma, 14; Cynics' view of, 98, 209; and Emmanuel's narrative, 35–36, 42, 55–57, 77, 100, 167, 219; and ethnographic method, 118; and existential imperative, 166; Faubion on, 237n32; and folktales, 11–12, 35–36, 78; and foreign aid, 214; Foucault on,

236n28; Hegel on, 237n34; and
Ibrahim's narrative, 166–67, 171; and
intersubjectivity, 9, 10, 11; Kant on, 9,
10, 11, 237n34; Kleinman on, 236n25;
Lambek on, 10–11, 236n25; and legal
status of immigrants, 219–20; Levinas
on, 9, 32; Løgstrup on, 55–56, 77–79, 86,
199, 240n28, 241–42nn36–37; and
migration, 7, 13, 219–20; and multiple
selves, 202; and mutuality, 86; paranomic, 237n32; and persecution, 56–57;
and phenomenology, 199–200; and
poverty, 201; and reciprocity, 36, 131;
Ricoeur on, 6, 101, 136, 237n34, 245n36;
and Roberto's narrative, 97, 167; Sartre
on, 9–10, 237n34; and sense of hope,
212; and sense of loss, 86; and social
crisis, 55–56; and social relations, 8–10,
209; and sovereign expressions of life,
77–79, 199, 240n28; Spinoza on, 6, 77,
136, 245n36; Zigon on, 236n26
ethnography, 117, 198, 237n38
European Union, 156
existential issues, 2, 3, 4, 6, 7, 24, 62, 118,
225, 244n17; and existential imperative,
166, 192, 228; and existential mobility,
202, 227–29, 234n14; and existential
reciprocity, 81–82, 83

face of the other, 9, 117
famine, 55, 76, 157, 159, 176, 179, 212,
240n27
Fanon, Frantz, 88
farm labor: Emmanuel's experience of, 25,
26; Ibrahim's experience of, 159, 164,
179; Roberto's experience of, 4, 88,
139–40, 143, 207, 215
Fasching, Darrell J., 12–13
Faubion, James, 237n32
Faulkner, William, 225, 254n82
Ferguson, James, 234–35n14
folktales, 11–12, 35–36, 79
food scarcity and sharing: Emmanuel's
experience of, 26–27, 28–29; Ibrahim's
experience of, 157, 159–60, 169, 175;
Roberto's experience of, 92, 106, 123
Fortes, Meyer, 246–47n14
Fortuyn, Pim, 241n30

Foucault, Michel, 236n28
Franco, Roberto, childhood of, in Mexico:
and border crossings into U.S., 88,
110–21, 124; and deportation from U.S.,
118–19, 215, 216; and fall from schoolbus,
100; and father's immigration to U.S.,
104–5; and food scarcity and sharing,
92, 106; and La Viña trash dump,
93–96; and longing to be elsewhere, 213,
219; and mother's illness, 102–4, 215;
and mother's immigration to U.S.,
106–9, 216–17; and mother's return
from U.S., 109–10; and reading ability,
99, 108; and residence in Apaxco, 101–5,
215; and residence in El Huizache,
105–10; and residence in la colonia
Higuera, 91; and residence in Las
Águilas, 92–101; and residence in San
Francisco Soyaniquilpan, 91; and
schooling, 99–100, 108; and snakes,
91–92; and social status, 95, 98–99; and
violence, 96
Franco, Roberto, family of: brothers, 91, 106,
107, 108, 114, 116, 122, 123, 149; father,
90–91, 92, 93, 99, 101, 102, 104–5, 110, 121,
122–23, 141–42, 149, 216; great-grandmother Candelaria, 88, 106, 108, 109, 136,
139; mother, 90–91, 92, 102–7, 109–12,
115, 120, 121, 123, 141–43, 144, 149, 213,
215, 216–18; sisters, 91, 98–99, 100, 104,
106, 108, 110, 114, 121, 122, 143, 149
Franco, Roberto, as immigrant in U.S.: and
adaptability, 208; and anti-immigrant
attitudes, 89, 124–27; and chance developments, 198, 219, 225; and construction
work, 149; and education at Bethany
College, 144–49, 216; and education at
Harvard University, 89, 148–50; and
education at high school, 131–33, 137–39;
and English language, 88, 132–33, 147;
and farm labor, 4, 88, 139–40, 143, 207,
215; and food scarcity and sharing, 123;
and gang activity, 133–36, 137; and green
card, 89, 141–43, 216; and meeting with
mother's friend Chava, 215–18; and
narrative indeterminacy, 198, 225; and
religious faith, 127–30, 136–37, 138,
143–44, 145, 147, 148, 198, 207, 224; and

Franco, Roberto (*continued*)
    residence in Bakersfield, 121–44; and
    state of exception, 222; and survivor
    guilt, 210; and U.S. citizenship, 88–89;
    and violence, 125–26; and visit to natal
    village, 221
Freire, Paulo, 124
French language, 62, 154, 167

Gandhi, Mahatma, 7, 13
Geertz, Clifford, 9
Geshiere, Peter, 241n30
Ghana: Mossi immigrants in, 246n12;
    NGO volunteers in, 151
Ghananian fishermen, as immigrants to
    Italy, 80–83, 131
Girard, René, 54–55
globalization, 4, 220, 234n14
God. *See* religion
Gogo people, 240n27
Good Samaritan, 215, 253n64
Gould, Stephen Jay, 255n4
Graeber, David, 11, 251n44, 253n55
Graw, Knut, 244–45n28
Great Depression, 175, 180
green card, 89, 141–43, 216
Groody, Daniel G., 128–29
Gurney, Edmund, 218
Guthrie, Woody, 87

Haarder, Bertel, 57
Han, Clara, 234n8
Harvard University, 89, 123, 148–50
Heald, Suzette, 239n15
Hegel, G. W. F., 237n34, 241n33
Heidegger, Martin, 7
Herzfeld, Michael, 195
hierarchy, social, 8, 95, 98–99, 209–10,
    251n44
HIV/AIDS, 27, 55
Hofmannsthal, Hugo von, 213–14
Hollande, François, 156
Holocaust, 117, 126, 198, 252n48
home, concept of, 157–58
hominids, migration of, 227–29
Homo Sacer, 222, 223
hope and hopelessness, 62, 69, 201, 212,
    241n35

horizon, migration as, 130, 244–45n28
horse, in Mossi legend, 181, 182
Hughes, Langston, 139
human rights, 7, 18, 119, 177, 199, 220,
    222–23
Huntington, Samuel, 124
Husserl, Edmund, 199, 201, 244–45n28
Hutu people, 16–17, 20, 97

Ibrahim. *See* Ouédraogo, Ibrahim
identity, human, 6, 8, 13, 24, 117, 124, 185,
    202, 206, 209, 211, 215, 223, 234n14,
    243n9
immigration: Danish policy on, 57; Dutch
    policy on, 241n30; ethical and legal
    aspects of, 219–20; of Ghananians to
    Naples, 80–83, 131; of Indonesians to
    Amsterdam, 155; and Israeli state,
    241n29; of Mossi people to Ghana,
    246n12; of Sierra Leoneans to London,
    68, 84, 113. *See also* California, immigra-
    tion to; Franco, Roberto, as immigrant
    in U.S.; Mulamila, Emmanuel, as
    immigrant in Denmark; Ouédraogo,
    Ibrahim, as immigrant in the
    Netherlands
improvisation, behavioral, 7, 202, 208,
    225
incest, 40
indeterminacy, narrative, 197–98
India, 201
Indonesians, as immigrants in Amsterdam,
    155
initiation rites, 27, 212
intersubjectivity, 9, 10, 11, 124, 211, 234n14
inwardness, cult of, 191, 192
Islam: Emmanuel's experience of, 53–54,
    75; Ibrahim's experience of, 165, 184, 195
Islamic fundamentalism, 241n30
Islamic University, Uganda, 53–54, 75
Israel, 241n29
Italy, African immigrants in, 80–83, 131
Iteso region, Uganda, 20, 33, 239n5

Jackson, Louisa, 151–52
Jackson, Stephen, 62
James, William, 136, 203, 218–19, 245n34,
    256n12

Jaspers, Karl, 123, 244n17
Jews, European, 86, 117, 126, 155

Kahneman, Daniel, 198, 248–49n6, 256n11
Kant, Immanuel, 9, 10, 11, 237n34
Kayibanda, Grégoire, 17
Keane, Webb, 237n38
Kenya, 16, 18, 27
Kidder, Tracy, 97
King, Martin Luther, Jr., 13
kinship: among Bagisu people, 21, 24, 239n15; among Nyole people, 239n15
Kivutien people, 62
Kleinman, Arthur, 236n25
Koroma, Sewa, 1–2, 68, 172, 205–6, 222
Kuipers, Evelien, 153–56, 164, 179–81, 186–89, 192–95
Kuranko folktales, 11–12, 35, 78, 185–86, 235n22
Kuranko people, 85, 141, 170, 173, 184–85, 209, 210–11, 251n43

Lakoff, George, 252n50
Lambek, Michael, 10–11
Lantigua, David M., 12–13
Lanzmann, Claude, 121–22, 242n50
Latour, Bruno, 233n6
Levi, Primo, 117, 126, 141, 198, 210, 252n48
Levinas, Emmanuel, 6, 9, 32, 117
Libya, 18
lifeworlds, 7, 117–18, 124, 137, 166, 186, 200, 212, 219, 233n7
Locker, Peter, 249n7
Lockwood, Douglas, 214
Løgstrup, K. E., 55–56, 77–79, 86, 199, 241–42nn36–37
London, Sierra Leonean immigrants in, 1–2, 68, 84, 113, 172, 195, 205–6, 222
Long, Jeremy, 214
loss, sense of, 85–86, 225
Lucht, Hans, 80–84, 131
Lugisu language, 23, 56

Makerere University, Uganda, 53–54
Malcolm X, 13
Mande societies, 240n21
manhood, Bagisu initiation rite for, 27
Marah, Noah, 84–85, 184–85

Marah, S. B., 62
Márquez, Gabriel García, 158
Marx, Karl, 7, 9, 241n33, 251n44
Masai people, 64–65
McMillan, Della, 156–57, 158, 184, 246n7, 246n11, 248n29
meaning, as existential imperative, 192
Melville, Herman, 203
Merleau-Ponty, Maurice, 10, 237n34
Mexico, migration from, 104, 106, 108–9, 142–43. *See also* Franco, Roberto, childhood of, in Mexico; Tijuana
Mexico City, 90, 91, 92, 93, 101, 142, 243n1
middle-class lifestyle, 191
migration: anthropological study of, 15, 157, 234n14; compared to transition to adulthood, 171–72; and drought in Burkina Faso, 157, 160–61, 246n9; ethical issues raised by, 7, 13, 219–20; existential issues raised by, 2–4, 6, 8; as horizon, 130, 244–45n28; and Hutu-Tutsi conflict, 16–17; and migrant imaginary, 185, 203; and Oedipal project, 212; prehistoric, 227–29; rural to urban, 26–27; and self-definition, 185, 201–8; and utopian yearning, 212–13, 221; West as destination of, 80. *See also* immigration
Mitchell, Stephen, 207
modernity, compared to traditional culture, 173–74, 176–77, 185, 189–92, 194, 195
Montaigne, Michel de, 202–3, 235n24
morality. *See* ethics
Morocco, 214
Mossi people, 152, 156, 173, 181–82, 209–10, 221, 246–48nn
Mulamila, Emmanuel, childhood and adolescence of: and education at primary school, 24–26, 34, 65; and education at secondary school, 25, 36–37, 46–53, 65; and education at university, 53–54, 59; and English language, 23, 25, 34, 65; and farm labor, 25, 26; and food scarcity and sharing, 26–27, 28–29, 49, 55, 79; and girlfriends, 46–47; and lack of latrines at school, 51–52; and longing to be elsewhere, 213, 219; and meaning

and father's death, 164; and food scarcity and sharing, 157, 159–60, 169; and importance of family relations, 183–84; and letter writing, 161–62; and longing to be elsewhere, 157–58, 213, 219; and mother's death, 152–53, 164–65; and physical abuse by teachers, 162–63; and residence in Bobo, 152, 165, 167; and residence in Damesma, 156–65, 168–71, 182–83; and residence in Ouagadougou, 152–53, 167–68, 172; and traditional culture, 158, 173, 174, 183, 209–10; and travel to Kaya, 158–59, 246n6; and work ethic, 178–79

Ouédraogo, Ibrahim, family of: brothers, 161, 169; daughter Karfo, 153, 155, 156, 164, 179, 181, 187, 192–93; father, 157–61, 168–72, 175, 182–83, 210, 246n11; mother, 152–53, 160, 162, 164–65, 168–70, 210; paternal grandfather, 168, 175; paternal uncle, 168; wife Evelien, 153–56, 164, 179–81, 186–89, 192–95

Ouédraogo, Ibrahim, as immigrant in the Netherlands: and anti-immigrant attitudes, 155, 156; and chance developments, 198, 219, 225; and consumerism, 175; and cultural comparisons, 171, 173–74, 186–90, 191, 194; and Dutch language, 155; and employment in concert-hall kitchen, 4, 156; and employment in post office, 154–55, 188; and food, 186, 187–88; and narrative indeterminacy, 198, 225; and ownership of townhouses in Ouagadougou, 222; and religious faith, 184; and residence in Amsterdam, 4, 153–55, 186, 192–96; and self-definition, 185, 205; and social equality, 173–74; and state of exception, 222

Palestinian people, 86, 241n29
paranomic ethics, 237n32
passivity, behavioral, 207–8, 251n41
pastoralism, 16–17, 20, 228, 240n27
patriarchal law, 211
Pentecostals, 102–4, 110, 120, 127–30, 136–37, 138, 176, 177, 216
persecution: ethical aspects of, 56–57; and persecution texts, 54–55, 57

Pessoa, Fernando, 203, 205
Peul people, 164
phenomenology, 199–200, 201, 234n14, 255n5
Piot, Charles, 176–77
politics: African, 189; Dutch, 156, 189; of language, 88; liberal vs. conservative, 252n50
Pottage, Alan, 251n46
poverty, ethical struggle entailed by, 201
prehistory, migration in, 227–29
protoethics. See ethics, beyond legal or moral codification
provocative impotence, Sartre's concept of, 36
psychoanalysis, 202, 204, 255n5

Qur'anic school, in Burkina Faso, 165–66, 167, 172, 184

racism, 44–45, 57, 125–26, 207
Ramos-Zayas, Ana Y., 243n9
Read, Kenneth, 251n45
reciprocity, 10, 36, 81–82, 83, 131, 237n34
reductionism, 166, 255n5, 256n12
refugees, 17, 20, 24, 56, 86, 199, 222, 223, 235n21, 243n10
religion, 9, 136–37, 245n34; and Ibrahim's narrative, 184; and Roberto's narrative, 127–30, 136–37, 138, 143–44, 145, 147, 148, 198, 207, 224. See also Buddhism; Christianity; Islam
Ricoeur, Paul, 6, 101, 136, 225, 237n34, 245n34
Rigby, Peter, 240n27
Roberto. See Franco, Roberto
Rospabé, Philippe, 212
Roy, Arundhati, 253n58
Rulfo, Juan, 221
Rushdie, Salman, 157–58
Rwanda: Hutu-Tutsi conflict in, 16–17, 20, 24, 76; as member of East African Community (EAC), 16

San Francisco, Latino immigrants in, 131, 219
Sarkozy, Nicolas, 156
Sartre, Jean-Paul, 9, 36, 237n34

The publisher gratefully acknowledges the generous support of the General Endowment Fund of the University of California Press Foundation.

Deborah Anne Kapchan
deborahkapchan@mac.com

The Wherewithal of Life